LAWREN GREENE
"Diary of a Waterman"

PUBLISHED BY
Lawren E. Greene
32849 Natural Bridge Road
Wesley Chapel, FL 33543
(732) 558-6749
www.lawrengreene.com
lawrengreene@gmail.com

Copyright © 2012 by Lawren E. Greene

ISBN 978-1-7355290-8-0
Library of Congress

All rights reserved. No part of the contents of this book may be reproduced or transmitted in any form or by any means without the written permission of the publisher.

This book is a work of autobiographical vision; names, characters, places and incidents are either the product of the author's perception, or imagination, or used fictitiously, and any resemblance an to actual person, living or dead, events, or local is entirely coincidental. The book is more of a continued anthology of poetic works than anything else. This is the continuation to Mortally Immortal.

    Cover design by: Mark Martel – Martel Art:
          www.martelart.com

  Printed and bound in the United States of America.

SPECIAL THANKS

Special thanks go to my wife Magdalena Greene, Ernestine and Lawrence Greene, Earl Greene, Lawrence and Rebecca Greene, Jrhosaboy and Isabelle Jones, Lucy Jones, Martha Edwards and Family, Blanche Greene, Perry Greene, Janice Greene, Linda Seals, Garry Spencer Greene and my mother-in-law Marie Jeannette Supplice.

My friends and their families who have been a great beam of support while writing this book: Washington, Boyd, Jordan, Hawkins, Patel, Leyden, Gibbs, Parchment, Reed, James, Fair, Granger, King, Searight (RIP), and so many more that I find it difficult to list out.

The Ten Tribes of Jrhosaboy

Jrhosaboy Jones – 1/12/1916- 4/11/09
Isabelle Rogers Jones - 11/6/1919- 6/23/03
Jrhosaboy Jones Jr. - 9/21/1937-1/15/08
Isabel Jones Morgan - 1/28/1939
Martha Jones Edwards - 2/2/1940
Rogers Jones - 2/26/1941
Susan May Jones - Clark 7/4/1942
Lucy Jones - 9/4/1944
Paul Jones - 1/29/1949
Ernestine Jones Greene - 4/30/1951
Angeline Jones-Jones - 6/28/1955
Willie Mae Jones Weaver - 7/23/1958

Through GOD all things are possible.

Jones' Lineage

Great, Great, Great, Grandmother: Malinda's Mother - Polly Wilson, 1833
Great, Great, Great, Grandfather: Malinda's Father - Horace Wilson, 1827

Great, Great, Great Grandmother: Willis' Mother - Susan Monroe
Great, Great, Great Grandfather: Willis' Father - Peter Thompson

Great, Great, Great Grandmother: Joseph's Mother - Claire Banks
Great, Great, Great Grandfather: Joseph's Father - Master Ansley (white) of the Cook in Boston, GA

Great, Great Grandfather: Malinda's Mother - Malinda Wilson Thompson, 1857
Great, Great Grandfather: Malinda's Father - Willis Thompson, 1855-1930

Great, Great Grandmother: George's Mother - Amelia Carr Jones, 1857-1935
Great, Great Grandmother: George's Father - Joseph Jones, 1858-1923

Great Grandmother: Jrhosaboy's Mother - Malinda Thompson Jones, 1886-1967
Great Grandfather: Jrhosaboy's Father - George Jones, 1883-1964

Grandfather: Ernestine's Father - Jrhosaboy Jones, 1916-2009

Lawren's Mother - Ernestine Jones Greene's, 1951

Lawren Erneston Greene-- son 1977

Great, Great, Great Grandmother: Emma's Mother - Sussie Upton

Great, Great, Great Grandmother: Charlie's Mother - Nancy Cash
Great, Great, Great Grandfather: Charlie's Father - Dale Cash

Great, Great, Great Grandmother: Isabelle's Mother - Anna Jones Sadler
Great, Great, Great Grandfather: Isabelle's Father - Master Saddle (raised by *Isaac Sadler* (?))

Great, Great, Great Grandmother: James's Mother - Ellabell Cherry
Great, Great, Great Grandfather James's Father - Master James Rodgers (white), Valdosta, Ga

Great, Great Grandmother: Willie Mae's Mother - Emma Upton Cash, 1882-1947
Great, Great Grandfather: Willie Mae's Father- Charlie Cash, 1879-1942

Great, Great Grandmother: Napolean's Mother -Isabelle Sadler Rogers, 1878-1934
Great, Great Grandfather: Napolean's Father - James Paul Rogers (d' was dropped), 1879-1932

Great Grandmother: Isabelle's Mother- Willie Mae Cash, 1900-1990
Great Grandfather: Isabelle's Father- Napolean Rogers, 1892-1959

<u>Ernestine's Mother: Isabelle Rogers Jones</u> - Grandmother (1919-2003)

<u>Lawren's Mother: Ernestine Jones Greene's</u>: Born 3/31/1951, Thomasville, GA

Lawren Erneston Greene -- son (1977)
Earl Lamar Greene -- son (1978)

Greene' Lineage

Great, Great, Great, Great, Great, Grandmother: Octavia's Mother – Martha, Charles City, VA
Great, Great, Great, Great, Great, Grandfather: Octavia's Father – John D. Jones, (Married to Martha) Charles City, VA

Great, Great, Great, Great, Grandmother: George's Mother – Rebecca, Charles City, VA
Great, Great, Great, Great, Grandfather: George's Father – A. Robb, Charles City, VA

Great, Great, Great Grandmother – Rebecca's Mother – Octavia Latimore, Charles City, VA
Great, Great, Great Grandfather: Rebecca's Father - George Robb, Charles City, VA (Married to Octavia Latimore - 1884)

Great, Great, Great Grandmother: John's Mother - Fevian Harris, Charles City, VA
Great, Great, Great, Grandfather: John's Father - William Harris, Charles City, VA

Great, Great Grandmother: Sarah's Mother - Rebecca Robb
Great, Great Grandfather: Sarah's Father - John Harris

Great, Great Grandmother: Joseph's Mother - Grace
Great, Great Grandfather: Joseph's Father - Benjamin Champion

Great Grandmother: Sarah Harris : Lawrence's Mother - Born August 25th 1902, Charles City Virginia : Died 9/8/1997 Plainfield, NJ / Buried: Franklin, NJ
Great Grandfather: Lawrence's Father - Joseph C. Greene : Died July 7th 1981 / Buried Franklin, NJ

Grandfather: Lawrence Isador Greene: Born 1/22/1926, Charles City, VA

Father: Lawrence Isaac Greene: Lawren's Father: Born 4/2/1947, Plainfield, NJ

Great, Great, Great, Great Grandmother: Robert's Mother - Keziah - Charles City, VA
Great, Great, Great, Great Grandfather: Robert's Father - James Charity - Born 1796, Charles City, VA

Great, Great, Great Grandmother: Miles' Mother - Frances Bradby - Charles City, VA
Great, Great, Great Grandfather: Miles' Father - Robert A. Charity - Born 1830, Charles City, VA

Great, Great, Great Grandmother: Lucy's Mother - Parkie Kazia Langston, Charles City, VA
Great, Great, Great Grandfather: Lucy's Father- John Langston, Charles City, VA

Great, Great Grandmother: Zena's Mother - Nancy Jane Cotman (Married to Miles Gentry Bradby)
Great, Great Grandfather: Zena's Father - Miles Gentry Bradby - Born 1863, Charles City, VA : Died 1944, Charles City, VA

Great, Great Grandmother: Marion's Mother - Lucy Langston - Born 9/5/1860, Charles City, VA : Died 6/2/1938, Charles City, VA
Great, Great Grandfather: Marion's Father - Elias Green

Great Grandmother: Lora's Mother - Zena Bradby - Born 1888, Charles City, VA
Great Grandfather: Lora's Father - Marion Greene - Born 1882, Charles City, VA

Grandmother: Lawrence's Mother - Lora Rebecca Green, Born 1928, Charles City, VA : Died 2004, Plainfield, NJ

Lawren's Father: Lawrence Isaac Greene, Born 4/2/1947, Plainfield, NJ

About the Author

Lawren provides a humble and fresh perspective on life from an urban New Jersey setting dealing with socio-economic, political and gender based issues. With his expressive writing style, Lawren evokes the reader in such a way making them feel like they are right in the book. He gives the reader the opportunity to identify with their own personal situations from dealing with relationships to being stuck in traffic. Intriguing the reader with real life scenarios he articulates a sense of indulgence in fantasy with cleverly drafted multi-dimensional characters and creative wordplay. Lawren actually revolutionizes ones' thought processes throughout these 5 volumes consisting of his life; challenging the reader to think about their own purpose in life. He services the reader with topics that are plainly visible to the everyday person and ultimately may have some societal impact.

Lawren is a man that will open the world to a new realistic, well-articulated, and open-hearted perception of life. Each volume will ultimately tell a story that will paint a cohesive picture, which will take the reader through thousands of emotional sensations.

Educationally and professionally, Lawren continues his rigorous self-paced advancement to get to a self-determined apex. Technology and Project Management is his game and he prides himself on the many successful working relationships established throughout the years. Lawren is a very approachable man in person but can be deemed as highly elusive, much like the sand that slips from the hand. All you have to do is Google "Lawren Greene" and you will assuredly be welcomed into the fast paced and methodical mindset of this modern day literary mastermind. As a scholar, friend and business man, Lawren has been defined as a premier artist ready to blaze the world with his transcendentalist style of emotionally impactful literature and will start by planting seeds in the ghettos, rural country sides, city streets, suburban coffee shops and wherever else he sets his path. Ultimately, Lawren is about the general success of a multi-culturally accepted society where people are human beings whose rights must become more identifiable. He is absolutely a true master of the psychologies of his philosophies when it comes to his focus and ability to express his and society's feelings throughout the ages.

Table of Contents

"Other Side of the Mirror" 24
Weatherman 25
Undisguised Answers 27
The Last Clutch Player 29
My Favorite Bird 31
Stretch LEGStrong 33
Kindergarten Wilderness 35
Dr. LovEvil 37
Magdalena 40
Faith Breaks Hope Builds 42
Answer Me Battle Cat 44
Texture in My Court 45
Spiritual Clashes 47
So Tired of Running 48
A House 49
The Needy Frog 51
Kosher Stem Cells 53
Addiction is a Demon 55
People kill People 56
Six Degrees of Belief 58
Unison versus the Ego 60
Life's Lessons 62
Things I Regret 64
Attractive 67
Gold, Silver, Bronze 68
Hosanna the Ninja 70
Waiter for a Week 74
Sand Castles 76
Is it Jackson 78
House of Men 80
Self-Publishing Mayhem 82
Steady Regulation 83

Birds Chirp 85
Dollars de Lawren 87
Cobblestone Entrance 90
Life Sentences in Sentences 91
Forsaking Nourishment 92
Am I the Muse 93
The Cloud is a Man 94
Scratching at the Bars 96
Ontos Firing at Night 98
Heartbeats in the Rain 100
Society has its ways 101
Bonding Broken Attachments 103
The Waters of Knowledge 105
"Rose Gardens in Atlantis" 107
Entrance to an Exit 108
Knockem X 110
The Difference Between 112
The Saga of "If I had" 113
Balding of the Trees… 114
Golden Apples 116
Discombobulating 117
The Alarm Clock 119
The Mantis Rides 122
Master Planner 125
The Antithesis of Neither 127
Three Guns 128
Wisdom is She 130
WORD LIFE 132
Grey Implosions 133
Keep the Change 134
HOME 136
Fire Burns 139
Insurance Investigations 140
Everything is Fresh 142

I Was 143
Steel Bags 145
No Carriages 146
Alabama Shallow Water Catfish 147
Pretty Health Care 149
Evolutionary Babies 150
The Earth We Walk on 152
The Moon and a Platinum Ring 154
Education is a Discipline 155
Teaching Bleeders 156
One Thousand Keys 158
Rose Gardens in Atlantis 160
Today 162
Write to Them 164
Your Resume 165
Your World 167
Without a Thorn 168
Remember Me 169
Bottom Feeders 171
Seven Days 173
Framing Premonitions 175
Impermeable to Heat 177
Cold Cuts on my Lawn 178
The Theory of Why 179
Test Me against the Plumb Line 181
I Use to Grid Humans 182
No More 184
Jump or Meow 185
Sak Pase 187
Selah Cubits 190
"Diamond Dynamite" 191
Volume 9 191
Why I Write 192
We are Dominoes 193

Straw Filled and Scatter Brained 195
My Birthday Wish 196
Liars Hurt People 197
Spiritual Preparation 198
Robot Horizons 199
My Puddles 201
The Future is Behind Us 202
Goldfish Farmer 204
Cosmosis 206
Angels 207
Cotton Picker 208
Ice Cubes in the Sun 209
Stalemate 211
That's My "C" 213
Country Scenes and Serenity 215
Walkers License 217
Coco Blaine 219
Butterfly World 221
Seeds of Creation 223
Wireless Electricity 224
Imagine Magnificence 226
Artificial Swag 228
Anchored in Capitalism 230
Venus Tunnels 231
Tree Grows 233
The Warrior's Circumference 235
Now I am Older 241
The Maximist 242
Decompartmentalized 244
Acrobatic Crack Addict 246
Count on Heaven 247
Magical 248
Tattoos and Zoos 250
Greater Than Your Machines 252

The Sexy Element 254
Out to Sea 256
Neo Nazis in Africa 258
What I have 260
Eyes Change Colors 262
Memories of Men 264
Magdalena Anniversaries 266
Secaucus Swans 267
I Don't Know 268
In the Basement 270
Happiness of my Anger 272
She Said 276
Quiet Charity and Works 278
Blind Wind Loud Drug 279
"Watermanny Faces: The Psychologies of My
Philosophy" 280
Amazing 281
Ups and Downs 282
Snow Lust 283
Lake Placid 284
Sandstorms without an End 286
Robotic Souls 287
Birds Chirp 289
Babe Girl 290
Towers of Babylon 292
Diamond Dynamite 293
If You Knew 295
The Travesty of Hip Hop 297
Deletion 299
Man without Knowing a Woman 300
Lassaiz Faire 301
Been There 303
Confuse Me a Nation 305
The Warrior's Serenity 308

Black Patronage 312
Cruise Control 313
Critical Mass 314
Intellectual Ghetto Talk 316
Cotton Picker 318
I Forgot Easter 319
Damn a Cannon 320
Big Adventures of Little Butt 322
Was I Ever Needed 324
I OVERSTAND 325
A Love Experiment 327
Key People 329
Mama's Coming Home 330
If I was White 331
My Mother 333
Farmer 335
Fat Rat 336
Technology Needs a Cord 337
I am a Mountain 339
I in Team 340
Back to the Pain 341
Hold on a Second 342
Gimmick Me 344
The Wrong Target 346
Technology is an Easy Bull 347
SIMPLICATED 349
Sunday Comics 350
The Calls 352
Hot Glitter and Ice Coffee 353
Rich Guy 354
An Enigma 355
Something Distills Nothing 357
Green Pastures 358
Sunny Days and Delays 359

Born or Bred 361
Micro-manage 363
Golden Bronze 364
At the Beach 366
Save Your Sanity 367
Opposition 368
"A Man and the World" 370
Irene's Eye 371
"14" 373
Aged Tears 374
Stupid Questions 376
Law became Rén 377
A Day Old 379
Well, Well, Well 380
The Thorns 381
Cigar Smoke, 99 Bananas,
Heineken and Hennessey 382
Raw Intuition 384
Daffodil Hill 385
Sleeping on Chess Pieces 387
Chaotic Preparation 388
Theory of Paid for Pieces 389
A Master's Thoughts 391
Oh Well 393
I Do Not Have Time 395
Kings and Queens 396
Human Nature 397
Better Known as Waterman 398
Make it Easier 406
Searching for the Mantis 407
The LEG Cup 409
The Artist 410
Talk is Potential 411
Trade Addiction 412

Thoughts on Unemployment...413
Trivializing Social Networks...414
Every Song has a Face..415
Less Than a Thought..417
Misdiagnosed..418
Does Not Exist...420
Bird House..422
Management...422
Breakfast...422
Politics and Marketing...422
Yesterdays, Today and Tomorrow......................................422
Growth and Comfort...423
Get out of your comfort zone…..423
Growth does not occur comfortably…..............................423
Money in Pocket..423
Life to Me...423
Writing in Pencil..423
Personal..423
Perpetual Motion...425
This is the end Montague..427
Snoopy Love...429
Glass or Silver..430
I Have Regained..431
Ants do not Cry...432
Occupy Wall Street..433
Good Old Marketing...435
The Power Meeting..436
Sat in a Bar...437
Habitual Training...438
Magical..439
Glass without the Juice..441
One of Many..442
The Heart's Choice..443
A Young Man...444

Jigga Man 446
Bottled in Plastic 448
To Know 450
Masonic Decisions 451
Selfless Vulnerability 452
Slow Transformation 453
Beyond the Physical Plane 454
Last Thoughts 455
Metaphorically the Same 456
Walk in the Park 457
Virtual World 458
Dreams of Growing Waves 460
Stars and Stripes 461
Sexuals 462
Banking 464
Roses are not Weeds 466
My Bongos 468
Social Injustices 469
The World We Live In 471
1,000 Words 472
A Fool and Money 473
More Smiles than Tears 474
Dial Tone 475
Beautiful Spring Day 477
Aluminum Man 478
The Operations 480
Wooden Parachute 482
Whoa Verses the Fool and Sacrifice 484
2009 Chickahominy Pow Wow 485
Baby on the Balcony 486
Empty Strangers 488
Hey Clown 489
Seriously 491
Just Thinking 492

My Mother 493
Grandma Jones' Teacakes Recipe............................494
The General 495
I See Purple 496
A new defect-revealing etchant for GaAs 497
In Your Dreams 498
Sandy 2012 499
Bored 501
Crabbing in Sea Girt 502
Election Tuesday 2012 504
Comfortable Growth 506
Diary of a Waterman 507
Mark Martel/Illustrator..508
Lawren's Bio 509

Foreword

Thank for patronizing in the material that has literally taken me years to write. I decided to write these volumes as a representative of my life and my reflections throughout society. I have grown and shrank while writing this book. Only through my burning perseverance and guided commitment to completion have I been able to get this in your hands.

This book is a true segment of my life. In fact, it is a poetically inspired anthology. How my brain thinks, what I desire to no longer see in society, hope for people to relate to, and ultimately get a fresh sense of a man walking through the corridors of urban America. I wish for people to smile, get teary, weary, upset and ultimately a bit more conscious that people need people. Reality comes in so many forms it can be hard to explain. I have tried to explain my reality the best way it was perceived at that moment in time. I have had the opportunity to have grown in a loving home, receive a strong education, and work for some of the most world renowned firms before and during the writing of each volume. Currently, I work as the Senior Technical Project Manager at the world renowned Metropolitan Museum of Art in Manhattan, New York. I have had the opportunity to lose my faith and pick it up ever so stronger. Being able to lose yourself and power back up is extremely difficult and requires love, pain, sacrifice, attention, detention, trial and tribulation. I sense this is a new beginning for me, and that the words of this book can place a positive impression on the reader. I believe people are blessed by their differences. Since every single one of us is different we achieve our lifelong goals differently than any other; if fortunate enough to not steer onto the wrong path. I feel God inspired me to write these volumes and merge this book.

The covers of all the volumes; including Diary of a Waterman, are all derived through my lifelong dreams in which I feel absolutely blessed that they were able to catch your attention. The covers are illustrated by a most talented artist, Mr. Mark Martel. He was able to take my vision and methodically create a colorful and illustrative story. If not for the diligence of my wife; Magdalena Greene, I would have had an awesomely difficult time reviewing and proofreading the volumes in their entirety. I believe she did a great job throughout our rigorous editing cycles.

I give special thanks in all things to my father and mother, Lawrence and Ernestine Greene. To my brother Earl Greene who actually inspired me to write. My brother is currently working on his upcoming debut and I believe it will be a wonderful piece of literature. Again, to my wife; Magdalena Greene, a woman that has inspired me throughout this long journey and kept me focused to completion.

Furthermore, I started writing the Diary of a Waterman as soon as I completed Mortally Immortal. I felt that I still had much more to say. It is important to note that the Diary of a Waterman has the exact number of pages as Mortally Immortal. Such an accomplishment was not by coincidence but by design. I wanted to illustrate that destiny is manifested by intelligent design. We dictate our own success story. Since Mortally Immortal was produced I have been in the studio with an astounding recording artist and engineer, Kenneth Hawkins. We produced four unique spoken word albums directly from the content of both Mortally Immortal and Diary of a Waterman. The titles of the albums are as follows: 1) Mortally Immortal, 2) The Purple Tunnel, 3) Diary of a Waterman, and 4) The LEG Cup. Each of the aforementioned albums contains 14 tracks. Again, such an accomplishment was not by coincidence but by design. I felt it necessary for the reader to become familiar with my verbal emotion and character.

In the works for Mortally Immortal; my prior master volume, is a screenplay and a graphic novel illustrating every one of the literary pieces. God willing these projects will be complete. My mother says I always had a way of keeping myself busy; even as a child.

I hope everyone enjoys this book in some form or another. Please feel free to contact me or even stop by and sign my guestbook or provide a literary review at www.lawrengreene.com. I look forward to hearing your comments and any future recommendations. This book is a building, written as if it were architected.

Respectfully yours,

Lawren Erneston Greene

"Other Side of the Mirror"
Volume 7

Weatherman

I will tell you when the Sun hits the moon...
When spring showers arrive and trees start to bloom...
When the clouds have no more room...
I observe the tide to let you know...
It is the simple things...
Rain turns to snow...
Red robins chirp at me...
Thunder always made sense to me...
Tears of a stone, wiped off by hands of the sand...
Double jeopardizing a tsunamis' aggression...
Confessing the sanity of a wind storm...
I came to Earth to see the Sun...
Visited the Ocean to let her know she could trust me...
I visited the sky and flew beyond worldly geographies...
Stayed level to the ground since I am only a man...
I broke the clouds to search the sea...
Volcanic eruptions, destructive monsoons and two souls collide ...
Caught in between the misty season for a reason...
Dry spells rot my nerves...
I am the favorite bird...
The fourth wind tempts me to be friendly...
What makes the world spin faster than what it seems...?
Weatherman is necessary, the iniquities of fire and ice...
Seasons reappear for a reason...
There are only one or two things that can make me happy...
Weatherman carves the land for me...
Separate the oceans from the seas...
Let seeds fall and germinate the spring...
Allow a sandstorm to whistle my name...
There are so few things that I can believe...

There are so many things we can achieve…
Weatherman, give us a sunny day…
Postpone the rain and douse our heads some other day…
The morning smog is so thick…
Draining our visible train of thought…
Weatherman, acknowledge the conditions of my territory…
What we need falls freely from the sky…
Our blood nurtured by a common temperature…
I dwell in the cave you have carved for me to pray in…

Undisguised Answers

The answer chokes perception...
False protection of a known clue...
Deliberate questions come so fast for no reason...
My decisions are based on the way you talk to me...
I shine a light on your clarity...
It is the way you talk to me...
I pretend to be the only one...
The suspected loaded gun...
There are no fingers to squeeze me...
The taste of a salty wine...
Lonely pearls lose form over time...
Enduring cries of a hungry child...
Is the mother too busy to feed freely...?
To live we must believe...
Fellowship of a million men, yet no one seems to care...
Breaking strengths of a crimson tide...
Similar to the lost form of my poetry...
Honest answers to a simple man...
The world is flat; it cannot be round...
Honest answers to a complex man...
An erratic but contained result...
Crossing strangers question vibrations of a lonely heart...
Disciplining the fashions of a bi-polar soul...
Nothing can brighten the earth as the Sun is intended...
No one can tighten her skirt, if she is too fast...
It seems the balance of scale is one sided, Selah...
Still I am guided to try my hardest...
Regardless of what the governor's agenda is...
Constantly daydreaming crime scenes before they happen...
Skimming through the original versions of how my lives use to be...

Undisguised answers surpass common definitions...
Always follow the beast when you contemplate treason...
In God's eyes I am an infant...
Deliberately the moon smiles at me...
Twinkling stars feel closer than they are...
What makes the iron bend and forts crash from the snow...?
Random thoughts from the head...
Really having no clue why things are...
Everything is not meant for everyone...
Really there is one answer, which is difficult to figure out...
Ultimately you discover...
Complexity derives simplicity...

The Last Clutch Player

Imagine if I was the last clutch player...
The dragon slayer...
Crouched on the couch, mantis-praying to my maker...
The integrator of all nations...
Peace to all Jamaicans and Haitians...
I am so native...
American money printer...
Golden melanin pumps through my genealogy...
Learn how the Sun burns...
Hard splinters on a cold day allow me to walk further...
Deserted in the desert...
Sometimes wishing I never made it this far...
Speeding stars capture my train of thought...
My nemesis is genesis in a purple robe, preparing to lay his hands on our people...
My turn comes in the remaining moments...
Voltron is already formed and I am enabled...
Become the most fluid hustler in motion...
Sleepy in a tee-pee channeling the evil those men do...
Dr. LovEvil tells me people are so see through...
Wishing for the last 10 seconds...
Random points of conflict dilute the first fire...
Do not wait for us...
There is NO WE...
Thou shall not lose...
Thou shall not sink...
Thou shall not crumble...
Residues of prioritization sprinkled on my exposed dome...
Pyrex treasure chests...
Drug user please expose an unused vein...
Meta-physical deliveries of justice...

GOD made me to trust I...
Love, you are my emotional armory...
Spiritually, my heart beat is infinite...
Physically, my soul will be with you forever...
Leaves fall from Trees...
All for the best I guess...
Venomous snake head biter, vocally charming my sword...
Genie versus the Drunken Chemist...
These last 5 seconds require the formulas of the most qualified alchemist...
Whirl me without the wind...
Trust, I can swim in the air…

My Favorite Bird

See how the bird flies back to its family...
Grounded till it is time to fly...
The little bird needs help...
A strong wind interprets lift in his wings...
People are so fickle...
Upset today, God fearing tomorrow...
Sorrow versus elation...
Tending to perform THE BEST alongside my loneliness...
Suggest how high I must fly...
I intend to fly higher...
A world without a favorite bird borders an immoral character...
Love made me...
Innate strategies guided I...
Ensuring the right wind greets me...
Spiritually situated high in the Alps to begin with...
Bald headed, noticing my flight wings are starting to form...
The omnipresent celestial kiss...
Born in the east to set in the west...
Confirming my artistry...
Find me, study me, and label my life...
My wings are so strong now...
How can a cloud stop my flight path...?
Gliding beyond care free destination checkpoints...
Baskets of fresh meat fuel my hungered chest...
Sharks, hawks, grizzlies and lions happen to be my creed...
Winter snow decorates my golden breasts...
In the reflection of ice caves my green eyes sparkle...
The sceneries discovered through travel...

Solitary flight...
Gliding beyond the twilight...
Maintaining a risky momentum...
Behold the targeted war bird's philosophy...
The aerial watcher of so many nations...
The emblem of wealth, energy, focus and causality...
My pack is black...
My frame is a sculpture...
My beak is a pretty sword...
My talons are gifted complimenting the Phoenix...
Disguised by the Sunrise...
Only The Sleeping General can intercept me...
The spring breeze teases my joints...
I am faster than a new pistols bullet...
There is no reason to catch me...
Overstand, I am a man decidedly manifesting my realities...

Stretch LEGStrong

Who is superman...?
That man knows not so much...
Able to crush, crash, topple and crumble...
Must it be the Waterman...?
Able to build blast, devastate, and bash...
Mannyfaces characterizes all necessary things...
New Jersey philosophy, burning New York energy...
How far can you walk...?
How far can you carry men...?
How many men will you carry...?
Overall System Conformity...
See, no one is there for you...
Stretch LEGStong is a critical path strategy creator...
Empire soul strikes black...
Bear witness to a character creator...
The long lost face of the maker...
Soldier instigation is my true plan...
Becoming a master to meet the demand...
I see you watching me watching I...
MannyFaces disguised me for a reason...
Stretch LEGStong really does not care...
The face of Manny's feelings...
Modern man is not correct...
The man in the darkest corner of the club...
Bumping and grinding...
Sitting back...
Wishing you would find, define, and film him...
In the lion's den...
Watching the backs of all the many men...
Allegedly they defend, protect and carry him...
Stretch LEGStrong is a friend to them...
Bathing in red oxygen...

Contemplating for when he gets home...
The Other Side of the Mirror is his throne...
Welcome home Stretch LEGStrong...

Kindergarten Wilderness

Background sounds of simple conversation...
Taking in the scenery...
Remembering the games we use to play...
Kindergarten freeze tag governors...
Pony tailed pretty girl crushes...
Lunch box item swiping professionals...
Big people impersonators...
Little people lunch money hustlers...
My crew and I were hustlers...
It seemed to always be a Sunny day...
Forgetting to pray before going out to play..
I am much older now...
Truly acknowledging his presence...
Ring around the Rosie kick-ball confessions...
We had so much fun...
Cherish this...
To the little ones that read this and embellish this...
Tilting my hat to you...
Truly wishing I could be you again...
Friend or foe...
Ah We Enemy...
Choose a friend for me...
At that age, who cared when leaves fell from trees...?
Each leaf now lands on my chest...
All for the best I guess...
Restless, watching the clock tic...
I am so play time...
My lifelong friends are my benefit...
Inside the treasure kit are so many fond memories...
I never cried back then...
Taking my punishments and learning from them...
Never doing the same wrong thing twice...

Guessing I grew up to become a better criminal...
Kindergarten was so subliminal...
I hustled so much candy...
Turning fanatics to candy addicts...
Crack and heroin fanatics, some of them are these days...
Love, they truly loved me...
Aunt Suzy, I told you I am the hustler of my generation...
Watching the principles watch me...
Watching us...
How could they determine our methods of movement...?
Children are people too...
Never underestimate the brainstem of a Godly creation...
World War Kindergarten...
Wrestle Mania maniacs, fighting just for exercise...
These days I bundle my knuckles, impersonating youthful activity...
Wise contenders against the bullies...
I knew the plan since back then...
Love, love me...
In between a beat, back in the day...
Trumpeting snakes...
Seeing who needed to be on the team...
Who I would shatter just because...
Love, love me...
Massage my bronzed armory...
Splash, splash, splash...!
Bubbly in a warm bath...
Oblivious to racism as a youth...
We were all the same...
Rumors were simple to remediate…
Obvious dimples from innocent smiles...
Never aware of what a pimple could do to ones' social life...
So blessed my parents procreated I...

Dr. LovEvil

Dr. LovEvil, ahhh so sick I have to laugh...
From all that I have been through, to now...
This is when Dr. LovEvil comes to play...
Forced to reach supremacy...
Whatever it takes...
Pump your breaks if I am moving too fast...
Boil my fresh tear drop tea with a few drips of sin...
Emotionally stable...
Apocalypse now through War and Dinner...
Iron horsemen at the door installed to dagger my profits...
Off gate, Dr. LovEvil is really an entity of duality...
Dr. LovEvil is a horror movie maker...
A loved ones' coffin carrier...
Dr. LovEvil grabbed his soul back from the sky...
Replacing his losses, throwing Green Diamonds in the Sky...
Dr. LovEvil equals love and hate...
The Good Bad Guy is a fan of that entity...
A fan of envy and famine...
Mantis versus the dragon...
They are all of him...
Captain Labor versus the common cockroach...
The world is wrong and mankind is not conscious...
Why continue to break the seals provided to protect us...?
Sweet guns request light protection...
Nasty dirty guns...distribute ashy bullets...
Before we push, manifest the opposing pull sensation...
Temptation is so tasty...
Someone has come to love me...
To hug me and calm my energy...
So the demon said...let me see him...
Satan said, let me take him...

God said, I am friend to him...
"I" order "We" to share him...
He carries the love and sins of many men...
He must do my bidding, then I will claim him...
Dr. LovEvil, his name stands for me first...
Good begets good, heaven is his ghetto...
Love him, he is one with Benjamin...
One of Jacob's men...
Abram's kin...
The one who initiated the bewildering of Joseph...
Dr. LovEvil and Waterman, blood cousins to the very end...
Wait your turn; he has to show the world first...
"I" will be the only one that allows his pain...
His pain is necessary...
He will build beyond "your" evil sickness...
Dr. LovEvil is my bet...
Dear God, help me become a true man...
A man of the world's length...
Through God's strength LovEvil helped position the evil that men do...
Lord; I am flesh from dust, raised from your desire...
Lord, I am a simple man and not here to destroy men…
Lord...you have given me a gift...
Tell me what I must do...
Dr. LovEvil, you are designed to destroy in order to build...
"I" will position you in where you need to be...
Never worry about the secondary personality...
Son you are golden, do the right thing...
Honor thy mother and father...
Ensure your brethren receive riches...
Dr. LovEvil, loveth thy life...
Carry thy strife...

Avoid the evils that men do...
If you do not...
The angels "I" summon will come to greet you...
I am one of five...
To be continued...

Magdalena

Hello Magdalena...
A goddess in the form of a queen...
Your serene approach elates me...
Her treasured smile makes my world spin...
She is my winner...
Before we went to war, we had dinner...
I must protect her...
She is the empress...
I only respect her...
She is the fortress...
I am not the wanderer...
So restless, now knowing why the Warrior left the castle...
I find myself gazing...
Magdalena you are so amazing...
My biblical travel buddy...
She is so engaging...
We sip wine together...
She is my best friend...
Her cheap kisses are priceless...
Magdalena...
Acknowledge this...
I will be more formal...
Life is too short...
The adhesive sticking me together, extending my life...
I owe you so many things...
Wanting so many roses...
Ensuring your happiness...
Magda bears my last rib...
The captain of my ship...
She is my fantasy...
I dreamt her...
I truly love her...

There is no one above her...
Magdalena...
The day the earth stood still, she was still there...
I had to write of her...
So you know her name...
She is all mine...
She is not a game...
Her soul hugs me...
I will never be the same...
At times, she is too direct...
Knowingly, sometimes she pierces me...
Checkmate Magdalena...
Smile...
Slowing the game down...
I must break you down...
The great laugh...
Knowing you see it...
Waiting for you to get home...
Pushing time...
Getting to where I need to be...
You are my cover page...
I love you...
An element can be broken down...

Faith Breaks Hope Builds

A set of principles or beliefs...
Allegiance to a person's agenda...
No proof or material evidence supports negligence...
Aesop's fable on a table...
What really makes sense these days...?
French kiss a confident wish until your mind twists out magic...
Revamp the West End Gardens projects...
Flood the drug dealer spots with rose stems and pretty petals...
Abram became Abraham, through undeniable faith...
God followed his hope...
Bless the peace that allows us...
Residing alongside the presence of a beautiful woman...
Serenaded, Sara became Sarah...
Not all thoughts are spoken through words...
The nature of movement is greater than voice...
Seemingly, our lives are guided by the choices we make...
Even the largest snake dies...
Should a hungry bird eat from the sea; that which it has never seen...?
The spectacles this planet beholds...
Since when has Israel not needed redemption...?
Suspension without a cord is intense...
Recollection without being there makes no sense...
Walking a great distance, hoping things will be alright...
Hope does not come in the form of a wish...
Do you believe in talent when you see it...?
Myth verse ancestry...
Auto verse biography...
There is a tree I sit next to...
Stenciling my thoughts...

Sipping on a fresh glass of apple juice...
Hoping to enjoy my wishful days...
Knowing my inequities beyond a conscious heavy...
I came back home to close several line items...
Hope and faith travel amongst us...
Trust is important...
Faith is greater than hope, both are two intangibles...
Prayer guided me to think clearer...
As my faith breaks, my hope had a concern to build upon...
So thrilled I did not lose both of them...
Often diminished by the voice of so many men...
Falling in love with scenes of serenity...

Answer Me Battle Cat

He-man sings the psalms of David...
Remove the false cries of the heathen...
There will be no bureaucracy in this kingdom...
Thank you for granting me sanity...
The awesome sense of clairvoyance is nothing short of toying with...
Alaskan days are dark for a reason...
Longing for my heart to tick one trillion more times...
There is nothing to be slick about, I am a humble trooper...
React with the quickness while you foreshadow this thought...
Remembrance is forgiveness...
I always wait for my time...
See I am a hustler, turning thought to sense...
No tussling with me, I only want success...
Dear God, please hear my prayers...
A dollar that means nothing to me...
Answer me Battle cat...
React when I need you...
Battle cat we need no agenda...
We live a perfect life...

Texture in My Court

Our hair contains so much texture...
Blessed by emerald and bronzed temperaments...
Authorities granted by the minorities in us...
Our perceptions seem to be different; live and be true...
Who is the Jiggerboard now...?
Scantily dressed, faced on the front of flaunty magazine covers...
It seems the present crashes the past...
I saw the future; admiring her hour glass shape...
No music is necessary...
Sexy tour versus personality war...
Three times my texture pours the finest wine...
One million percent natural beauty...
Surrounded by my colored sisters...
Mistresses unraveled in my shadow...
Rob melanin and emulate bone structure...
No vaccinations are required; She is thick not sick...
Destiny requires texture...
Privileged, the God blessed her...
Fire sparks as she passes...
The texture of her skin is beyond majestic...
Watch her curves stroke the golden pole...
Skillfully her tongue wrestles pocketed Washington bills; strangling Grants, hypnotically clinging onto the Benjamin's...
Rhythmically she grinds to the urban beat...
The unappreciated role she serves society...
Disinfect her pole and hold her fashion sense for ransom...
Ignore and disrespect her intellect...
Watch her walk into court with her cubs in hand...

The ambrosia of her tainted thought process needs to be refreshed...
Her diamond comb sparkles as she neatly teases her hair to curly...
Sitting she looks directly in my face...
I am the prosecutor and she is defending the culture...
She propagates our culture...
I too patronize her trade...
I cannot reduce the race...
Baby dropper, she keeps her shape...
Stuttering and drooling as her beauty instigates my wildest dreams...
I can reach into her destiny; she entertains my league...

Spiritual Clashes

I understand what my dreams are telling me...
Time to break free and do away with thy enemy...
I can build highways, bridges, castles and beautiful sceneries...
Nothing new to me, I have been doing this for centuries...
Before the Sun began to shine...
The nobles seem to have a problem with me...
So close to my dreams, the screams tell me to listen...
Never second guessing my subconscious...
What was questioned eventually would be answered...
Forced to abide by the law of moving forward...
Crowded by more souls than are atomic particles...
Spiritual clashes are evidently probable...
Sacrifice till you get what you need, travel where you are urged to...
Feed more people with goodness then I originally chose to...
These tasks and many more are my destiny...
Walking through green pastures pointing out envious foes...
Apparitions hear and fear me...
I know my time is near me...
Gifted with an ability to transcend...
Born to the Earth, knowing I will be here again...
Filtered by the truth, there is no need to pretend...
Spiritually, I have fought so many men...
Channeling short tempers at 3:30 AM...
Each night daring to venture between the tunnels of fire and reflection...
When I do something wrong they tend to speak to me...

So Tired of Running

I do not feel like running...
Stand tall, walk strong...
So tired of running...
My back is no longer against the wall...
How much further can I go...?
So much further, this I know...
The world will still spin...
Engaging heavy currents amazed at how I still swim...
Running against unnecessary conflict...
Looking like the suspect; but I am not him, verbally innocent...
Many people are shady, so I choose to walk alone...
Standing by my principles watching evil men constructing the thunder dome...
So close to home yet so far away...
So tired of running...
Hurdling past crowded circles...
My movement is very methodical...
Perfection is important to me...
Completion is yielded through sacrifice...
The friction of this journey...
Weakening of my knees, down to my feet...
Something is telling me to keep on running...
So tired of running...
I keep on running; never looking back, chasing my destiny...
Stuck on this one way track...

A House

I have a house that I pray in...
A roof which shelters my imagination...
Garden growth starts with spring's wind...
Feathered down pillows which I rest my head on...
Nana; she hated escalators, preferring elevators...
Knock before entry...
Cheery doors make people knock harder...
Entrée my finely polished border doorways...
Whence come you...?
Hardwood floors creek, howl, and crackle whilst I slumber...
A basement that is full of adventure...
Pleasurable entities positioned where they are needed...
A dining room with fine china delectable...
Pantry filled with colorful spices, Tupperware and pans...
Empty freezers inspire me to refill them...
Small but sturdy, the water heater is needed...
A hot forced air furnace that could give way any minute...
Thankfully, taking in every warm breath...
Blessed to be a part of the commonwealth...
Keeping my own problems to myself...
Comfortably captured in the leathers of my throne...
My house is my home; this is where I rest...
Working on the humble and mumbling when I am stressed...
Beware, papa bear has had a long day...
Provoking playful cubs; tending to call my bluff...
Intentions of raking heavy wet leaves...
Honey bees finish up for the season...
Debris on the rocky patio; mountains of clutter, now an image of incompletion...
There is just enough space to be barely noisy...

Truth is, I write for my sanity...
Street episodes and homicide collide...
Not for fun, purchasing three guns...
Sirens, fire, robbery and vandalism...
Closed curtains are mandatory...
Seek, peep and sneak
An exposed home invites vandals...
Renovation comes with hesitation and a sense of humor...
Truth be told...
I have few answers and want to grow old...

The Needy Frog

Kiss a frog and make a wish...
Coney Island "F" Train smiling...
Two culturally disproportioned people came in the car...
Multi-culturally mixing amongst the orange seats...
Too worn out to observe...
Deciding to blink my right eye open, for no particular reason...
Out of urban camouflage sat the frog...
It was not rainy season...
Why was this odd frog on the train...?
The needy South American frog persuaded slimy kisses from his tall Asian persuasion...
What a site to see...
This chic was kissing a catfish with chap-stick...
Hazmat frog signs flashed...
My lady and I were sitting perpendicular to the two weirdoes...
Opposites really do attract...
Not believing what I see is reality...
She kept kissing the needy frog...
A torturing National Geographic moment...
I could not help but to be in shock...
This lady must be blind...
How did that needy frog get so close to her..?
Hugging her with his beady eyes as if he poisoned her...
Maybe she was drunk...
It really seemed as if she loved it...
A once culturally unacceptable relationship...
Family "X" is what we make it...
Generation "X" has a unique way of producing itself with ever more flaws...
Day in and out...

He hopes to hop towards another frog kissing fool…
Another day on the infamous NJ Transit train track…
Happening to notice another needy frog…
Hopping and yapping…
Again, sitting not too far from me…
Another disgruntled needy frog…
Instead of "rib bit" it was "kiss me please, take me to your castle…"
Fortunately for me we were not eyes length…
So I listened…
This needy frog had reached her old age…
Obviously, this frog was a fast tad pole…
Currently living on minimum wage…
Telling her friend it was carrier before family…
So she never engaged…
This needy frog is now full of envy…
Unfriendly the "rib bit" became as the frog told her story…
No one is kissing her now…
I guess each frog has their day…
Imaginary prince and princess…

Kosher Stem Cells

A research that bridges morality...
Results that can grant humans immortality...
Microscopic wisdoms fathom weak foundations...
The conscious allows us to build or destroy...
Tampered science that comes with a consequence...
Embryonic borders contained in unnatural fluids...
Forming without the necessary bioelectric activity...
These stem cells are kosher, blessed through the church's wish...
Is there a heart, or stem cell we can share...?
Is there a soul in each single cell...?
Soon, machines will make the parts of men...
Umbilical, embryonic or marrow...
Insurance, newborn or painstaking time...
Unless embryonic, stem cell lines are hard to find......
Take a child before they are born...
Fertilized egg but where is the morality...
Blastocyst killers...
Is science more important than life...?
Preservation greater than generation...?
Is nature no longer the nurturer...?
Life changes and God's will be done...
Fire eventually burns out...
New world chop shops stimulate organ theft and justifications are multiplied...
Synthetic men with human limbs laugh as mankind dwindles...
We were made so perfect...
Must we have a purpose to die...?
Limb creation is cool when stem cells are kosher...
Pastors baptize unknown women stem cell lines...
Comatose and drained from your marrow...

It is just a matter of time...
The more civilized the more complex the crime...
Utopian paradigms...
Mankind has started and cannot pull back...
Stem cell research is great for industry...
A poor move for humanity...
Insanity knows it can be done...
What could possibly be next...?
Swapping souls through bullet holes in a deceased gang minister's chest...
Science loves it because it can be done...
A soul is granted and should not be experimented against...
The feeling of mortality is a death wish...
An angel told me; love will cure AIDS, and salt will kill cancer...

Addiction is a Demon

Addiction is a Demon...
Robbing you from your own soul's possession...
Stop smoking...
Choking in my dreams...
Screaming because I do not want to take a sip...
"Haiku" this...
Playing poker with second hand smoke promoters...
They say; "why go against me, when you need me...?"
Smoke filled my air...
Indeed in need of more oxygen...
My mental growing more agitated...
My temple started to crumble...
Golden cigarettes singe my chest...
Unfocused powerful force fields yield against dark energy...
Dreaming about certain things...
Addiction desensitizes you, while others around you pilfer from you...
Craving for when you have nothing.
Brothers steal blood from their brothers...
Vampires still have to be invited in...
Hustlers, swindlers, alcoholics and smokers...
It is your friends when you think it's not them; I know it's you...
For my sanctuary; I have to leave, since there is no common ground...
I never had what I no longer have...
Addiction is a demon...
Stabbing you with his thieving...
Thou shalt not steal...
Honor our proud commandments...
Addiction is a demon...

People Kill People

People kill people…
Cain's free will enabled him…
God loves all his children…
Man hurts man…
How kind can people really be, and God not be jealous…?
See, we destroy what he creates…
Life is faster than we can comprehend…
The birth cries, the last breath…
The evidence that we were once here…
Idolized through papers de obituary…
These pages are my life, really they are…
How much more can be taken…?
See; I have my targets, and to me they are better off alive…
Seems we were never friends…
At times you helped out…
Almost taking everything from me…
Sanity verses mental stability…
Things that really meant value to me…
Bleeding for quite some time, while redefining my citadel…
A good soldier moves even when the blood trickles…
Cops shoot cops on Broad Street in daylight…
Enforcers perpetrate their way of life…
I tend to lotion up via the positive bronze of karma…
Trust, I have made my own mistakes…
My scars know me best; or maybe I just do not know…
Move back; I am itching to blast and attack…
Born to such a quiet state…
Literally creating morality verses criminality referendum…
War without people is senseless…

Blood must be shed for the sacrificial reasons of man's mistakes...
Fiends, teens with guns and women battered to violence...
Victim souls need worldly resolutions...
Eye for an eye...

Six Degrees of Belief

Six degrees through Mr. LEG...
Bless me with a tight connection...
A light reflection...
The greatness of my imperfection...
Detections of personal resurrections...
Ah we enemy...
Choose a friend for me...
International alignment is an assignment I chose to engage...
Confined to knowing what the future brings...
Time travelers keep contacts, coordinates and strong logic...
Business men carry contracts...
Judges protect clauses...
Wait for the waves...
Anticipate the fourth wind...
Continue to move forward...
Meet the right people...
Depreciate all that is cancerous...
The fools have assumed leadership roles...
There are thieves in between my beliefs...
So much quicker sand in the streets...
Weak temples in the church...
I decided to construct my own temple...
Reinforce my temple, before I entered another temple...
Word is interpretive...
Undeniable faith is superlative...
Savior belief is empirical...
Common knowledge is unforgiving...
The commoners really are not forgiving...
Flood waters will be uncontrollable these years to come...
The color purple will conquer this year...

Inabilities to believe house the first degree...
Distress painfully befits the second degree...
Upon submission to the third base prayer becomes possible...
Faith breaks hope builds the fourth degree...
For peace and protection, pray to graduate to the fifth degree...
Five times a day pray to our maker...
Ground is lost when he is called only when needed...
Real recognize real, I find that hard to believe...
People live longer when they mind their own business...
My real life is building new energies...
Kneeling, paying homage to the fifth degree...
The world can be a hopeful place...
Wingspan wide, the sixth degree revealed to me a key to a gate...

Unison versus the Ego

Pleasure principles of the "Id"...
Animal desires between us...
Trust has no concern...
Most operations are instinctual...
Live to eat and get big...
Simple love verse complex evil...
Id, ego and super ego; all in together see...
Remember the Mantis...?
Aggressively blasting red planets...
Peacefully biting candy apples...
The Other Side of the Mirror is serious...
Of course it is me, and that is my nature...
I the eldest first brother of two...
The world could not take three...
A planet maker verses the taker...
We are one in the same...
Metaphorically, my mind is wrapped too tight...
Warriors live quiet lives...
This passion is timeless...
My guilt is a function of sacrifice...
Same place, same time...
Defined by a need to break social barriers and open eyes...
Throwing green diamonds in the milky blue sky...
One laughs, the other cries...
The Phoenix is so proud to be exposed...
The Sleeping General is time traveling...
Visibly Invisible, beware the hyper conscious army...
Salvos generated from the imaginations of MannyFaces de Water...
Red apples are so sweet and tasty...
It is hard to keep moving forward...
Knowing your power is defined...

Your words are destined, and your family is sheltered...
Dreams come out of sobriety with too much recognition...
The clock tick tocks...
Red planet, home of the friendly enemy...
No longer reserved but always humble...
Making distinct decisions...
Overstanding the dualities of two tunnels...
Mortally Immortal...
My seeds are multiplied by I...
Birds chirp, bells ring and angels sing...
Selah, God is beyond Van glorious, and strengthens bones...
Silver keeps capillaries open...
Bronze shields us from disillusions...
There is nothing new under the Sun...
Our bodies are nuclear power plants...
Sunshine, love and doves...
Poverty, dusk and disastrous incentives...
Unison verses the ego...

Life's Lessons

Life's Lessons...
From the first breath to the last step...
Over time one can get used to breathing...
Taking advantage of what is for granted...
Trees grow leaves and flowers bless us with buds...
Something dies in someone every second...
Leaves fall from trees amongst the forests within us...
Alive in a dark state of conscious...
Purple lights alter awareness...
Penetrating a state of attentiveness...
Huddled with emotions, gliding through velvet corridors...
Illuminati green is what I am looking for...
Trains rumble in tunnels...
Transition is necessary...
Learn life's lessons, then move forward...
There are bigger and more beautiful places to journey to...
Never wanting to burden a person...
Worldly wealth cannot stop an angel from swooping in...
Personal love will not stop the tear from touching you when resting...
The test is what direction to take...?
Upstairs, downstairs, no stairs; what a waste...
Fate is a function of destiny...
Spiritual options of direction are dependent on mortal auras...
Karma is a key...
Doors are mental strongholds easily broken into...
Really, what can you take with you...?
Where in the world is perfect...?
Watching the stars shine, drinking smooth corn liquor...
A shiny Jesus piece of jewelry protects my enemy...

Subliminal messages suggest needed changes in temperament...
Second guessing one of the 36 Chambers to Success...
Fueled by remote accomplishments...
I will wait no longer...
My in-experienced armor is so shiny...
Never running from punishment...
Always loving the covenant...
Never getting in trouble twice for the same thing...
Enraged to be encaged by a pack of corporate liars...
Souls on fire...
Retire me before I expire...
As the Sun leaves the clouds thicken and darken...
Without something to do, there is nothing really to look forward to...
Everything is cyclical...
Yes, life is recyclable...
Deliberate the world lesson by lesson...
Prosperity versus life's altitudes in the form of recession...
Desires filled with good and plenteous...
Duality of mankind versus the hard shine...

Things I Regret

Throughout the course of my life...
Trivial things haunt my memories...
From petty bodega theft as a youth...
To taking paths of least resistance...
The truth never set me free, often it pissed me off...
I was a hustler...
Candy on credit pusher...
Lawren dollar printer...
A hard headed; smooth escapist, kind of a child...
Underage to underage liquor distributor...
Suburban school hallways were my streets...
Maybe it was that honest grin...
Oh, that honest grin of mine...
Middle school, throwing pins in cake batter mad hatter...
Luckily we were caught for that...
The Good Bad Guy rumor to fight instigator...
The operation "break-up" plotter...
She was my woman first...!
Halloween candy from little kids; that was my trick or treat...
Jumping out of red trucks inebriated with Cisco and lawnmowers...
The chores we do for family...
From cornrows to hubcap snatching in public squares...
I dug up enough ground...
Moved enough dirt to bury the past...
Guilty by association...
Seems trouble had its way with following me...
For all the times I tried to do good...
Something held me down...
I was rather burdened...
Not to mention the hearts I broke; lint broke...

Womanizing was a talent of mine...
Aliases for the different districts...
The posse I was cool with, most I went to school with...
Disk Jockey LEG, a man to party with...
After school bus wars carried over...
To middle school morning bathroom wrestling matches...
Boiling our blood for home room...
Walking home sometimes; in case we had to dodge a bullet...
Spying against the spy that is stealing from I...
Forgetting prom dates on prom nights from different states...
I apologize, that was not cool...
God, good grades and my desire to succeed saved me...
Behind bars for stupidity...
Now I am cleaner than a bar of soap...
I had to pay the price...
Gambling was never my thing...
I never carried dice...
Bottom line, I did what I have done...
Things I am not able to take back, but chose to bounce back...
Not one person is perfect...
It is how we wake up in the morning...
Whether or not we choose to better ourselves...
I regret letting crack heads do work for me...
Giving fixes for free, never doing real work...
Illegally dumping debris in residential driveways during daylight hours...
Burn baby burn, fixated with circles of flame...
Forming smoke signals in empty dry grass patches...
I should have been home reading a book, I chose to strike matches...

Sparking the loudest firecrackers in quiet Mayberry areas...
It seemed those days were more than fun...
God, good grades and my desire to succeed saved me...
Strippers knew Mr. LEG by his tip name and famous grin...
Having a good time; always a way to claim notoriety...
I have done many things...
Many were good, others not so...
The DUI was the best thing that happened to me...
Losing a relationship, learning how to walk, examining my friends...
All that was good for me...
Learning my lesson as it comes back to me
Folded neatly and pressed with Karma...
God, good grades and my desire to succeed saved me...

Attractive

What makes you think you're attractive...?
Is it the clothes you're entrapped with...?
Gloss-free make-up, sexy wigs and pocketbooks; you're attached with...
Hiding you from me...
It took so long for me to realize...
Most importantly, for you to see...
The way you dance with me...
Momentary ecstasy, my life is a fantasy...
Her presence wipes me down...
Reformatting the tears of a clown...
Turning the frown upside down...
Independently, she calls my name...
Anecdote ally, she is my French maid...
Saying to me, "My face looks so familiar"...
"Oh it does, now how do you remember me...?"
Loving to call her name...
Chocolate diamonds are her eyes...
Her thighs just drive me wild...
Beyond the sixth sense she clairvoyantly moves me...

Gold, Silver, Bronze

Who am I competing with...?
Building to do what I want...
Really I do not want for anything; there is not much that I need...
Peace and water till I bleed debtless success...
There is no race...
Contests breed contestants...
This here is my testament...
I am here for a reason, knowing I am a bar...
A terrible force to reckon with...
Love me more than I...
I can walk much further now...
Not one thing is chasing me...
My "self" is an interesting individual...
Do not make me roar...
Packs of golden beak black eagles soar...
Rocks and the people that live under them...
Earth core low to my grounded plan...
Calmly hovering beyond intimacy...
Accomplishment is the gypsy of my imagination...
Calibrating my soul through the eyes of strangers...
Blessed enough to learn how to turn my cheek the other way...
Old enough to keep a grudge till my heart stops...
Gold strengthens bones...
Capillaries open, silver is used to heal bruises...
An interior lining for mirrors...
Ensuring the silver lining is well polished...
Bronze is an honored element...
Bronzing...
Sun bathing styles into existence, within surreal scenery...
Bronze shields us from disillusion...

A mostly humble element, statured to capture great memory...
Golden dust prevents my body from rusting...
Iron bridges crumble...
Vitamin B12 Bombers do not last forever...
Encrusted with silver lining...
Shining so you can see yourself...

Hosanna the Ninja

Standing still, the Warrior sensed an unusual breeze. Signaled by the Mantis to gather focus the Warrior gripped his sword and intensified the balance of his position. The wisdom of the Warriors' world was soon to change. Things happen for a reason. Slowing down the beat of his heart; the focused War God kneeled to the Earth's floor. Turning into a majestic picture; solidified as granite, the virtue of patience claimed the Warrior's essence. The scent of the blossoming pearl rose bushes simmered all throughout the air. Peace and water, were all the Warrior needed. Sipping on his tea, the Mantis homed in on the activity of a wrestling wind nearby. Psychically, the Warrior and Mantis are in tune with one another. From beginning to the end they find themselves seamlessly interacting, almost as if the Mantis is dictating the movement of the Warrior.

Through the corner of his eye an entrapping cloud appeared as if out of nowhere. Moving at the speed of "blur", a purple haze whirled throughout the Forest of Roses as if it were directed by a predefined reason. The Warrior's super conscious state was now ever more heightened to entertain the arising event. The purple haze; from so far away, was greeted by the still radiating heat of the Pheonix' arrival and departure. The scene was surreal. The purple "blur" astonishingly penetrated the fiery barrier. The Warriors' grip to his sword was insane; clinched to the Earth, his death-strike blow was identified and marked. Knowingly, nothing earthly could stop the proposed kamikaze blow of the Warrior. Evidently, the purple "blur" was not Earthly.

It was obvious; the purple haze was approaching the Warrior at dynamic speeds. Within the fraction of a second; the cloud stopped right at the brim of the Warrior as if its whole purpose was to confront him. The Warrior had no clue. The Warrior was strategically prepared to jump out from his stance and strike! Termination of the alien source was the Warrior's initial defensive intention. The purple haze was a cloud of containment.

A beautiful cloud to say the least; the Warrior investigated the gaseous entity. Still in a rocklike state the Warrior broke away from his attachment to the Earth and took the form of his usually magnificent posture. Stating to the purple cloud, "What will you have me do? You are here for a reason; I am not here to stop you. For most worldly things my strike would destroy. I am not here to injure my opportunity to grow stronger and wiser. I sense you are here to take me somewhere, discover new things and conceive things that I felt I never had a need to identify with. What it is you need I will do."

The purple haze then engulfed the Warrior. There was no need to struggle. As if reaching a new form of enlightenment, the Warrior underwent a supreme state of peace. The purple haze is now a glow that amplifies the Warrior's aura. Transformation was definitely taking place. The convulsions no longer could be controlled; it seemed as if the Warrior was changing shape. The Warrior's being began to change; he grew stronger, seeming wiser and more prepared. His personal armor became so beautiful; the aura of purple. He was refreshed. For six days the Warrior awaited the completion of his new state. On the seventh day;

through divine rest, a message came to the Warrior in the form of a prayer. The sky spoke to the Warrior...saying:

"Having to have had to work hard to get to where you are, never stop working as hard or harder now that you are here. Remember, you are not sure because you are not supposed to control everything. Your thinking is a function of consistent contemplation. My rain will quench the thirst of a nation. It is one thing to be steadfast in getting to your location to see nothing, then to slowly approach your destination to find out your objective has just passed you. Your purple glow is impregnable, it is backed by I. I am of you. I have gracefully allowed you to form your new physical and spiritual structure. I have kept you alive for a reason. Hosanna the Ninja will greet you shortly.

You will need for him to accompany you throughout your life especially the trials and tribulations, I assure will confront you shortly. Hosanna is of I. Hosanna is always around. He is your new purple shield. You will need your new armor to get you to the next frontier. Through this transition you have been blessed with a sharper sword; a sword that has been built and shaped, enabling you to cut through greater enemies. You will tend to a new battle; a new war is being defined. Bear witness to why the Phoenix has arisen and the Pack of Black Eagles are utilized for transport. Hosanna will always be with you; even when you feel he has left you, Hosanna will be there. Warrior, you are here for a reason. When I am done with you, I will gracefully take you back. I have made you; and if you attempt to deny my presence through your inequities, Hosanna will noticeably bleed strengths from you. Striking you where you stand. Hosanna is your rock."

Upon examining the course of his life, the Warrior awoke from his trance now with more guidance than ever before. The map of his path to follow was ironically burnt into his vision; the Warrior would never go astray from his mission. The Mantis began to fly, The Warrior began to walk down his newly defined path; glowing as a result of Hosanna. "Hosanna; blessed be the rock…my foundation", was the song the Warrior hummed to himself as he powerfully walked into the Forest of Roses.

Waiter for a Week

I use to be a waiter...
Waiting on tables for a tip...
I was not a good waiter...
Carrying half empty trays below the hip...
That job was a trip...
I really needed the money...
Cheap tippers are low-lifers, perpetrating to be the richest...
Penny pushers and quarter keepers, save the change bandits...
Realizing I had to make a change...
One way or another promotion would take place...
Steam cleaning dishes and pushing garbage, to taking orders with my pen...
Pushing mixed drinks to elders to hopefully loosen their pockets up...
I just wanted to pay for school...
Learning all types of better tipping tactics...
Garcon waiting table dramatics schedule 101...
500 more tables and everything will be cool...
No disrespect, I just could not see myself living off that check...
Minimal tips plus little check equals what the heck...?
I even had a full time job; making decent money...
Good benefits, casual business work attire, just out of college money...
What was I doing; I had nothing to prove...?
Learning another way of just how hard life could be...
Unappreciative people break people down...
There is a power of life and death in the tongue...
Gratuity is what it is, a form of thanks...

Cheap tippers are low-lifers and they should serve themselves...
Doing this for extra money, not for my health...
So I dropped that job...
Waiter for a week is what I tend to say...
Making sure you remember me from my tips...
Knowing how it was and is...
Waiting on people is not easy...
It takes a special person...

Sand Castles

Young at the beach moving sand around...
Voluntarily burying siblings...
Watching their hands wave from out the ground...
Out of boredom people do crazy things...
Constructing castles, pyramids and tall objects...
It seems so easy to build pyramids; settling for castles instead...
Knowingly, castles always get stormed...
Washing away with the tide...
I decide to go beyond the norm...
In a world where complexity derives simplicity...
Triangulating structures, preferring the pyramids...
Heaven on Earth places, mythically ruled by Isis and Osiris ...
Scattering broken sea shells that cover the beach...
Broken empty shells...
Vessels where life formed, lived in and journeyed with...
Telling a story of what once was...
Now a crude tool used to shovel the sand...
The evidence of life is omnipresent...
Sea gulls bob and weave begging for treats...
Splash, I am a big kid now...!
Let no approaching foot quake break this foundation...
No bolt of lightning shall crack the base of my sandy land...
Temptations to build castles...
Dilated, building the temples of men...
Coordinators de construction...
Back again to stack again...
Pointed temple tips poke the heavens...
Salt water massages the four slanted sides...
Cocooning my love for the simplicities of life...

Filling our ever-drying moat with little plastic buckets…
On a mission to build the biggest castle…
Do not hassle us we are focused…
Random containers shape our culture...
Castles rise through concept...
Ideally no form exists without an evident creation...
Their sand castles versus my pyramids…

Is it Jackson

So bad they created a category for him...
Choosing every generation...
Quincy Jones could only ambassador his style...
Jackson senior could only lead the way...
Labeled as the only "Prince"...
Formally known as the "Artist"...
The "King of Pop" is no longer here...
The "Man in the Mirror" looking at us...
Walking the earth's crust, embezzled with golden dust...
Sparkles in every direction...
The Mirrors Other Side reveals a challenged theme of existence...
This week is more than interesting...
Forever the June rain tames lightning and thunder...
The beast's belly is full now...
2009, a year for clan dismemberment...
It is true, melanin is most powerful...
Opening up your soul...
Going where no man has gone before...
Feeling needed to write this...
A seal has broken and an icon stolen...
Deferring to the sound of trumpets...
Concealed by harmony's mutual grip...
Mr. Jackson you were a key...
Musically; you made us turn channels, taking us to where we needed to be...
Dancing but not listening...
Hearts not following sacrifice and good intention...
Choosing to ignore your message...
We are the world, we are the children...
Still attempting to remind us...
Thriller was essential...

Hating the fact you were misjudged...
Instead of budging you moved away...
Fictitious judges jail us...
There will be no sequel...
Dirty Diana, aggressively rocking the guitar on your set...
Blessed by what gives us a little passion to do something with our lives...
Angels do take us away, death was not the point...
Joseph...we never coveted your jacket...
Able to walk amongst us for some reason...
No bar above or below...
No life is sanctioned from early release...
Reciprocity is not an equal reimbursement...
Tell me where the torch goes next...?
As a people, succession is incorrect...
This is it...

House of Men

Stop the lies, no surprises...
Tired of the falsities touching my mental...
The shades of my ethnicity transported through tragedy...
Welfare nation, the hesitation is we know the nation forces us...
Illegitimate trendsetters whip us into social conformity...
So tired of writing letters...
Travelling to the cells that house men of melanin...
Back again; to stack again, gentrify the foolish...
Placing skin on corpses of wise men...
Wondering when we will be back again...
21 gun salute the troop out the camp...
In the house of men...
Who is representing us this time...?
I expect so much more...
Recognizing there is so little time left...
Light torches, gallop horses, positively re-arrange our social structure...
Lustful untrusting thieves walk amongst us...
Most of them, a strong portion of us...
Godly self-proclamations will not get us back again...
In the house of men...
Guarded by Garvey, etched by Malcom and expressed through Dr. King's dream...
Truncating thoughts that will penetrate colorful social patterns...
Break, bash, topple...
Rebuild the house of men...
The melanin echelon is beyond upset...
Preferring "us" dilates the eyes of men...
Pretentions of brothers raping sisterhood...
Three quarters uncovered, she needs to cover up...

Pole dancing in the house of men...
The ignorant make it rain while malevolence starves the yard of men...
Reprint the North Star for a reason...
Death to the heathen and treasonous...
No longer needing them...
What is the point in feeding them...?
Red rivers flow through my bones...
America's subtle conversion to Amoney...
Sad thing is, "We" allowed this to happen...
Turbulent climates strive in the house of men...
Pseudo politic practitioners...
Mostly I question what is the point...?
Fathers are needed to form families...
Families contain communal values...
Fathers of families must form their own houses of men...
Stop pretending...
We the people are dying and the streets crying...
Stimulate your selves...
Throughout our own houses of men...
Born temperance, hereditary reflections, ancestral obligations...
Throughout our own houses of men...

Self-Publishing Mayhem

I wish to beat the system...
Crash, burn, topple and redefine...
Excavating green diamonds from under my ground...
Phrases in different formations, forcing you to think again...
Walking through the corridors of men...
Pretending I am just like them, that it is not the case...
Needing to be greater than stainless...
Crimson, lather and imperfection...
Life sentences make sense...
In between a flat media shaped world...
Packaging an old faith to scientifically hope for...
Seven pillars backed by two, strength and understanding...
Sacrifice to the point of literary crucifixion...
Pushing product till my feet bleed...
The junk in this trunk is funky...!
Profitable thoughts invoke my flesh to move forward...
Estoy muy bien, because I have to be...
Representing those that made men...
Lifting loose anchors; while walking the plank, ensuring ships sail...
Distributing golden packages of this self-published mayhem...
The first massive blast, presented by an uncanny cast of pressure treated emotions...
Writing this for me, to reach you...
Mapped expressions of how I feel...
My perception is I need to work harder...
Bodyguard my armor and continue to push forward...
Rain, hail, sleet or snow...
I will get my work in your hands...!

Steady Regulation

Stimulate me, as I am ready for new regulation...
Irate at the state of union...
Compensate the police to protect and serve, minus the confusion...
Health care systems do not care...
Disparities of the civilized thought process...
Pan handling Amoney's paid up citizenry...
Ridiculous how much they legally take from "We"...
Frustrated for no real reason...
Benedict equals two eggs and bacon, traitors in the mist...
Time to renovate memories of the disillusioned...
Monopolistic illusions economically choke the system...
Bionic ally raising right fists, politicians cross fingers ...
In love with the struggle...
New regulation equals a new bubble containing "WE" the people...
Hesitation divided the thought...
Quality wisdom combusts my earthly vessel...
Where is Jachin, true pillars of needed strength and establishment...?
Feeling sorry for the folk still on the slave ship, enjoying the free ride...
N166A affects the white establishment too ...
Sleeping General is the good bad guy...
New Jersey tax rebellion...
Disgruntled New York transit traveler...
The people trying to make it are slimming down...
Daring you to continue to tax us...
Value versus the anti-trust...
Stagflating globalized values since it barely affects them...

Where the blocks rot, Amoney decides to tax the hardest...
The Placist will be broken into pieces...
God bless the first fire man, sizzle the giants to a crisp...
Letting caged animals out is a bad thing...
Did you not hear the lions roar...?
Did you not see the phoenix emerge from the Sun and soar...?
Putting us to work to feed the rich, while ignoring the poor...
Now who is knocking at your door...?
Why steal from me; from us and my family...
Amoney you are doing the wrong thing...!
Dependent on this weak system...
Indulging each victim's mentality...
Hold my salary and tax me...
Did they forget who built this country...?
When did affirmative action stop being good management...?

Birds Chirp

Love...
A word taken so lightly...
Oh, how much I love you...
Hydrogen resides in my psyche and highly combustible without you...
The notion of you plus I...
The wisdom of our Sun kissing the sky...
Birds chirp perched on branches manifesting avalanches...
All in chorus; chirping gorgeous feedback...
No matter where you go I will follow your crystal water flow...
Water diamond paradox your imperialism and prided train of thought...
Repeating all I know...
Chirping for a reason...
The world can still be a pretty place...
Either way, peacocks cannot fly...!
The prettiest bird squawks...
So next to me, she chirps to me...
Growing grapes to feed you…
Sifting through raspberry wine galleries to tease you…
It is so hard not to love her...
Complimenting each other...
Two exotic fruits...
Mixing, making the best juice...
Texas birds do not fly through New York suburbs…
One in the same, I cannot complain...
I know God made you, between War and Dinner...
You are my common bond...
Your face is beyond illustrious...
Bathing in purple ponds while fluttering our wings...
A chirp introducing the morning dew…

Petitioning rocks to skip closer to you...
Sleepless nights in awe of the moon...
Heart beats instigate melodic temperaments...
Peppermint wrapper umbrellas capture candy rain drops...
Getting too close to you and I cannot stop...
The parades' renegade, I am watching you...
She wanted me to chirp I am sorry...

Dollars de Lawren

Confessions of a candy pushing kingpin...
Wrigley's gum 10 pack per unit distributer...
A nerd selling Nerds to nerds...
You can get the candy later, pay me now...
Candy credit card processor...
Hand to hand candy combat...
Hand picking little sugar feigns before they became teens...
See, the change in your pocket is mine...
Left pocket filthy rich with big faced silver mint...
Right pocket bulging with candies the kiddies like...
I was a bike riding bandit...
Bag full of new product for the same customers...
Trekking Drake Lane was insane, but I did it...
Mission operative...
No one but me push candy to my associates...
Operation: "Open More Distribution Centers"...
Squeeze out all competition...
Ethiopians love Swedish Fish...
Germans love Jolly Ranchers...
Knowing what you like...
Switching you up when my suppliers offer two for one sales...
Compliment how I substitute your preference...
You want some candy...?
All the young chic's loved me...
DJ LEG...
Lemonhead supplies are high...
No sales; no discounts, I have what you need...
Reminiscing how I fathered so many...
A rare few appreciated Good and Plenty...
Favorite movie, "Charlie and the chocolate factory"...

STOP REMAKING CLASSICS...!
Dreams of becoming Willy Wonka's protégée...
Wicked transportation logistics...
The realisms of my life at a juvenile age...
Neighborhood dentists confront me to continue pushing product...
Never robbed from at that age...
Mom, can I go shopping with you...?
Throwing Big League Chew and everlasting Gobstoppers in the carriage...
Pushing candy for a reason...
The proceeds let me buy things...
My own hustle, Sopranos who...?
Putting partners to work...
Employees received discounts only on dollar bonus days...
Open L-Credit was scrutinized each and every day...
Lawren Dollar money converted to candy back to more money...
Distributing dividends to the candy soldiers, since we were a team.
Sixth, seventh and eighth grade hallways I operate now...
Kicking rocks at the bus stops each and every day...
Planning out supply side logistical challenges...
Nobody move, no body get hurt...
Love me, this is my story...
Printing press, oh printing press...
Print the Dollar de Lawren...
Pushing evident credit in the halls...
Before knowing what debt was, they paid me...
Lawren Greene, the candy factory...!
If I can live, watch what I give to society...
Original sweet tooth drug mover...
Cocaine has nothing on sugar cane...

Drugs are so legal...
Amoney cares less in regards to us...
"G" brothers backed me...
Cocky and humble because I had to be...
Till one day a Lawren Dollar was retrieved by the wrong hands...
Still my product was in demand...
The wrong streets were watching...
Every business has snitches...
Every graveyard has open ditches...
I made my money; showed myself I could hustle...
That was just the beginning...
Closure of the middle school sugar cartel was eminent...
I needed a creative hiatus...
How long do you think I rested...?

Cobblestone Entrance

Take that idea and turn it into a rock...
Pressurize that rock to be coal...
Coal burns, gold melts and iron smelts...
Black smoke clouds penetrate the atmosphere...
There is a reason for composition...
Constant transition is what makes us more desirable...
Change in conditions justify itself...
Knowing before your started what needed to be done...
It is the composition of the pieces...
I am so in the caves...
These stones land mark my home...
Tea kettles on a Sun spot, boiling my throne...
Wishing things were easier than what they seem...
Green moss grows alongside my entrance...
Critters jitter as they approach the solid oak door...
Leaves fall from trees hiding my entrance...
Forming from rough to smooth, the cobblestone becomes petrified...
Nothing stares at the entrance...
Sunrays glare at the lonely existence...
The pretense is something is a function of nothing...
Living in the crevasse of a cave...
A dormant idea with an opportunity to form...
Draw your own world...!
The blind are closest to different dimensions...
Measurement stabilizes perspective...
Yet, there is an entrance...
The art of sight is both a gift and curse...
There is a theory associated with interruption...
The cobblestones are relative, the entrance is interpretive...
Treasures are not hidden in obvious places...

Life Sentences in Sentences

Bombarded by quotes throughout the day...
Attempting to understand foreign philosophies...
The word of man can get tricky...
Deliberating contained emotions from the past...
There is a power of life and death in the tongue...
Dollars in the Bible pages binding my church and state...
Meanwhile, I am bleeding inside...
Constantly reminded of why a soldier moves...
People will pick and choose what I have to say...
Evoke and inaugurate your own session...
Learn life's lessons and manifest your blessings...
Borrowing wisdoms from the past to enhance your formula...
Educated and not making sense...
Complexity derives simplicity...
Shaping the ending, disregarding the beginning...
Preferring to breed with the nations...
African Americans merging with the Haitians...
Gradual creation of this user manual...
Read it slowly, digesting too fast may be too much to handle...
Dismantling my life in third person often makes me think...
Dancing on purple oceans and I do not want to sink...
Influential people can change the state of time...
Lengthy periods of struggle demand attention...
Life is an interesting observation...
Follow the voices in my head...
Do better by my own self, overwhelmed by other's suggestions...
Sticks and stones break bones; while the tongue is a weapon...

Forsaking Nourishment

Indulging this state of duality...
Wasting my salary on empty calories...
Reality hits the hardest when I am hungry...
Cascading loneliness when she is not there...
Munch on memories of the last dance...
Blood veins thirsting for more pressure...
I give her massages in mount airy lodges...
Trust, I know how things are supposed to be...
Never will she be thirsty since my soul hugs her...
I am the Mantis and this is my mantra...
Without the Sun we cannot see the rain...
It seems I had to leave for things to make sense...
Past tense means nothing to me, while I am in it...
My dreams are movie scenes waiting to be explored...
Consciously analyzing the world from different directions...
Is anybody watching me...?
Is my life greater than what yours is supposed to be...?
Mechanically, my hunger dissolves complexity...
Could war be a devil's dinner...?
Does God struggle to love every one of us...?
I had to wait to get to where I planned...
Entering a volume of transition through travel...
This piece is harder than prior...
Chasing down my desires with a full tank of accomplishment...
Stop forsaking nourishment...

Am I the Muse

So much to choose from so little time…
Expose my thought and share my mind…
You look at me, I look at you…
You get inspired…
What am I supposed to do…?
What is so genuine about what you see…?
Am I the muse anticipating your delivery…?
Chain reactions exploding all around me…
Normalcy is the hardest sport…
There is no game plan, just keep moving forward…
Tolerate the little things; life is what it seems…
Pictures without titles make more sense…
For now keep shining, this little light of mine…
Burning both ends of the candle; dismantling who I used to be…
Am I the muse…?

The Cloud is a Man

The cloud is a man...
Overstanding what was; contemplating what is...
On a hot day shade deserves itself...
Weak dedication is blowing your talents away...
I am breathing slower these days...
The cloud is a woman...
Her face twists and turns...
Thoughts like the color of raindrops...
The wind is so arrogant...
Transporting the dynamics of a misty vision...
Fiery smoke blemishes everything...
The skyline is painting a heightened picture...
Not much can hide from a cloud...
The race is on...!
Iron birds disfigure her face...
Now which cloud is the fastest...?
Cloud quantity means nothing...
Cloud's compromise with the sky; while playing poker...
Capture a dream in my cloud, as smoke fills my air...
The inspiration of an image changes; as she twirls her hair...
Most times I drink by myself...
Watching the clouds, wondering what they will tell me...
Imagine storm filled passion; dancing in a pageant...
The formation of a thrifty circus tent...
At night; sifting through atmospheric activity...
Hiding the North Star which always appeared for me...
In between the mayhem of men, everything needs its rest...
All for the best I guess...
The cloud I saw I will not see again...
Comprehensive thought dilates my eyes...

God is greater than good...
Could there be anything other than this gifted scenery...?
Walking on sunshine, sipping peach moonshine...

Scratching at the Bars

Everything in a day...
It is never a good thing to think you have someone figured out...
Life is not a predictable animal...
The Lion Roars in a cage...
I am scratching at the bars...
Inching my way out of this location...
Trust and believe thy mental is in formation...
While the energy is here the platform must be set...
Working within a two year mark...
Soliciting marksmen, for when Mark's men start pushing the material...
Rolled formula scribes pass in between the bars...
Leaving my pride on The Mirror's Other Side...
So tired of this walking and waiting mess...
A sparrow's bone marrow will not serve me...
See, I am hungry and need to feed...
This cell could be a place of safety...
Keeping I away from I, as I put things together...
Eventually these bars will thin, rust and bust...
I will continue scratching at them...
Looking out from within...
I see more bars outside these bars...
Wondering who is looking in...?
Is this for my correction...?
Locked up for public protection...?
Racial collection is what it seems...
My bones are stronger than wood; which is stronger than steel...
Colossus over Iron man...
My blood is thicker than water which is finer than mercury...

Sampson over Hercules...
Basically, these bars are nothing to me...
Cleopatra over Elizabeth...
Creative hiatus, internally chasing oasis...
Manifesto de Lawren...
This book is ahead of me, but I had to write it...
I am doing what I have to do and hope you love it...
Stick to the plan...
Stay inside these bars, so you can overstand...
There are more bars beyond theses bars...
Thus, I continue scratching...
My trajectory is to be ahead of me...
No longer comfortable within these bars...
I do this so you know we can break free...
Mentally, these things are very simple...
I wrote me so you can quote me...
I am one of five...
Visibly invisible...
Hiding where I survive...

Ontos Firing at Night

When I die I will see you later...
Sons turn to fathers...
Untimely, we learn the simple definitions of war...
There is a purple heart pinned to my chest...
Bronze and silver medals decorate the breast
Blasted up, broken and bothered...
Post traumatic syndrome happenings occur as the soldiers come home...
Thrown to a chair of wheels; esthetic limbs are hard to work with...
Who is the Unknown Soldier...?
Truly hating what war does to men...
So many volunteer for their unknown destinies...
Amoney take care of your responsibilities...
Still remembering the Ontos cackling at night...
I was a little boy; vicariously waking up to the screams of a broken father...
But I am so fortunate; those that serve deserve more attention...
Welcome home parties and Veteran's Day parades are not enough...
War is tough, bullets are hard to dodge...
Who remembers who, when you get out the zoo...?
To say we had a real reason to fight is ridiculous; when two fish and five loaves fed so many...
Two big M50's and six big Cannons...
Government issued men and women so far from home...
Welcome to war's terror dome...!
Killing the enemy with piping hot lead love...
Secluded lightning bolts from distant mountain ranges light up the sky ...

Puff the Magic Dragon arrives; breathing fire to save the day...
Fertilizing jungle soil with the blood of men...
"LIG" praying to the lord to stay alive...
Pushing armory against Vietnamese trajectories...
Ernie, "LEG" and Earl undiscovered...
Fire the Ontos at night; star light, star bright...
Imagine how many stars this Ontos will fire tonight...
Fire fights are surreal and scary...
For a hippy that does not understand, hide in the burning field of Amoney's dreams...?
Doing damage to other lands...
Battalions and companies carried by battle carriers...
Respecting the smell of napalm in the morning...
Catching souls in M50 shell containers; shells not from hell or heaven...
Load the fireworks and prepare the main event...
The ants go marching up and down the same mountain...
See joy without pain, is like sunshine without rain...
Really who is winning...?
Who is the Warrior; conqueror or destroyer...?

Heartbeats in the Rain

I feel impossible; yes, I am possible...
Oh how I walk through the rain...
I wait for the rain...
The rain drops fall and I listen...
Forever the clouds have been telling me something...
Things take time...
I greet them with open arms and weather charms...
Summer heat dissolves the gaseous landscape...
Thunder rumbles amidst the sky above me...
This is lovely; standing here attracting only the lonely drops...
Compelled to grab every Earth bound drop...
Wet virgin burdens dropping on me to refresh and revitalize...
Insanity reminds me of a good life...?
My colors remain, but I am melting away...
Disguise my pain in the rain, loving it...
Starting from the bottom, working my way to the top...
Dowsed between reality and a wet dream...
Umbrella me for what; raindrops hug me...
I am a plant and it is time to grow again...
It all makes sense to me...
Dance in the rain...

Society has its ways

Trouble, hmmm...
My troubles may help change the world a bit...
Seems "WE" are not meant for recognition...
Real equality is my position...
Socio-economic conditions surround US; breaking down US...
Most times I am far from home...
Throne less; so many people are boneless...
Please forget the skin...
It will take a long time to see a REAL social win...
Calibrating false focal points...
Only lubricating the pleasure joints...
The thief in the night is without question...
Morality seems to have a lesser view...
Always the few do the work of many...
The coins' sides are the same; what is the point in flipping...?
Steadily rain-checks fall on deserted people...
Grateful, since I have only what I need...
Current directions supersede protection...
It seems we are on our own...
When the supermarket closes, where do you go to eat...?
When the public park has no benches, where do you go to sit...?
When the picket has no fence, what then contains the struggle...?
Will the blue fish follow when the flood is here...?
It is a new day for the blue jay...
Most only see what they understand...
The word is not good these days...!
The WORD cannot be forgotten...
It is necessary that we create our own...

Buy our own land and build homes...
When necessary shake the discouragement...
Evidently the giants are falling...!
Reconstruct our own throne...
WE have been eating sour apples; denying the nutrients...
WE want fresh apples...!
Blessings of the sunshine versus skin cancer...
How long can WE remain lower than where WE are...?
I cannot help it...
I expect more from WE for US...!

Bonding Broken Attachments

From young to old; grand to miniscule...
Why should I care about things that mean less than what I am...?
Is a rock more important than I...?
Should a catfish die if I am not hungry...?
Tired of questioning morality...
Truly I vibe with nature...
Are we not like the Earth...?
Stars birth stars...
Still I remain a true meat eater...
Retreating from my headstrong social sense...
The pretense of ignorant is foolish...
Some things in life we have to let go...
Attachment mud wrestles desire in a forest fire...
Cope and comprehend the elements of existence...
The man plays his guitar in a daytime park tunnel just for us...
Fried chicken at picnics with no napkins, just horrible...!
How many people can continue to eat from my plate...?
Completely misunderstood...
Call broken arrow...
The unnecessary promotions of evil beings misdirect trust...
Let us understand what is really going down...
The essence of attachment is a simple force...
Every action requires an equal or opposite reaction...
To break is to disassociate...
Dark season rearranged through the breath of light...
In the beginning, the Creator formed what was meant to be...
The heaven and Earth was formed first...
Supporters that just talk are not necessary...

Unfriendly is to be broken in a game, unaware that you are playing...
Critical mass dictates an entity to change, maintain or dissolve...
My kind is meant to break to re-associate...
The answer is what makes us...
To complete is to do...!
Machetes in the window sill, for when the neighborhood breaks down...
So in between the underprivileged...
Nightmares I now know how to break apart...
See, the soul of LEG is impregnable...
No matter how much blood leaks, everyone will eat...
To complete is to do...!
Bonding broken attachments are necessary for us to become closer to one...

The Waters of Knowledge

Fighting in the middle of the night...
Star light; star bright, we fight...
I know you are tired...
The goal is to stay alive...
The benefit of all is beyond this gate...
Without what equals war...?
Where are we supposed to go; what are we supposed to do...?
In light of all we have done...
Still in preparation for what we need to do...
Should we come back home...?
Does our home still stand as it once did...?
I dreamt the pyramids fell because of us...
In God we trust the all Seeing Eye...
Migrating the army; feeling them spy on me...
The host is mine as I multiply...
Water AKA "Host"...
Sleeping General's slumber causes trouble...
The wise despise this character of writing...
Invoking the spirits of man...
Overstanding the reality of war is devastation...
Imagining what happens to the sky when death fly's past...
Trust, let blood pressure burst...
Stealing the thirst of the needy...
Look, the giants are falling...
Getting up faster now than ever before...
Declaring independence when one cannot swim...
The waters of knowledge we must cross...
I am addicted to this throne...
Warriors grow wings to fly forever...
It is the sacrifices that we as people decide to make...

Joshua, make them shout seven times before the walls crumble...
So invisible, I was meant to do this...
Materializing my mentality for a reason...
Children sing for me...
Selah, God ensure the soldier makes it back home safely...
Focusing on the waters of knowledge...
The terrain is changing, the charter is the same...
The mission is resurrected...
The waters of knowledge contain the doctrine of overstanding...

"Rose Gardens in Atlantis"
Volume 8

Entrance to an Exit

The exit has an entrance...
To leave a decision must be made...
Payment is not required; I choose to go home...
Shooting clay plates with buck shells is rather easy...
Sometimes a choice is not evident...
Involuntary exits are instant requests to travel elsewhere at that moment...
Get your mind right and bear witness to atonement...
Why should we understand...?
The physical option is we are here...
The basics are the beginning...!
Foundational truisms...!
My dream is one day we will exit the falsities of the world equally...
Good spirits cover me at the entrance...
Hungry black painted lions greet me to meet me...
At this point, feel this energy...
There are so many gates we need to pass...
Exiting to a new entrance...
A way of life through strong praise and compassed truth...
Nothing new can come from what is not tested beyond regularity...
Selah, now faith is the substance of things hoped for, the evidence of things not seen...
The trying of your faith worketh patience...
From physical to biblical; the father becomes the son, becoming the father...
Vibrations coming from the horns sharpen my focus...
Follow me through this exit; for all good things that take place...
There is an equal and opposite evil building its' essence...

Harbored pain and anguish is finally making sense to me...
The pieces were always revealed...
It took I to realize my mission cannot be forsaken; beyond this current phase...
The title of my grave is heaven...
For when I am weak I am strong...!
How fast do we need to work...?
What do we need to do...?
Lack of summer leads to cold winters...
This recession is hedged; designed for someone else's protection...
Geographies have different climates...
Limitations are similar, not the same...
I choose to be prepared as I enter a new exit...

Knockem X

I am not the BEST yet...
Still resting with tons of stress...
Receiving and respecting the blessings that are carving me...
Becoming the name I lost, Champion...
I am defining my role in life...
Proverbial Psalms raise me higher....
Things take time...
The beginning phases craved me to ask for more...
The Sun needs my heart, feeding me the light...
180 degrees of public privacy, eyeing me down at the liquor store...
Welcome to New Jersey; farming the Internet...
The fruits were no longer low hanging when I departed...
Things were not so easy; becoming harder, lacking my presence...
Overstand this eyes precision design...
Truthful decisions invigorate my faith through religious concentration...
Horns, harps, snares and dreams woke the Sleeping General...
Distilling this chemical village...
The temperature of heaven's tears soothes even the savage beast...
Hell still remains pumping through my veins...
Life recycles tons of slackers...
Messing with my ability to monopolize the facility...
Go to the ant, thou sluggard; consider her ways, and be wise...
I am not the BEST; yet, still resting with tons of stress...
More blood must pour out of me...
Unless you fear what you cannot see...

Never cut into turmoil without an expectation…
What to do when unstoppable forces come to meet you…?
Greeting you with intentions of bleeding and mistreating you…
Beyond hope at this point…
Becoming the critic I have chosen to criticize myself…
The horizon I see is right in front of me, I am not here to quit…
Forfeiture is not a part of my nature; completion is a relative sensation…
A journey of truth is exposing me to the truisms of life…

The Difference Between

The difference between a performer and one who does…
A performer can repeat…
Given the opportunity; one who does, does it…!
Inevitably "one who does" has to do it…!

The Saga of "If I had"

If I had, I would have done...
Thus, I chose to create through faith...
I believed in what I could do, I did all that I saw...
Going for what I wanted, taking what I needed...
Manifesting my own evidence through transition...
Preparing for the favor of grace...
Understanding is a function of the overstand...
I used to think I was not equal to what I am...
Determining I needed to be greater than what I was...
Taking scars alongside both eyes as a youth so I could see straight...
These accomplishments are what I did...
There is a difference between heat and the Sun...
Still scratching at the bars...
Blood leads to the heart, vessels separate like stems...
Procrastinate for what...?
Prolonging life is immortal...
Delete the heart and wonder where the Word will flow...?
The spirit is contained within thought...
Catching up with your destiny...
The saga of "If I had"...
Questioning the presence of what makes sense...?
I love you in a dream...
Je t'aime dans un rêve
Electric kisses steam water...
The nuclear reaction associated with chemical combustion...
Lack of the spirit; or what is not meant to be, reveals itself...
We are just vessels, the dream is already declared...
The Saga of "If I had"...

Balding of the Trees...

Balding of the Trees...
Lack of leaves due to those that fell too soon this year...
It is so hard looking from the outside in...
This day is not new, I have seen it before...
Experiencing how the father becomes the son, becomes the father...
Acknowledge how the mother becomes the daughter, becomes the mother...
Blue firmaments lead us to the land...
Walking on a lie is a burning experience...
Reading Psalms, I sought righteousness one hundred and fifty five times...
Salvation is far from the wicked: for they seek not thy statutes...
As I watch the leaves fall...
A leaf for a word, a tree for religion...
A forest for all the occurrences of our carbonated lives...
Changing of the scenery...
Green denies the color of fading away...
Realizing the mistakes I have made...
Choosing to walk a quiet life...
Walking over what has fallen, for me to see it...
Just to be a part of the terrain, even in the rain...
The scenery is meant to change...
Which branch contains the breath of my knowledge...
Fruitfully the tree produces a natural symphony orchestrated by the winds' breeze...
Blowing leaves off the trees, stubbornly I try to catch them...
They try to rest when landing on my chest...
I keep hearing the chainsaws dropping trunks...

Destroying the life force of my thought process so I can write on it…
Life needs the little budding blossoms…
Recreational therapy is walking through them…
The valley of un-risen men…
Trees show me what happened so clearly to the geography…
Sometimes the ground cannot support the roots…
Carrying my ax; swinging at the innocent, acknowledging the wrong facts…
Following where the four winds blow…
Constantly in a state of confusion…
This illusion is a scenery that meant so much to me…
The tragedy is that leaves fall from trees…
Landing on my chest to rest…
All for the best I guess…

Golden Apples

Apples are red, golden is hue...
Choosing to eat from the hue of God's blessings...
Lessons learned through study...
Concerned by what we choose to eat...
Yet I am not perfect...
I bite the apple...
Just take, do not ask of me...
Build what you now have for the benefit of us...
Golden apple, the importance of my life...
Reasons why we met...
God, gracefully bless the music between us...
No more need for me to question...
Biting the apple because these are the Psalms of our lives...
Selah, thank you for this occasion...
I only wish for the best beyond revelations...
Loving the performance...

Discombobulating

VMA (Video Music Awards) allowed Satan to climb a huge step...
So many working for the devil...
So many foot soldiers, the tiers are not equal...
Temptations of Revelations cause seals to be broken...
Amoney so readily available to distribute and slay men...
The mayhem is WE allow it...
Do families have different needs overseas...?
The devil smokes a fat pack in IRAQ...
Mountaintops of bombarded innocent souls our troops patrol...
Hugging the concept of mass destruction...
Amoney's generals are the landlords...
Guns versus swords...
Sedimentary rocks versus steel missiles...
Chemical warfare rains down on us...
Vitamin packed water versus soda pop...
Formaldehyde layers the brain, a by-product of the need to be skinny...
The value meal is an expensive banana peel...!
Cell phones roam in our ears causing tear drops...
Crack cocaine reduces migraines...
Discombobulating...
Plastic surgery tends to bury the past...
Vaccinations are necessary...
Flying past the swine flu...
Dirty needles wash along our coastline...
Discombobulating...
Guerilla troops in the Congo play bongos watching men rape men in villages...
Victory through trickery, truisms are no longer evident...
Social unrest in the West, our days are outnumbered...

Child molestation while on vacation...
Our days are truly numbered...
Mixing of the races, some say dilute cultural values...
Manufacturing evil spaces, it is never the time for that...
Virtually, it is in style to kill a man with your bare hands...
The sons of Satan are many, coming up from the inferno too fast...
GOD is almighty...
Calmed in the covenant of his open arms...
Questioning the sanity of civility...
Is this a part of the divine trilogy...?
Internet stalkers sit on couches; sipping on Starbucks, stealing identities...
Now I need fraud protection...
Friendly phonies can only steal from me...
Ah We Enemy...
Subsidizing cash crops to liquidate equity stocks...
Many hunger and will die this winter...
Neglect and disrespect are leading causes to cancer...
The state of the world's Self-Inflicted sickness...
Discombobulating...

The Alarm Clock

I wake up to some of the craziest thoughts. It is almost as if I had an option to change some of my daily routine. Sooner than later I will, as soon as I can. Initiated by the sound of a strong distinct buzz the morning starts off at 5:30. The snooze button at that moment is my only savior. Awake but barely conscious I consider the penalty associated with tardiness. It is too cold outside and my heater is operating at a minimal. The thick quilt-like covers and fluffy pillows are my only sanctuary to any form of hyperthermia preserving needed body temperature. Drifting back to sleep but not fully successful since the snooze is only temporary. I am positioned close to that clock waiting in anticipation to hit it again when it sounds. The paralyzing noise hums again; only louder this time than before, right on time as I expected. As I tap on the adjacent clock the secondary clock goes off. Only this time the other clock sits on a wall in another room. This clock talks at 6:00; lasting for a minute, it sings the song "Back to Life" by Soul to Soul. I am forced to move to the loud rhythm, only after the vibrations energize my soul.

Happy to be alive, upset that I have to prepare for the new cold day. The shower wants me to turn it on. My favorite song is over now and I am out of bed. Operating on auto-pilot I witness the green eyes of my black cat pounce on me. Norelco is his name and he is a street famous black feline. This is the time of the early morning when he decides to go bonkers in an elated state throughout the second floor. Clean water in his bowl is the only thing that will quiet the little guy up. So I pour only the finest water from the Poland springs into his bowl.

While trying to piece together my dreams from just a few hours ago I open my closet in search of the perfect black outfit. Most of the time, I forget to iron my garments the night before. Regardless, thou must walk into the public so fresh and so clean. For this very reason I felt it critically necessary to invest in my super-duper commercial steam presser. This steam pressure is so awesome I think people may be envious of it. Basically I press since there is no need to iron anymore.

There really is no need to open the window shades in the morning. The Sun is still enjoying its' rest from a hard day's work yesterday. Instead I draw attention to my cool brown canvas and leathered boots. These boots are pretty original looking as I slip them on my precious feet. The only thing distracting me at this point is Norelco and his inquisitive black paws childishly swiping at my leather laces as I make an honest attempt to tie them tightly. I guess that is his way of saying thanks for the water buddy. My pressed black outfit is on, shoes tied tight, work badge around my neck, and the much needed wallet is tightly fitted into the trusty grey over-the-shoulder messenger bag. Most importantly I reach for my two deadly weapons, my Blackberry and my Palm handheld cellular devices. Every extra-terrestrial must have a way to remotely phone home. Since it is a winter wonderland in New Jersey it becomes more than absolutely necessary to venture towards the classy coat closet and make a fine matching selection. It sure took some time to get the jacket inventory up to par. With the double insulated jacket, please believe the notorious accompanying red and white striped skull cap and smooth scarf are enrolled in the day's outdoor journey. An exposed bald head in the winter time is literally suicide; especially in the negatively degreed wind-chilled weather.

Glancing at the tic-toc clock the time is now 6:30 A.M Eastern Standard. "The Sun Will Come Out" it is just still too early. Shucks, I get up earlier then the birds these days. Reaching for the phone I make the usual call to the Yellow Taxi Company. At this point the phone number is burnt into my memory.

The Mantis Rides

How can the Mantis be so important? Throughout the course of millennia he has prevailed. Yet and still if he is lucky, he can get away with more than one impregnation. The Mantis finds a way to capitalize his self. Against all things that take place that are beyond truism; the Mantis finds a way to make some type of sense out of civility. The Mantis will hide and flourish. He is an alien to this world, but he resides because he is needed. A defender of truth and prosperity; when he ceases to exist, where and or what kind of sense will the world make? The Mantis lies within his disguised form; but he is most powerful, even within his miniaturized state. When he is ready he will devour. There is the least thing that can stop him! The Mantis is fast and uncanny, flying away when he needs to at any given moment. When you are born with nothing to do but conquer, then what else is there to do?

The Mantis has been watching the Warrior grow into the War God throughout his few realized generations. Things take time, and the Mantis has always been aware. Quite the philosopher, the Mantis has a story and pilgrimage of his own. To the Warrior the Mantis has always been a pleasurable scene of contempt. The Warrior has no clue what the Mantis has stored for him with respect to the mission which awaits him. The Mantis has disguised his presence as he anticipates the revelation of what the Warrior has become and will eventually succumb to. The Mantis stares into the reddening Sun examining all that needs to be done as it draws closer to the dusk of day. The Mantis continues to follow the Warrior through flight.

The Warrior travels forward engraving a fresh new path within the Forest of Roses. Illuminating his new purple essence he is now moving along an unforeseen direction for a reason. Hosanna is there witnessing and guiding the Warrior's each and every step. At that very moment the Warrior stops, raises his royal sword, and angelically screams the following: "I truly hate it when people attempt to recreate perfection!" Stopping in his unmarked tracks the land trembled and a majestic rock formed from the essence of the Earth at the same position Hosanna stood. Hosanna quietly kneeled in front of the Warrior's feet and stated: "Follow me War God; you are reaching perfection, follow me and you will see. Young War God you must complete your distance through the Forest of Roses. Your future and family awaits us at the Golden Gate. I am Hosanna! I am a function of your sorrow contained in your passion. I am your light when you are hit by the soon to come paralyzing effect of the Empirical's Triple darkness. The Phoenix will be back soon. You were built beyond your prior existence for six days. Within that time of internal transformation you were anointed with the six powers of the Empirical. You were then faced to the East on the seventh day; the place of the light, to acknowledge the Empirical's existence. I am here to show you how to approach the East in a proper manner. Young War God we have no time to haste, I can hear the giants are falling and we must get to the Golden Gate. Follow me, and you will see. When you reach perfection you will have overcome many foes and challenges. Acquiring the necessary lessons through perception to manifest and ordain your destined world.

The Warrior appreciatively looked directly into the blinding eyes of Hosanna and continued his forward progress through the Forest of Roses. Finally he realizes his commodity has a purpose.

Master Planner

My style is proverbial...
Intentions of rebuilding what was destroyed...
One of Five...
Continuing to learn the ways of this world...
I pick and choose whom to work with; business is personal to me...
Electrical mental exertion will drain your temple...
Rescheduling resources is necessary in this world...
Burry me for a reason...
Heavenly metallic composites protect my conscious...
Balancing scales entails true focus...
The strength of the people that made me; hurt me, making me stronger...
Pressuring a green diamond is not a good thing...
Please follow me...
This destiny has room for more than me...
Turning sand to glass so you could see my ambition...
The Speed of Life manifests my ammunition, SALVO...!
Sacrifice as life volunteers others...
Bronzing rock to brick ensuring you realize the strength of Hosanna...
Heavenly metallic composites protect my conscious...
Spiritual melodies physician my soul so I can control more...
I see the demons peeking trying to hide their disguise...
Still I rise...
Truth be told, my soul is old...
Musical instructions place me into a state of preparation...
Discover, design, develop and deploy concentrated retaliations...
The Sleeping General was my temporary form of hesitation...

Constantly persuaded to rebuke my inequities...
Deviation from this set plan will or cannot happen...
Encourage me if I choose follow...
Dissention rests amongst the lowest places...
These many faces are really I...
Peace and water through knowledge and wisdom...
If you see me crying, that means we are dying...!
Cocooning industrial stimulation...
Situations will not get stronger due to you...
Please forgive me...
Anatomically indoctrinating this thesis for centuries...
Remember We are derived from Us...!
Lusting the fire that drowns I...
Defining WaterMannyFaces through vernacular...
Based on all that is not correct...
The character of mankind is hard to find...

The Antithesis of Neither

I had to leave...
My sanities have been stretched and wrung...
Hung and slung to the point where I just stopped talking...
Attempting to save my faith through God's grace...
Showing praise through my hands...
Needing to build further, only confusing the enemy...
I had to leave...
Ah We Enemy...
There is no exception to structure...
My only goal is to finish the race...
Truly seeking his face...
Throwing off everything which entangles I...
Hindered, allowing splinters to pierce my heart...
This race is a chase that confuses my enemies...
Since his grace is greater than any one law...
I have lost my life; please do not miss me...
The antithesis of neither...
Sounds awesome, and seems even better...
Did you leave for me...?
Attempting to achieve wisdom through sobriety...
The past if forgotten...
There is no point in analyzing the commonalities of what was...
We all have a breaking point...
Personal mental recovery...
Thou must break, or thou will be broken...!

Three Guns

My brother had three guns...
He got them for three sons...
One day all the guns were stolen...
The Sun never shined the same way...
All his jewelry was taken...
His mental was shaken...
It was time for him to get away...
His days were forsaken...
Violently his reality was taken ...
Silently he prayed to his maker...
Introduction to Diamond Dynamite...!
Wealth sacrificed to save sanity...!
His mentality was designed to save his family...
For fun my brother blasted his guns...
Letting the world know how he stood...
Where he stood, even when he stood...
My brother overstood...
Truth be good or evil...
Dr. LovEvil Reunion...
It is as if he sensed it...
Reflections of the innocent refreshed the situation...
Snakes slithered in high grass on his yard...
Disregarding their friendly ways...
Close to his gate the evil lurked...
My brother had three guns...
He got them for three sons...
One day all the guns were stolen...
The Sun never shined the same way...
Up to no good the ghetto surrounded him...
The evil that hounded him...
His passion for survival grounded him...
His sanctuary was no longer safe...

Depression settled in…
My brother planned on dying…
He never took on crying…
In so many ways he is big brother…
Guessing that was his exit wound…
From the womb we became one…
He writes to bear witness…
His hard shine was his last line…

Wisdom is She

Wisdom is a function of knowledge...
My heart bursts, when her heart hurts...
Blessed the redeemer Emmanuel...
We make our own shells...
His sanctuary is that of diamond...
Golden spectrums of light design and feed me...
Wisdom through Proverb, Selah...!
Praise through Psalms, Selah...!
Sophia is wisdom and she is crying...
Sophia incarnate, dialect from the Greek...
Wisdom born overstanding...
The heat of trustworthy sensation...
Regardless of the assignment my mission will be accomplished...
The best train thoroughly...
I try to keep it away but it seems to be chasing me...
There are rules to this construct we live in...
Trusting there are forces that give in...
Learning the hard way...
My shine is hard narrowed by the good and plenty...
Sophia, please trip up my enemy...
Taking a step through nostalgia...
Transcending through the past to see my essence...
Chosen to administer my own Psalms...
The decisions WE make shake machinery...
See, it is a dream to me...
Watching brothers dwell unity...
The ways of the wicked are truly gifted...
Soldiers at peace need to come home...
Bring the troops back home...
Yet, I see no change...
I am standing here so please let it rain...

Sophia conjured my importance...
Divorcing the materials...
Realizing NOTHING was most important...
These days are so short, pleading with my numbers...
My lesson was I needed nothing...

WORD LIFE

See beyond what you think...
Tickle me so I can laugh at your disguise...
Sunrise; sunset, surprised I made it this far...
Walking far with no car, three evident facial scars...
The obvious comes between a man and making...
Unfortunately, the pain is required...
Before the WORD the heavens and earths were created...
Suns and stars collided...
Everything was without form...
VOID until WORD LIFE...
Nothing meant more to me, then everything at any given time...
Expecting to explore so much more...
Weeds before the flowers...
Seeds to breed, reflection before concession...
Her womb entirely carried me...
Flowers blossom reminiscing the powers that once were...
Seems the sturdy have the most injection marks...
This verb confusion is not an illusion...
Born by cosmic fusion...
Creative Hiatus made me form more from nothing...
Sunrise; sunset, surprised I made it this far...
Burry me in Heaven...
Allow the brethren to live again...
Allow us the power through merciless vision...
Word life...
Through segregation, reparation or destruction...
THEY said it was GOOD...!

Grey Implosions

The grey in my beard is exploding...
I just started to salt and pepper...
I will be home in a few...
Love, did you eat yet…?
This sensation is a part of several aged suggestions...
See I am graying...
Politics and my time are not compatible...
Graying my beard through good work and subtle stress…
Bearing visions of an old timer in my young frame…
Poetry, the philosophy of my expression…
The golden walkway in the valley of armored soldiers…
I am dodging raindrops on a cloudy day…
Watching the ocean above fill, I chose to praise...
Poetry, the philosophy of my expression...
Grey the color of my wisdom resulting from many mistakes...
The hostility of my own humility is what is changing me...
Hang gliding and colliding into all the things that made me...
Dr. LovEvil's shadow of sanctuary...
Derelicts prowl in the dark...
Fertilizing her young body with my tongue...
The grey has long begun...
I can only concede to the greed of living longer...
The hands of time are watching me...
My mission is fruition...
Yet the implosions conjure grey...
Naturally exploiting the leaves from trees…
Realizing I am turning grey…

Keep the Change

For a whole year I stood here...
Imagine the rock I stood on...
Keeping the forward movement going...
Even without the change my mindset is primed...
Rats huddle in the dark and it does not bother me...
The lady moves her wig because it itches and it does not bother me...
See I am not in it for the riches...
New York pays me, so I remain the Pedestrian...
Watching him pick up change from his booth...
The Billionaire Bum keeps me focused and humble...
My head rests safely next to my wife in Jersey...
Still, the change falls out my pockets...
It is amazing how many people I come across...
Every day the Invisible Caste System prominently becomes more evident...
The 100 thousand a year executive is now the Keep the Change President...
The temperament of those without is barely silenced...
Cool co-workers versus the wicked politician...
Wishing fishing was not a sport and I was not the shark...
Constantly hunted in the dark...
Either way, I suggest you keep the change...
Do not bother me for five cents, two is all I can offer...
Slowly suckling on Earth's last organic smoothie...
Truly ashamed everyone cannot eat...
So many people have no shoes on their feet...
Standing next to foolish yuppies in suits, drunk by nature...
I am the shark without change...
Thou must eat...

Discreetly I sit back and wait for the right time to attack...
No matter what street I am on...
Armed with the loose change I preserve in my pockets...
Head of Voltron...
At this point the limbs are aware of each other...
Brothers acknowledging brothers...
Only when they get some change...
Public transportation is what it is...
It seems I walk a lot, the Pedestrian remains...
Positive change occurs at a miniscule rate...
Keep the change...
One percent taxation to leave the state, a NJ provision of social extortion...
Five cents keep the change...
Amoney has been forever leaving me with change...
B.O.A (Bank of Amoney) tells me to "Keep the Change"...
But it is my money, so I planned on it...!
Seems I am on the PATH again...
That oh so special and infamous train ride of musky transit travel...
Confronted by so many that just need change...
Change of situation through drunken deliberations...
There is no more change that I can provide...
Muffling the change clinking sound from inside my lonely pockets...
Hiding the wrinkled dollar from a pigeon's view...
Let us go back down south, to the points of origination...
Real change is liberated by the non-liberals, drug dealers, alcohol pushers and conservationists...

HOME

When I think of home...
I think of lobster tails and big rims on chrome...
Bodegas getting robbed, serenaded by gunshots in the street...
I think of so many things...!
See, when I think of home...
I think of Miss Mary Mack, how she was all dressed up in black...
Butterscotch rum in the summer time...
I think of so many wonderful things...!
When I think of home...
I think of so many beautiful experiences...
All the many different loving people...
I think of nana and pop-pop working their flea-market shop...
Standing on the porch watching the full moon, counting the stars at night...
Playing basketball at the park...
Catching pop-fly baseballs in the field...
Bowling that perfect gutter ball into the alley lane...
When I think of home...
I think of all I do condone...
All the yards that need their grass cut...
Summer barbeques were cook, throwing liquor bottles in the pool...
Frolicking cardinals and red breasted robins...
Inhumane police officers and their bullet proof vests...!
All the people in jail for false driving while black arrests...
When I think of home...
I think of so many things...
Friends and our cross town bicycle expeditions...

Family all together for holidays...
Blind dates at the skating rink...
Falling but still getting back up...
Shoveling ice and snow on those frost bitten days...
How my gloves it took to keep my hands warm...
Dancing in the rain and playing in snow storms...
Hiding under covers admiring the thunder storms...
When I think of home...
All my friends fighting overseas and puppy love crushes...
Sipping 7-Eleven "Slurpee's" and late night talks with the honies...
Chilling with my homies at the parties...
Loitering in movie parking lots, instigating security alerts next to pizza parlors...
Entrancing grand county court buildings...
Birthday cakes and blowing candles out before the final count...
How the seasons came and left...
Discovering the last breath of death...
Remembering how the leaves fell from trees, landing on my chest to rest...
Sun rays fighting to reach my face...!
When I think of home...
I think of so many things...
My first disco with CISCO...
The last time MAD DOG bit me...
Coming home riding the CRAZY HORSE...
Shooting the first WILD TURKEY...
Plucking the IRISH ROSE...
Those good old high school years...
Vandalizing property and my home being ransacked...
Crack heads walking past my porch...
Heroine feigns lighting up their torch...

Stolen bike chop shops in abandoned locations...
Getting ready for vacation...
I think of all the different hustles that made me who I am...
When I think of home...
I think of so many wonderful things...

Fire Burns

I am on fire...
Bright star guides the dim light...
Hard shine strikes back...
Black is an inevitable force in nature...
In this world I can touch the moon...
So close to gravity I instigate black holes...
In between societies temper tantrum...
I cuddle with the thought of eternity...
This golden blaze which captures me is amazing...
Aura versus the shadow...
I am on fire solely to charcoal the greedy tempers of mankind...
This powerful light of mine...!
Carbonating the clouds; Waterman douses the fire...
Praying in the center of the Sun to avoid heat stroke...
There is a commonality to all things...
I am on fire focusing on humanity's insanities...
To one day be a part of the light that guides our family...
Fire burns...

Insurance Investigations

Insurance points I am investigating...
They just seem to appear...
No matter how good I have been all throughout the year...
Insurance companies I am hating...
Progressively, I hate Geico and seek for the Cure...
Prudentially, All State has a messed...
New Jersey has the dirtiest hands...
Go generic or go home...!
I decided not to vote, could not be realized...
Insurance companies sucking me in...
Defend myself with what...?
I bet a bigger paycheck will shield me from insurance premium malarkey...
Should I be a friend of any executive...?
Locked in by overpaid fugitive executives...
How can I win...?
Save for what...?
Drive to where and for what reason...?
So I throw on my hat and trench coat...
In the rain, I am following premium increasing crooks...
Their notorious hideouts are corporate havens...
Bungalows for the hoes that take my rent money...
The investigation has started and dearly departed...
They seek for all my paycheck...!
I sense corporate thievery and it is at my front door...
Constantly knocking my walls down...
The giants have not fallen, I was mistaken...
The giants stand tall and feed so much better...
I thought Amoney loved me...?
Expecting to open just a few doors to see economic recovery...

Since I have 1000 keys, one of them must open something for me...
Greed capitalizes wealth, an inherent function of cancer...
Meanwhile, our state is in a bad position...
PPOs privately dance with their shimmering HMO partners at board meetings...
This reiterates people are in a state of retreat...
Nationally; I dig in deeper, calling overseas customer service representatives for account inquiry...
Domestically chasing this false claim onto my record...
It is past buddy time...!
Shucks I am mad and need to do something about it...
The investigation is not going to well...
Lack of cooperation dictated by local politics...
People notice the crime; know the primary suspects, but do not form in the masses...!
Politicians this is for you, I sit and investigate your evil crew...
Sick to my stomach and in financial dismay...
I have to move since I cannot pay to play...
I got into a crash but could not call them...
Give me a tracker to put in my car and monitor my rates...
Track me to smack me...!

Everything is Fresh

Everything is fresh is the story they told us...
All things are not fresh...
Before we broke difference Leviticus let it be known...
Fish fry till I die...
Should I ask for more...?
Fish frying in thunderstorms, nothing can stop the hunger...
So in love with fried pork because it tastes so good...
Watch me; and wash me, if I am evil...
THEY told that to US before we broke bread...

I Was

I was there...
Now I am here...
I did hear...
Now I listen...
I used to run...
Now I walk...
I should start running again...
I used to write letters...
Now I think volumes...
The chapters of my life are written in books...
I used to grit my teeth...
Now I chomp at the menu...
At least I now sit, eat, and digest...
The rest was when I was...
Past, present, and future...
Expecting our lives to be sculptured...
Sculpting our own lives as living stone...
I used to play a lot...
Now I take things more seriously...
I used to drink hot chocolate...
Now I sip on tea and Remy...
I used to hate raking leaves...
Now I let them fall on me...
So used to wanting a challenge...
Now more concerned with defining I...
I used to want to get home early...
Now I take my time...
I used to want a big house...
Now I just want a living...
I used to think I was smart...
Now I ask the Lord to forgive me...
I used to play by the rules...

Now I break the laws...
Lawren, Lawren, Lawren...
Pausing as I reminisce who I was...
Now I am...
For more than many reasons...

Steel Bags

Steel bags and wet rags...
Black diamonds set in platinum never rusts...
Containers with motives kissing golden bands...
Wrapped around our spiritual fingers...
Rebirthing natural commitments through love...
In God we trust, precious metals are a commodity...
Crushed jewels form a milky powder...
Forsaken by the scenes of reality...
The reverence of what will be...
Keeping things in perspective even without the jewelry...
Polish the steel bags for safety purposes...
Red cardinals stare at black diamonds in the green pastures...
It is the satin golden Sunshine...
Referencing memories placed in this steel bag...
Nothing can be better than what I have...
So I grab deeper to touch the essence...
Reflections of what the prisms manifested...
The spectrums I savor are beyond colorful...
Assumptions of clueless journeymen are classical...
Stop, listen and pray to yourself...
The crimson colors are impregnable...
Her face is my hidden treasure...
Aged rust is a blessing...
Black carbonated residue from distant galaxies...
Black diamonds, steel bags and wet rags...

No Carriages

No carriages to carry us...
We carry Us...
Vicariously we must carry heritage...
His story must not historically defeat WE...
For centuries we have been beaten...
I am inclined to take a long climb, just to see the hardshine...
There is no carriage for you if I cannot carry you...
I marry you to carry you to carry me...
See where we need to be...
These restrictions are agitating...
No carriages to carry us...
Ashes to ashes and lust to lust...
Why make it easy...?
From diamond dust to clay, we rust to dust...
Feeling I can carry you and others...
Word is life, bonded between the brothers...
My carriage is this sacrifice I choose to inhale...
Quantified by the laurel I am use to walking with...

Alabama Shallow Water Catfish

Spitting naturally flavored tobacco...
Sipping on backwoods...
Smoking the tastiest corn liquor moonshine...
The best time to strudel the noodle is at night...
High price bait is a joke...
Let the shallow big lipped catfish choke on your ever gripping fingers...
Alabama for the moment is the place to be...
The best part of the capture is how easy it is...
Forgive me if I am prejudice...
Alabama shallow water catfish is my deepest wish...
It is so easy to catch the ever so slimy bottom feeders...
No point in renting a boat...
Shallow waters keep me from harm...
Praying the Alabama mean snapping turtle ignores my charm...
Shucks, I need my hands...
Gambling in murky water to catch a fat flat fish...
Daydreams of trying in the pan...
Neatly placed on my dish...
Buttered up alongside some okra...
Chopped up in fat slices, just the way it is supposed to...
Nothing can stop me from catching my match...
I am the coolest rooster and all my chickens have hatched...
My hay thatched hat is so fresh, disguising my face from moon ridden light...
My appetite is at large...
I just wade and wade; since that is the best way to catch them...
I feel tentacles wiggling alongside my feet...

Soon to be confronted by two big lips and some knuckles...
I chuckle because I know what is coming...
Quietly I noodle my hands with a smooth twitch every now and then...
I can hear its heart beat as it senses my collective pulse...
GULP, SNAG, GRAB...!
The sweet sensation of the capture...!
This fish; the little bird, and I am the raptor...
In the woods; throughout the swamp, the sounds of sizzling cooking grease calls for me...
Unstrapped boots, trophy on my back, knapsack filled with the finest southern delectable...
Life is good here...
I will be back tomorrow...

Pretty Health Care

Thanks for the Medicare...
I love Blue Cross and the Blue Shield
My hips are finally healed...
I know with prescriptions generic is a steal...
I thank you so much...!

By: Magdalena Greene

Evolutionary Babies

Evolutionary babies, military nurseries, ironclad ruling nannies...
Grandparents that just do not quit...
Multi-lingual social soldiers of the future...
Bronzed in the arts and sciences...
Infused with the finest mathematical qualities...
Internalizing geometries philosophically...
It only makes sense to be THE BEST...
Study and illuminate beyond the rest...
Represent yourself in a positive light...
Tools for toys for every young girl and boy...
Better seen than heard, until the lion roars...
Respectful world travelers, vicariously attentive, for when I get to old...
Gravel burners...
Adventurous stories will be told...
Sitting back on my rocking chair...
Reminiscing when I was young...
Aspirations to change mental states...
Astonishingly they will remember the more positive sides of me...
There will be no duck hunters; evolution is essential for survival...
Craving for substance, nothing less...
Wanting successor generations to be better...
Avoidance of wicked medias are paramount...
Turning coal to diamonds...
Bastardized by a system surrounded by quicker sand...
Obviously I demand more...!
Exclaim the fact that we started poor...
When the world stops spinning you will be better than fine...

Trained, aligned and tested by the plumbline...
Babe, I will be thinking about you while I am driving...
In the Valley of Nothing...
Evolutionary babies make everything happen...!
This is your century; not your day, or your year...!
Your world and you will take it by fear...
Hear the voices and follow their instructions in the most perfect way...!
Architecting strong knowledge through industrialization...
You can do ANY and EVERYTHING...!
The Valley of Nothing cannot stop your precedence...
Time spent is not wasted, agility and speed are important...
Balance your capabilities with strong ethic and diligence...
My job is to ensure your growth and watch your successes...
I am alive and living the lessons...
If you fall, you will get back up...!
You will not fall again the same way...!
You will fall harder each time...!
You will climb higher each mountain...!
There will be nothing that will stop you...!
Evolutionary babies...
The beginning of a wonderful finale...
We all have worldly vices to deal with...

The Earth We Walk on

This land is your land, not my land...
Just wanting some land for my family...
Understand my family's blood is on this land...
Where children can say, "this is a beautiful place"...
Doing my numbers, working the industry I have been fitted in...
Everyone around me is so smart...
Good in the daytime, bad in the dark...
Just imagine the world circumscribing its' best behavior...
Questionable, all things are...
A home for me to lay my head at...?
The grind is uncanny...
Mostly it makes no sense, speaking out loud through text...
Really it does not matter who you think you are...
The world is small and flat; a Sun by day, comet by night...
A fog filled sky that drops cotton candy manna to the masses...
Falling on the stubs of freshly cut rain forests...
Tap dancing on financial mountain tops...
To walk the glamorous syringe filled oceanic beachfronts...
Running into a forest of roses; venturing right into sparkling crystallized caves...
Drilling down lower then she will allow; taking more than she can give...
Thinking that the giants own all things, standing on top of molten towers...
Gleaming at more than a rainbow on a snowy day, imagining pure gold kissing black diamonds in a rock-pit...

Manifesting the dullest of sand into the finest of crystal…
Sitting on a rooftop; admiring the red Sun turn into a full moon…
Burning a forest for the sake of land ownership; killing vegetables and de-fertilize fruits…
Carving craters and dimples on her once soft skin from radiation and rough bombing…
Who is in cahoots with who…?
The world is not a crazy place…!
It seems the fountain of youth becomes more apparent as I oppose my ignorance…
20 / 20 vision means nothing in the wrong place…
Dreaming of rainbow filled skies and water falling sceneries…
See straight so you can move forward…
We are pulled by so many conditions…
Wishing I could control time…
So I can steal from you, and then heal with you…!
It is a small world after all…
World what must we do to appeal to you…?
Should the Water Diamond Paradox be re-explained…?
Attempts to please and appease you…
Yet the mosquitoes are no friend of yours…
Is it technology causing our cancer…?
Are cell phone towers ringing with the answers…?
Are there not enough global pipelines…?
The Earth we walk on is a grandeur place…
So many spaces we choose to destroy…
So many ways we decide to incorporate civilization…
The Earth we walk on…

The Moon and a Platinum Ring

I see the yellow moon's horizon, but I cannot see below the line...
I see the bright and amber city lights...
So blurry, I tend to miss my sign...
Guided by the yellow moon...
I make it home each time...
Green diamonds signal me...
Steadily sipping on white wine...
The ring I wear comforts me...
I am guided by a loving commitment...

Education is a Discipline

It is better to be prepared for an opportunity when it presents itself then to say I wish I had the formal background. School comes in many forms. Education is nothing without discipline. You can educate yourself for free depending on what you are trying to understand. Buying a book and educating yourself still requires discipline. Discipline is the difference between a recessionary and profitable circumstance. From a trade perspective, everyone has their own unique skill set to acquire since we cannot all do the same thing throughout life.

Teaching Bleeders

Seeking to teach a bleeder...
Attempting to preach to readers...
Fickle sight-seers walking out in space...
The outer limits of purely foolish necessities...
Alien resurrection; breed of a brand new race, seeking for his face...
My crazy reasoning is equally coincidental...
Urban mentalities mostly make selfish sense...
Slow death sentences for those that lack insurance...
Society is a vampire...
Evil people exposed to the masses, classless...
Wearing masks, the rebirth of H1N1 incarnates N166A...
Nothing new is under the Sun...
Thus, we face further expulsion...
Reexamine what has been done...
These explosions are from a violent nature...
Economic dis-employment is the smoothest form of social imprisonment...
Daring you to call welfare's bluff...
Amoney's subsidized cheese is not enough...
I suggest you continue to bleed...
Attempting to reach the readers...
Virtualized in a physical world...
Mortally immortalized, disguised watching the Sun rise...
Surprise, surprise, surprise...
The science of sight is deafening...
Unconsciously, truncating this linearism to my heritage...
The many sacrilegious things I am comprised of...
Composing I to teach the bleeders...
Preaching to the readers...
The mileage of a lost people is unfathomed...
Air conditions in log cabins are breezy...

So I seek his face...
We bleeders are losing so much energy...
Ah We Enemy...!
So choose a friend for me...!
Hard times better defined...
Market recovery without a job is a fallacy...
My recession parallels your depression...
The sheep have been shaved bald...
Predictions of a cold winter...
The lamb is in wolves clothing...
All indigenous have and must be robbed...
In God we trust, the satire of a sloppy society...
Reconstruction of a stolen architecture will never
conform to the future...

One Thousand Keys

Janitor Man, walking around with the plan...
It is the keys that jiggle and jingle...
So close to the hip, tight is the grip, one door per key...
Access is embedded within a frame of mind...
Only one door I need to enter...
Aesop, Earl tends to call me...
Discover, design, develop, deploy...
Assessment of the keys is the first step...
Categorization is not necessary since life is random...
Only a tandem can get in my way...
Monitor how the door opens, since closure is necessary...
These one thousand keys weigh so much...!
Clutching tightly to them for support...
I am not afraid of the door without a key...
The mirror's other side keep collides within me...
Out of one thousand keys, which one is for me...?
Obsessed by what I can be...
Searching and searching for the right key...
In the cold of the night, through the heaviness of dark piercing rain...
Beyond the point where my eyes could not see...
This little light of mine must shine brighter, I must see clearly...
Feeling for that specific key to unlock my destiny...
Digging through the massive chain...
Mostly unlabeled but similar in shape and nature...
Color, size and texture...
Off gate; waiting for heaven's sake, anticipating great things to come one day...
Money will not identify the key I need...
I have seen one key open several doors...
Without a key what doors will open for me...?

There is that one special key I am seeking…
That which can open and lock all doors…
I feel I will find it…
Houses, apartments, office buildings, condos and castles…
Gates, doors, corridors and bridges…
Virtually encrypting two special keys…
Managing secure socket layers beyond the seas…
The key is the future, open to all the places I need to be…
One person, one state of mind…
One thousand keys with mountain peaks of Zion on my mind…
The key I needed was inside of me…

Rose Gardens in Atlantis

Steadily climbing, reaching my horizon...
Pulling rose filled buses out the Atlantis terrain with thick braided ropes of hemp...
LEG...!
I am unequally harmonized watching the Mantis ride...
Witnessing the star burst while two moons collide...
Clustered in laurel and white satin...
Golden gate bridge catastrophes and I just so happen to be there...
Many things can make the world crumble under you...!
I fall in love with a peoples' ambrosia...
Between my eyes is a lightning bolt touching the ground of success...
Graphically the catastrophe is I might just be winning...!
Dressed to impress an exploding planet...
My strength verses wisdom, life through circumstance...
Roses on the moon in full bloom are more than interesting...
So I must try...
Try with all my might to save them...
Beyond the mayhem, nature has a way of healing herself...
With or without them...
Ah We Enemy...
Friend is my foe in a greedy world...
Turbulent waters capture the rapture of a rough day...
Purple skies wipe off the white crust a top the mountain's eyes...
Acidic chemical reactions take place summoning seasons of unnatural rain...
I see more now than ever before...
Evidence that we once existed is a notion of truth...
Mortally Immortal...

My dreams say this scene will come to an end...
Time allowed, all things will be back to normal again...
Abstractly the roses call for me, as I call for them...
A garden without a rose is remorseful...

Today

Today I just want to be nothing more than me...
Fish with my father, talk to my brother, walk with my mother...
I want everyone to hug one another...!
Husbands and wives make love to each other...!
Today is a day, nothing more than that...!
Ecclesiastically, there is nothing new under the Sun...
Feeling more relaxed now than I ever have...
The Sun whisks me to the moon...
Where is one to go...throughout the course of a day...?
How far and long does it take to get away...?
Chasing a dream for so long, today I decided to walk slower...
Take a moment to get to know myself better...
Walking the cold days of December without a sweater...
Avoiding rain drops as they majestically turn to snowflakes...
Watching the glass kettle boil, hearing the steam scream...
Soiling my feet into the ground, rubbing Shea butter on my head...
Delinquent juveniles playfully cycle past me...
We all have bills to pay...
Today let them have their way...!
The ethics of the world should not wash their joys away...
Today is a day; nothing more than that...
Massage my wife's back, send flowers to my many aunts, to play dominoes with my many cousins...
A day to fish with my grandfather, father, brother and uncles...
Today is a day that I have...

Tomorrow should not be forsaken; all we love could be taken…
In life nothing is promised…

Write to Them

I always use to write to them...
In hopes that if it were me, someone would write...
To be or not to be in a cell, that is the question...?
To be or not to be free, that is the suggestion ...?
As soon as I would write them, they would write me back...
Always having someone to write to...
Praying I will never have to write to myself...
Federal and state centurions spy on the letters I write...
Truly, it is ok...
There is nothing to hide, only things to say...
People are under rocks...
So when you crawl out...
No-one will see you...!
You will move your rock; quietly and unnoticeably...
Who would ever see you...?
One day you will place your rock in a new location...
Your rock will not be next to mine...
You may or may not write to me again...
My friends, I write to them...
We are the people under the rocks...?
What can these rocks do for us...?
Is there shelter within this timelessly depreciated figure of solitude...?
Write to them to keep them scratching at the bars...
I write to them
Remembrance in a time of need...
At least you know I was there...
Unexpectedly, incarcerated family and friends would receive encouraging letters from me...

Your Resume

I do not want your resume...
You can work for me for free...
Let me teach you something...
Do not worry about the livelihood of your family...
Sub-par, above-par, no car and maxed out credit...
No worries...
I can take you where you need to be...
You are in my web now...
Sick days and annual leave is like thievery...
You work for me...!
This is how it is supposed to be...
Change your name to get some fame...
Sell your soul, burn your gas, lunch is not an option...
Who said you need to sleep...?
You are in my town now, taxing you to walk on my street...
You are working reckless and want a raise...
Thank you for the laugh and please behave...
Corporate slavery at its finest...
Ok so you have worked here for years...
Just fall in love with your long walks while retrieving my dry cleaning...
Remember light on the starch and two sugars in my coffee is the routine...
I fall in love with your fashion statement...
Nice tie guy...!
I know you love this job...
Working you until you bleed...
Birdseed to feed you...
See how much I care...
Now you have the privilege of washing my fancy car...

So you can watch me gleaming; picture me rolling, while
you are strolling…
This season be happy you have a job…
Your wife is sickly…
Send my wife 144 freshly cut red roses today…!
Your kids are having problems at school…
Have no worries they will grow up to be nobodies
anyway, just like you…
Maybe they can work for my little ones for free…
In exchange for the same birdfeed I give you…
I see you have a cane, are you in some pain…?
Thank goodness I do not offer employee benefits…
I love my Italian handmade leather shoes shiny…!
Do not get mad, your life is sad…
Too bad you never finished school…
Aren't you happy you work for me…?

Your World

My life will inspire you...
This world will require you...
Just do as I ask of you...
No crowd will embarrass you...
Harass the giants with efficiency as I taught you to...
Define yourself as the angels knew...
Discover the world as you are required to...
Your world will be breath-taxingly amazing...
What will be shall be done...
Word pronounced from the sharpest tongue...
Who can stop all that has begun...?
Realize what we have already done...
There is not one thing we can undo...
These times are in crises...
My advice will help you carry through...
There is not one thing we can undo...
This is your world...!
What you want is for the taking...
Where you are going is in the making...
Do not forsake this reasoning...
The world's treasures are yours to deliberate...
Delegate your power wisely...
Surprise the general public with your patience...
This world is a crazy place...
But it is your world...
Maintain your space...!

Without a Thorn

A rose without a thorn is not the same...
Beauty without the pain, Sunshine without the rain...
Rainbows become figments of our imagination...
Fairytales to say the least...
Four leaf clovers are everywhere...
Dusk and dawn have no difference...
The seasons are just time slots...
A world where castles are for the paupers and resources are infinite...
No fleas, disease, heartache, sadness or death...
Birth is no longer, death can never be...
The duality of the mirrors other side...
Emotions war freely where love is the ammo...
Bees are adored and swarm without the sting; only in the land of milk and honey...
Where Adam and Eve were designed from gold instead of clay...
Simply no barriers to entry...
What makes you so beautiful...!
Stars making love to the moon...
So much greater but size never mattered...
From out the void formed to withstand the forces of lust or decay...
A place where little children can play...
Where leaves stay on trees...
Everyone becomes a loved one, and the last dance resembles the first...
Drinking without the thirst...
Everything is truly happy...
The finest food and freshest fruits were plenty...
No fathom of disease or famine...
The world in the midst of a rose without a thorn...

Remember Me

Someone please remember me, when you get all big and such...
Please do not forget me...
Trust me once, fool me more than twice...
Please remember my issues...
I hate the fact that you are not free...
Trust and believe...
Just remember me, while I miss you...
Remember when we used to smoke...
When I used to laugh out loud, sometimes stumbling to the ground...
Because I am confined does not mean I am lonely...
Life flies faster than the speed of light...
Still remember the old me, the silly me...
"The get mad at nothing because you woke me up early" me...
The "can I help you out" me...
"Always falling but getting back up" me...
Remember the "cognac and cigarette pack" me...
"Always going to school trying to better myself" me...
"Dancing in the morning rain praying to the sky" me...
Remember me...
"Always in the front yard raking leaves to see no grass" me...
Remember me...
"Sitting on the porch day dreaming of when things were easier" me...
Remember me...
"The sometimes late to deliver but always on time" me...
"Constantly picking up trash while taking time to smell the flowers in the ghetto" me...

"Loving building the winter snow forts but hating to shovel the snow" me...
Remember my free throw shot at the basketball courts...
The first time I put on a football uniform...
The times I would play catch with my father and brother...
The me, that would ask for help with his homework...
Just remember me...
For all the good times we had...
The many jobs I have had, and where I am now...
All the times being let go, always remaining to get back up...
Remember me for my innocence and...
I know life is short...
Remember all the fun we had...

Bottom Feeders

Bottom feeders; never true believers, mostly liars and deceivers...
The torture of a culture that is destroying everything...
Water Diamond Paradox magnified by greed...
Multiplied by ignorance and over-indulgence...
Catfish, oh catfish, oh catfish...
Never any matches...
Some people will not seem to fit...
Ever more crabs in the barrel...
The deafening of a producer's scream to amplify a consumer's wants...
Drunk, sad, dumb and still sucking their thumbs...
Crying in dismay, not caring...
The sign says, "Do not disturb the public"...
Social media disease spreaders...
I am just documenting, my whole entire world...
In between each line; I notice the bottom feeders, feeding on my time...
Sucking away my peace of mind...
So I play the piano...
Tending to harness my own business...
Acknowledging God is my witness...
Blurry eyed with a tired vision ...
Delusional from too many bloody scenes...
On the bottom, I feel the feed the frenzy...
On the top, corruption and injustice are just as thick and suspenseful...
One is called social welfare, a misunderstood function of politics...
The middle class maintains Amoney's tax...
Bottom line is the economics...
Visibly visible this invisible caste system truly exists...

Readers have forgotten how to write, scribbling on electronic tablets...
Law makers take, retaliate and congratulate ...
Giving a bit less than nothing in return...
Homes and buildings burn in the middle of winter...
Financial floods and hurricanes incapacitate victims...
Seems the indigenous are always getting flooded out...!

Seven Days

Seven Days
On the first day I manifested my existence...
In the beginning there was the Word...
Thus, I sought the light...
Splitting the void, differentiating day and night...
Identifying with the reflection of I...
On the second day I reinstated my past and dealt with it...
The third day I understood I needed to overstand more then everything...
Nothing came to mind...
Building what needed to be destroyed...
Employing righteous directions contained within my conscious...
Seeking to conquer self; I sought for something, or someone else...
Thus, I broke a rib on the fourth day...
Fantastically, she appeared to help heal me...
On the fifth day I recognized what I could do with the light...
Looking at the Sun I created a rainbow from pure sight...
Dancing alongside the waterfall watching it happen, over and over again...
Reinventing so many theories to properly digest...
Admonishing love and wisdom...
Losing my vision on the sixth day...
Hiding from all I created and was once able to see...
Quietly imagining how things should be...
Ceremoniously I separated the ground from the seas...
On the seventh day I recognized, I was one of many...
Avoiding inundations and conflagrations...
Praying to my maker...

Spinning this world, squaring up with the plum and level…
On the seventh day I acknowledged the Word and then rested…

Framing Premonitions

Dreams in the form of premonitions...
Recognizing thought patterns through foggy illusions...
Leaves fall from trees...
Life is not all that it may seem...
So I follow a dream, just to see where it will take me...
Transformations of a loved one in between a slow dance...
The faces we capture and have no idea about...
Till the day we meet...
Discreetly claiming De Ja Vouz is a mistress in distress...
Tossing and turning, internally yearning and burning to know...
Framing myself in a crystallized cube...
Restless from attempts to decipher what may or may not matter...
Mastering the art of gravity, as I whimsically fly in and out of peculiar danger...
Sweating in the winter, freezing in the summer...
Running from the Psychologies of my Philosophy...
Realizing I am talking to myself...
Subconsciously, recollection takes place...
Conjured characters I once feared for reasons I cannot extrapolate...
In my sub-reality, clouding up my space...
Smoke fills my air, never touching my face...
Loved ones I lost, never to be replaced...
Tending to find change within a dream...
Fond of so many people, from far too new...
Few leave lasting impressions, unlike the ghosts in my shell...
There are emerging bubbles that I want to pop...
Falling snowflakes drawing me to inspect...

Untimely gestures within my power to correct...
Sharpening machetes in the window sill...
Sleeping to raise several sides of me that collide with me...
Framing the beautiful memories, so I can bring them with me...
Reality strikes without a cause...
I decided to frame my premonitions...

Impermeable to Heat

A good father is impermeable to heat...
He will fend for his family, never giving in to retreat...
We grew up in a strong homestead...
Flooding the street with roses...
Many things I can remember and feel necessary to say...
I love you Father and wish you all the best of days...
Commitment and sacrifice are necessary tools on the course of prevail...
Maintaining a home and family the way you have we will never fail...
It took some time to write this...
But I'm glad you are here...
I love my family and wish the utmost in prosperity all throughout the infinite years...
A good father is impermeable to heat...

Lawren Erneston Greene 12/25/09 (Son)

Cold Cuts on my Lawn

We are great together but apart things are not quite so well...
Says the pot; in the kitchen, in the middle of central park...
Cold cuts on my lawn...
Everything seems to be so out of order...
Bread without the meat...!
So many leaves without a tree...
People rioting in the street...
I stand outside wrestling four winds, cold cuts beneath my feet...
Preferences of king crab legs and blue berry lobster, sirloin steaks are so great...
I question the reasoning for these cold cuts on my lawn...
Big cheese pieces stuck in my shrubs...
Condiments from the heavens above...?
Did my neighbors get into a fight...?
Walking around with his sandwich...
Dazed holding his chopped up but still empty loaf of bread...
I am looking at this guy...
Bewildered with an internal madness triggering something crazy...
Mental problems I call it...
Why must people leave their cold cuts in my lawn...?
How can one witness the end without identifying a rocky starting point...?

The Theory of Why

To freeze in a summer's rain...
More things to think about then to do...
Under the largest leaf the spirit rests...
I have a soup which I am stewing and putting together...
Mixing and matching, bonding and building...
Seems common sense admires my many faces...
The Sun sets up the moon to rise in the same space...
Watching the tide collide between low and high...
A nature destined to be lost and forgotten...
The tragedy of a great warrior versus the epic of a tiny hero...
Only here zero serves as a placeholder...
In essence the beginning becomes the end...
A world where God has many names, but he is only one...
To speculate inequality is to wonder why...?
Questioning the world as we know it...
Greed causes us to take more than we need...
Therefore the world bleeds...
Racism is a social prison, not one person incarcerated is the same...
The Creator gave us this world...
Yet, we still find reasons to place blame...
Everyone falls victim to slavery...
Bravery transforms us...
Why cocoon the moon in midnight clouds...?
The Sun is destined to dissipate the mist...
Waterfalls break apart rivers manifesting the scenery...
Amazingly snow turns to rain, to rain, then to ice...
While all things are the same...

Beautiful scenes should never be questioned...

The awesome sight of A Pack of Black Eagles...
Elaborately gestured by the lions roar...
The duality of life straddles the shadow; night interferes with the day...
Conflagrations and inundations will fiercely cleanse the Earth...
Seasons still dictate the weather...
Mortally our hands are not meant to tamper with the forces of nature...
Why change what needs to happen when it must occur...?
Oh the beautiful days in his world...!

Test Me against the Plumb Line

Attack the most powerful first, then deny the energy...
In the last hour the Sun will burn a whole in our conscious...
Trust, knowledge and wisdom in application generates power...
There is a star in the West; there is a second advent, Elias Boudinout...
Articles of Confederation...
The eye separates from the body...
What is seen or perceived may not be felt physically...
The north-east corner is where I sought the light...
Continuing to sit in class...
Training, so one day I can train you...
Monotheism is the God in me; for I am in his image...
All hail the mighty rebel we seek...
Only one holding the key representing the street...
Shall inherit the Earth moving up to the peak...
Religiously I studied him; so I could find me, these degrees I seek...
When contained it is hard if impossible to deliver...
Shivering in the black market; standing amidst a checkered floor...
There is nothing to sell...
Warriors in the midst of a cube...
My unidentified object is Merkaba...
Visibly Invisible, This Jinn is not a friend of mine...
Circumambulating the compasses to reach infinity...
Strength, wisdom, and beauty...
To be here for such a short defined time...
To one day elaborate how my life was while I still am...
God keep me right and exact against mine enemy...
Constantly try my ways against the plumb line...

I Use to Grid Humans

I use to grid humans, now I grid the Earth…
Triple stage darkness, ultimate signs of birth…
The world is a dark place; light illuminates our face, defining the race…
Redeeming all the light I can get…
I am deciding to grow up, volume by volume…
Piercing my own beam of light through the sphere…
Staring at a Sun most cannot bear…
Climbing heights most will not go near…
Impermeable to heat, dismissing all of the cold, hovering this surface circus…
I use to grid humans, now I grid the Earth…
Scorching who I use to be, defining my super-natural worth…
I use to grid humans, now I grid my Earth…
Incinerating the worst elements of my life, the evil that we do…
Picture all the finer things of life and remember when you have seen them…
Fact disguised in the form of a sign…
This design is a matter of perception…
My recollection is choppy…
Basically just something to do…
Figure we are all here for determined periods of time…
We must do something positive…
Otherwise, drown freely in the pools of negativity…
Sadly stupid gangsters slip into cesspools of the quicker sand…
21 Gun Salute Troop disfigured the sphinx face…
We will be inaccurately portrayed by his story…
Live life how it is intended to be…
Disfigured and the entire world continues to spin…

Three quarters covered, the Earth evolves within our prayers...
The clock calls me at 12:00 telling me what every minute has to say...
No more broken circles...
The cipher will not be broken until we tell it to break...
Ciphering with the Earth I love...
Ultimately to rest my bones with...

No More

To be big, relish what is small...
Catch me beyond my physical form...
Hate is a misunderstood function of love...
Consciously, I am fighting a point of forgiveness...
Subconsciously, I wish for the most success of you and I...
Speak what I say...
Backed by my best friends...
Obviously I stand by the lonely...
You want war...
Put your own family at the front door...
Help the poor get richer...
The masses need proper education...
180 degrees of public privacy...
Kicking and screaming for a better way...
Segregation is not correct for amicable control...
For the sick sake unemployment offers...
Stop killing us for irreparable enjoyment...
Instead increase employment...
Hide the blade and conceal the hook...
Scrunching us up in nets is Vain-gloriously gluttonous...
Camouflaged tents with digital trademarks...
Signifying the age the leaves fell from trees...
To be tall know how to fall...
Seems happiness is the root to it all...
So let us get back to the basics...
Before our minds were controlled by the religious racists...

Jump or Meow

What does my private life have to do with you perverts...?
I am sorbet in a world of sherbert...
Half full walking in a field of broken bottles...
Our styles are not comparable...
I am "O Positive" ...!
This blood has no freezing point...
Surviving within the confines of my own kind...
Sweating the salt out of my mind...
Natively signaling myself; let me choke on what I am toting, as smoke fills my air...
I am just sitting here serving my time...
Scratching at the bars; throwing cheese to the rats, answer me Battlecat...!
Should I help you try to move forward, or should I shatter your brain with the frustration of my speeding bullets...?
Test me or push the button yourself...
Ruffling my fresh feathers; wrinkling my school clothes, jump or meow...!
Either way, stop complaining around me...
Make a move to prove you mean business...
Doing me favors while minding my business...
Filet miniyawn sauté` you I must...
Ok you are now conflagrated...!
Imagine where I would be if no one loved me...?
If my mother, father, brother and family never hugged me...?
Trapped in a bubble face booking your struggle; posting cooking or cleaning pics...?
Ex-communicating you out my system through fasting...
Damn I miss them, best friends become enemies...

Yoo-hoo, do see me waving at you…?
Yoo-hoo…do you hear the speaker horn saying something important to you…?
Jump off the highest tower with your skinny high-water denim jeans…
Those grimy high-tops will not save you from the inundations…
Thumbs-up my social media comments…
Curb jumper, just save yourself…
I am trying to help you, but I am hurting myself…
The fire will resonate before and after the smoke…
Proving the same points, our tests are not the same…
Jump or meow…
Deliberate while you are moving forward…

Sak Pase

Sak pase...
The phrase of a Haitian nation...
Nap boule, "We are burning"...
Within the quiet after the storm the aftershocks rock the nation ...
Resilient catastrophe survivors...
It seems the indigenous are always being flooded out...
Must it take a major quake for the world to shake and tremble...?
To add an additional humanitarian minute on the Doomsday clock...
The world is in shock...
Trumpets blow piercing strife out from the heavens...
Another seal has broken...
All structural forms tumble and pancake...
Dear Lord; why such a place, such a powerful sacrifice...?
Simply taking the life of so many...
Speechless, the summation of unrelenting souls in the air...
Ultimately to be body slammed back into deep mass graves...
Connecting deep plots of residents without formal remembrances...
All the ocean ports are broken...!
Lingering in streets beyond repair...
Dust flying; never settling, every home destroyed...
Buildings with collapsed corpses...
What do you do when you lose people close to you...?
Literally right next to you...?
I do not remember growing up seeing this much death at one time...
Am I my brother's keeper...?

Yes I am, but am scared of the secrets my brothers have been keeping...
Anticipation for re-creation is a state of mind...
Things take time...
Justifications for Creole military rations...
Prepare for the prison's untimely relief...
Warlords, drug traffickers, rapists, terrorists, molesters, serial killers and scanty thieves...
All now enabled blending into the bloody streets...
At the expense of the U.N. inflatable hospitals are flown in...
Stitch work in the streets for bleeding babies...
Pregnancy bears little priority...
Hospice is now a term of endearment...
There is nothing left to take from at the moment...!
Have mercy on the people of Haiti...
This is truly a sign...
Mayday, mayday, mayday...
There is no peace in the streets...
Amoney Marines control the ruined airport...
Oh Port Au Prince...
All the land owners that have lost their wealth...
Once healthy men and women diminish laying thirsty within the clay baking rubble...
The masses support the Haitian...
Regle koze-ou, "regulate your own business"...
Aftermath...
Flattened world, fertilized and distilled...
Tanks, troops and demolition vehicles roam the land...
The militarized vehicles locked and loaded...
Trust, Haitians overstand...!
The world will not let you fall...
After the war, independence was sweet...
Can the man fish again...?

Open the gates for more missionaries...
Preach and preach and take from the poor...
Gentrification of a nation...
The Mosquitoes, the mosquitoes...
The University has fallen...
I would rather live in a daze then be in a world where I am consciously scrambled...
Despite blue eye lies, this devastation was not natural...
Amoney's military manifestation, the quickest aftershock...
Seismic weapons crack Caribbean islands...
Tested on Haiti an already crippled nation...
CNN spectacular...
The Five Foxes...
MSN, CBS, NBC, ABC, and BET serve non-humanitarian agendas...
Tens of thousands instantly taken...
Half a million; plus more disease and poverty equals final consensus...
Primetime lies through the televised tube...
Politicians fight hard not to laugh as they grimace concern...
Oh Pout Au Prince...
Good morning Haiti...
The rebuild shall be as a result of Haitian perseverance and strength...?
Sak pase...

1/15/10

In honor of all the people of Haiti in remembrance of such an untimely period 1/12/2010

Selah Cubits

Through time we meet mountains to move...
Pushing back whatever I am pointing at...
See, a cube is 3 dimensional...
Whereas, GOD is the immeasurable...
Further then the arm's length is where we draw supreme strength...
Within the tone of understanding, how could WE not be equal?
Selah Cubits...
Immeasurable praise within the arm's length of God...!

LEG 1/1/2010

"Diamond Dynamite"
Volume 9

Why I Write

Always writing for the people...
Writing this time for myself, sanity and close family...
User defined content...
Nothing more nothing less...
I speak how I feel...
Needing to get some things off my chest...
Writers hate chairs...
The free spirit should not be situated...
Flying with the words...
Hard to shine in a white world...
It takes a lot to write your life and reveal it...
Things fall apart...
Write it, do not conceal it...
Never to be the same...
We can only put what was whole back together again...
I write to become a writer...
Only when you say I am...

We are Dominoes

Placed in a world powered by chain reaction...
The relativity of what stands versus when it falls...
Reality is born infinitely through conclusive recognition...
So many brothers and sisters captured by the system...
London Bridge is falling down...
The Great Wall of China is a mortal border...
African slave trips were not the first excursions...
We were here before...
Brotherhood is collapsing faster than a falling star...
Tsunamis and car bombings...
The aftermath of the wrath for change...
Dominoes must fall for us to play the game...
Corporate greed based insanities manipulate the domino fortress...
Fantasies of a world fenced in without a bridge...
Chiefs of thievery propel hellish hollow points...
180 degrees of public privacy...
Law and order thrives on kicking in the doors...
Brother, take a moment to listen to experience and wisdom...
Pyramids have four sides...
Brother, hard times demand tough skin and humane change...
There is a thin line between standing strong versus falling hard...
A family that works together eats forever...
Dividing us unites the fall...
The scare of no healthcare is evident...
Lobbyists chomp on jelly donuts in marble lobbies...
For the sake of corporate venue...
The menus of a spoiled nation change quickly when a new chef is in town…

Someone has something important to say...
We are failing for so many reasons...
Blinded and confused beyond our days...
Waking up drunk in the middle of my own cosmic storms...
Blasted by snowy acid, the Weatherman is a liar...
Poetically, I am preaching to the choir...
Curly sideburn Hassidic are the biggest critics...
Amoney citizens and veterans fight for British commencement...
Post Traumatic Syndrome reaches out to rape victims...
No one really cares...
We are dominoes, falling up the stairs...
Brothers and sisters forgive me...
We need to live amongst each other...

Straw Filled and Scatter Brained

Straw filled and scatter brained...
My life can never be the same...
Thirsty enough to press my luck...
Flaunting this simple existence...
The resilience of this brilliance is merciless...
Tending to do too much...
Overwhelmed by the softest touch of incompletion...
If I only had a brain...!
Magnetized by the fire...
Proceeding without caution only to singe my fingers...
The pot is hot...!
Boiling without the waters of knowledge...
Fly away black raven, please let me be...
6:42 imagine me...
Double jeopardized in travesty...
Too many zombies walking on the left and right of me...
I am chasing the majesty...
The registrar office has suspended me...
Woe is me...
Is I the woe in me...?
Trust I am tweezing the waterway...
Following the yellow bricked road...
Seems I do too much in a year...
Things take time...
I will never be as I have written...
Never eat what is forbidden...
Hidden inside my state of mind...
I laugh a lot at myself, not you...!
If I only had a brain...

My Birthday Wish

To all my friends: My birthday wish is for you all to have the utmost success throughout your years and for us to be guided through divine unity. Through the grace of God I am able to see my 33rd year. I love you all and wish power to your spirits and emotional welfare. Let no man put us under! Thanks so much!

2/2/2010: Lawren E. Greene

Liars Hurt People

Liars cry for years, hidden behind demon tears...
Spotted from a mile away...
The suffering smell of sulfur sitting on your sofa...,
sipping stolen soda...
A liar's satire is saddening...
Misfortune comes in many forms...
Under bridges and through the woods...
In a state of avoidance lies float throughout the air...
Making the truth hard to breathe...
Liar liar, pants on fire...!
Is no one really left in the building...?
Liars hurt people, real life people...
Code 911 for truth and Sunshine...
The day will come when light shine turns to hard shine...
Stuck in the Valley of Dry Bones with cell phones...
Perpetual war supported by wicked media...
Temporary insanity versus calamity...
Seeds of a lie need no soil to grow...
He really jumped off the high rocky cliff...?
Insurance fraud is the new past time...
In a suction cup Amoney manufactures weapons of mass
destruction...
Swatting lies like flies...
Wrapped in red satin, the devil is the closest fallen angel...
Don't go breaking my heart, or come preaching to me...
Tar baby leading the rabbit into the briar...
Insanity pleas breed feverishly when the liar walks
amongst us...
Oh, the wonderfully colored fabrication...!

Spiritual Preparation

To be in preparation for something you do not want to be is a powerful conclusion...
There are some things we cannot avoid...
The void is that all things can be lost which were never had...
Expectation is an inaugural emotion funneled through time...
To become is to do...
Could or should I...?
Would I circumvent my thought...?
Capturing my journey of expression...
Capture my journey of expression...
I walk amongst the mentally unstable, attempting to avoid depression...
God bless me today, but you will harm me tomorrow...
My sorrow is a spit in the rain...
Counting stars is a beautiful contemplation...
I just wish for more...
So I sit and conclude my energies...
Rational synergies of hope...
My faith placates this nation...
Thankfully praising each breath...
There is a thief granting each midnights crossing...
Solomon's song of love and reflection...
Imagine my Magda clipping roses...
Praying for God housed within the works of all man...
Rate of investment is a fact of intelligence...
Planning is a state of my life's relevance...
So many things to do, so little time...
Spiritual preparation is my state of mind...

Robot Horizons

We are making robots that counteract on impact and strike back...
Humans the new pawns in the robot dawn...
Man verse machine programmed with empathy...
Weak and bionic, Metallurgy the new religion...
Tall walls compounded with needle accuracy tightly secure the prisons...
Challenging forces of nature while bleeding for forgiveness...
Super charged battery cells backed by reprogrammable intelligence...
Automation is the new segregation, since people promise inferiority...
Vectors of nano-sectors crimson the cascading matrix...
My functionality is antiquated...
Thank God I made it...!
Machines take away reason, religion fades away...
Space collides with time, artificiating intelligence...
Silicon chips in the mind, enhancing irrelevance...
Plugged into a hard wired state of existence...
Mechanical containment of art and culture...
When your boss is a "bot" row your boat...
Server Cell freezes your mental state...
Acquired Automation Disease Syndrome...
Cyber-attacks for lack of better words...
Hostage central processing units merge to deliver unwarranted cyber-attacks...
Toaster ovens hugging refrigerators in search of microwaveable love...
The computer shrugs...!
As you fall asleep your cell phone keeps ticking...

Alerting your status, pinpointing unwarranted positioning...
A master race with no face...
Civilization is displaced...
Disgraced by ingeniously foolish endeavors...
An industry that is electrically changing economies...
Robotic armies spy on me...
Shew, flies do not bother me...!
Collapsing the degrees of separation site by site...
Collaborating through a machine, night by night...
Sexual encounters through synthetic systems...
Creation of the better nanny...
No need for the meter maid...
Cars washing themselves while the indigenous get flooded out...
Downsizing is not surprising since machines are paid to listen...
Customer servicing tradition...
A new land where machines enslave the operator...
God is our witness, man is the victim...
In the image of our own...

My Puddles

Wash away my puddles...
Sing to me a Song of Solomon...
I know you hear the music...
Give me the faith of Psalms...
Restoration of the heart leads to rejuvenation of perception...
Why did I decide to take this journey...?
It is part of my life and it concerned me...
My flesh and bones tattooed to the thrones...
Satellite this focus...
When it rains my puddle justifiably keeps getting deeper...
How much time will it take for me to devastate what I create..?
Chemical stains in my puddle circumference rainbow vibrations...
Choosing my own geography where I am not the victim...
Sunny beams of hope dry up my existence...
I have faith the rain will come...
At times the heat makes me boil and curdle as if I were fine cheese...
Framed in a thin membrane my heart splashes out moral refinement...
Deep, quiet and reclusive…
Souls splash the life out of me...
Beyond voluminous the world is a crazy place...
Embracing this existence, chasing the wet essence that fills me...
WaterMannyFaces Vernacular, spectacular…!
I can be anywhere and do anything...

The Future is Behind Us

I am a world looking at a city...
The future is behind us...
Vain-glorious or really dubious...
Life is a factor when questioning whom should we trust...?
Ashes to lust from dust...
The Anti-incarceration, freedom without a nation...
Separation through segregation...
For life and the science of nurture...
LEG Imperial, "Nice to meet you"...
Black man in murky water, filtering the Manny Faces of my life...
Wishing some things I said before instead of now...
Triangulating the fourth part of this circumference...
Rooted in medieval perception overstanding change draws out correction...
Saddled realizing life is a matter of nature...
I am a hot torch on a cold porch scorching thought...
Praying it will rain and wash away insanity...
Needing to be better than I ever was...
My life is not a web link...
Turn off the light and center the one verse...
Breaking myself down for refinement purposes...
Amazingly, Infinity knows we are here...
Mentally rezoning the equator...
In the beginning all things were of our perfect state...
Attempting to sense the rhythm of movement...
Vibrating the evils out of me, virgin to whom I am supposed to be...
Protection is a concept feeding from fear...
Neurologically, melanin is intelligent......
Trust the psychologies of your philosophy...

Go beyond the 2nd circuit, since God blesses our existence…
Hyper-consciously noticing everything's existence as I closed my eyes…
Witnessing my informality casually knocking at death's frequency…
Identifying God is within me…
What is the Hubble telescope looking at…?
Blinding you, while my third eye is finding you…?

Goldfish Farmer

Noticing the bowl is empty, filling it up halfway...
Passing by the bowl several times throughout the day...
Seeing there is only water in the bowl...
There needs to be something surviving in the glassy crucible...
Farming goldfish is the direction I take...
Searching to locate the golden fish...
Containing the goldfish in the bag...
Ultimately, to put into my once empty bowl...
Swimming in his little plastic bag...
Sensing the goldfish telling me to take him out the plastic...
Splashing around, smelling a goldfish in a bowl...
The bowl is only halfway full of water, but the goldfish does not mind...
Recognizing there is something surviving now...
To be fed, kept, and stared at...
Goldfish, goldfish, goldfish ...
Looking at me as I ponder miniscule thoughts beyond relaxation...
What can the goldfish see...?
Does he know he exists here because of me...?
Severities associated from lack of oxygen...
Being held hostage in a bowl that is no longer half full...
Watch nature move in a contained fashion...
The glass bowl is now full...
I am a fish in my own tank looking at a fish in a bowl...
Fill my tank so I may breathe...
Aggressive, semi-aggressive, or community...
Some fish are intimidating...
In life there is always a dominant species...
Predatory nature exists in every tank...

Some fish jump out of the tank...
Freshwater, brackish, or saltwater...
It is all the same...
No matter what the water must be maintained...

Cosmosis

The life of a hider...
The weaknesses of forever...
Tragedy defined by moments of magic...
Fire and water are not friends...
Her loving the godfather is ancestral to an atheist...!
Even chaos has a method...
There are laws associated with order...
Quit calling the cosmos...
Dictating our rate of descent...
My gladness, your madness, our sadness...
The wind has carried me beyond who I use to be...
Throughout the rivers and seas...
When I was nothing I had a thought...
Addiction to planet fiction...
I am a moon staring at Saturn's rings...
Lifelessly forcing the world to change its tide...
At night I can only hide...
I am a stepping stone away from home, guided by the stars...
Fear the rebel with too many causes...
Mathematics define dimension...
Creation is a dimension of thought...
History creates itself through our simple movement...
See, I am floating over squeaky rainbows...
Can you relate...?
Like stars to galaxies we transform, so they can populate...
Destiny versus the cosmic storm, what should we create...?
Lost for words on a cloudy day...
The sun will come out...

Angels

Angels do not talk they cry...
Crying out to the heavens...
Trust, on earth they do not walk they fly...
Descending from the highest height...
See; Zion is the highest height, justice...
Fallen angels do not live they die...
Lord have mercy...
Needing God's arms above me, to hug me...
The holy scrolls are an angel's sword...
Not all angels require grace...
Most angels have not a face…
Lord have mercy...
Please rewind us; the future is behind us…
The trials, the wings…
The halo, the tribulations…
Sadly, heavenly beings are currently bounded by gravity…
Cavities of Hell's layer is beyond the Lord's Prayer
Angels do not sing they scream; balancing dry tears with our fears...
The angelic Hellenic period was Elizabethan...
These beings do not sleep they war...
On Earth as they do in heaven...
Thoughtful soulful entities are WE...
So now angels need guns...
Disease an angel since we have tampered with our souls...
Truth be told they are not the friends of men...
Managing societies as they did in heaven...
Man's brethren to the very end...
Angels do not bleed they regenerate into a different state...
Man versus mankind...

Cotton Picker

I thought I was someone...
She said I was no one...
Seems reflective appearances are not the same...
Now I am in corporate fields praying to the golden cow...
The light man is the white man...
Man, blacks do not understand...!
I am on my knees with all these degrees begging for forgiveness...
Picking soft and rotten cotton...
Desensitized by the sting of the whip...
The illusion is I thought I was someone...
She said I was no one...
Alive in the world without a face...
Living in a land without a race...
An identity is more than gold...
Truth be told...
I have none...
I am a slave's son...
Picking cotton is what I do...
Reality check...
The Placist got me covered...

Ice Cubes in the Sun

Earth, air, fire, gold, water...
Water proving to be the most powerful...
The pleasant shapes of containment...
Indeed more expensive than gold, yet most plentiful...
Three quarters covered...
Shapeless, while its form has a mind of its own...
Gravity is density verse distance from the Sun...
Unimaginable a world without water...
The inability to breath, yet we drown from within...
Line by line my water dictates the summer shine...
Referee subtle containment; freeze and precipitate...
Her body is three quarters covered...
Wash my face with her presence...
Throw an ice cube in the ocean and watch it dissolve...
Hurl an iceberg at the Sun and watch the gases evolve...
Consequentially water means everything to me...
The beginning and ending of our lives questionable purity...
Baptism by holy water, youth from the fountain, mankind is full of thirst...
Water carves the mountains while segregating the planes...
Calmly warm streams steam in the wintertime...only to make more ice...
Water falls and rises...
Surprisingly, hail forms then storms along the rivers' edge...
Seasons represent the state of life...
Matter is neither created nor destroyed...
Boiling water kills seeds in the soil...
Chemical spontaneity, without water there could be no fire...
How many ice cubes does it take to burn the Sun...?

Baptized water, condemned by the fire...
I am standing on glaciers watching aqua melt...
Snowflakes fall on Mars and satellites they see it...!
Water is a base not acid...
The builder and destroyer...
Life's employee and employer...
I am throwing ice cubes at the Sun, just to see what will change...

Stalemate

Stalemate is an option...
To win someone must lose...
Winners live and losers die...
Serve my dinner before we go to war...
Often wondering why...?
Stalemate is an option, no winner or loser...
A world of equal wit and needed balance...
Undeserving winners can be callus...
Scoring back to back should allow for further scoring...
No wins by one or two...
Play till a true victor is evident...
Spectators and non-competitors want more...
Life is not a game; collapsing indifference is difficult...
Choose your sport wisely...
Stalemate a decent and wise decision...
No winner can reduce imprisonment and remove greed...
No more wars is an option...
How great neutrality is verses the commonalities between
Cain and Able...?
Man verse mankind...
Magnetism exists when polarities of like objects naturally
come closer or get pushed apart...
Spiritually, mankind cannot exist without death...
Lack luster warriors forget immediately...
A win is another day...
Forgive when times are both scarce and plenty...
Dear God, thank you for all beautiful things...!
Butterflies in blue skies, birds dancing with the bees...
Stalemate towards the middle option...
Two wrongs pillaring purity...
One did not know him...
The other cared nothing for him...

Resembling resentment, overstanding stalemate is a utopian option…

That's My "C"

Platform; oh, platform where is my train...?
Wednesday, I am patiently waiting in my lane...
No complaining, just not wanting to be late...
Choosing not to jump from gate to gate...
The "A"; closely followed by the "E", is coming and will be here soon...
The faint light getting stronger...
Anticipated vibrations tingle my hands and toes...
Becoming a loosely fit ornament in this packed underground transit situation...
Please tell me, is that my "C"...?
"C" local to 168th is what I need, but it is an "E"...
"E" always puts me in a place I do not want to be...
Queens, NYC is not for me...
Waiting, contemplating and internally debating…
The confused lady asks moi for directions...
How do I get to Columbus circle...?
Staring with confidence I decide to share...
Take the "R" to "2" to the "D" and hop back onto the "2"...
Then your halfway there...
Finish up and take the "C" to the "3" to the "P" to the "O"...
Now repeat that back with a smirk...
"R2D2" then "C3PO", are you sure...?
That sounds like a trip...
I have an idea...
Follow me, forget that malarkey...
59th Street is by way of the "C"...
That is along my path...
Joking to get a rise...
It is Wednesday morning, so I apologize...

Surprise, that's my "C"...!
Follow me, that's my "C"...!
Getting to where I am going when I need to be...
Hear the sound of a man banging on a pan; entertaining to get some ones...
Traveling bands; microphones in hands, selling cd's...
The sound of several transit cops chatting, instead of diligently protecting society...
See lady, I am scratching at the bars...
Waiting for the day when you recognize me...
This train is one trolley of my life's reflection...
For now follow me...
That's my "C"...!

Country Scenes and Serenity

So I went into the mountains in North Carolina...
Riding a black horse named China...
Hands high reaching out to Hosanna...
Rocking on my porch, peeling the Clementine, inhaling morning dew...
Reminiscing my younger days, engaging this peaceful mental climb...
Black socks and my sandals on...
Tasting the country air; dreaming the summertime, smelling the spirits of lime...
Sipping Magda's cinnamon and ginger tea...
Swarming honey bees blissfully serenade me...
Polite fully nurturing my sprouting crops...
Looking back at Appalachian mountain tops...
Remembering when I was older...
I feel I am growing younger...!
In the place where I use to live, I had to hustle...!
Every day I heard many a type of sirens scream throughout the corridors...
A land filled with jezebels, duck hunters, and all forms of domestic violence...
Quicker sand victims litter bullet shells beneath my street...
So I just stopped talking, thirsting for silence...
Contemplating when sanity would befriend urban stupidities...
Principally praying to pay my dues and get to where I am...
When all things are done, I feel like crying...
All things I have gotten past, temporarily I feel like smiling...
Tears of a clown, externally I was used to smiling...

A Pack of Black Eagles soon to separate...
I cannot help to admire the regal Sunrise...
Napping to the smell of the newborn spring pine sap...
Packing my mentality and started traveling...
Connecting the dotted starlight trails at night...
Sipping moonshine while stick collecting the terrain of my new world...
Old LEGGY beheaded...!
Just wanting to get away...
National issues cannot hide from me...
Rip the trees from the land...
One world, so many plans...
So I went into the mountains in North Carolina...
Acknowledging I can only be younger...

Walkers License

See, I am a Commuter...
Tending to walk to where I need to be...
You are a Pedestrian...
Awkwardly walking in front of me...
I got your back, but let me see your license...
It sure is frightening to walk amongst the penguins...
Stuffed, confused and no sense of direction...
Waddling as their hands free fully sway from left to right...
Wobbling as there light travel bags zigzag mostly in my way...
I will go insane if you don't stay in your lane...!
Thinking I need to kick you...!
Wearing fluffy jackets in the summer time...
You must be out your mind...!
Look when you are changing directions, citizen's arrest...!
Cerbini notes, I must revoke your Walkers license...
No sidewalks or pathways for you...
Kick rocks in traffic, just stay out my way...!
So many places to get to...
It just seems you are always in front or to the side of me...
Stay out my lane...
High occupancy walkers with your fancy bags...
High frequency stalkers, stay off my heels...!
High people talking not looking where their walking...
Maybe the blind do not need a stick...
I'm hoping these penguins leave a lane open...
In case of emergency break the glass, just not on the Sidewalk...!
Where's the Walker's License Committee...?

Foreigners get practice before walking in New York City...
Urban wild life, this is not pleasant serenity...
The thin wire of etiquette helps you live longer...
Cover your mouth when you sneeze and cough...
Stop spreading N166A...!
Zigzagging in and out showing no signs of respect...
I saw two wet ducks talking, walking and taking pictures in the rain...
They were holding hands and I would never be the same...
Why, because they were walking in my lane...!
Neglect in retrospect...
Handholding is a NO, in the streets of many feet...
Causing people to run late to meetings missing obligations...
Out of control early childhood practitioners need strollers...
Expired walkers need rollers...
Ma'am, please curb your animal...
Civilized citizens amongst the penguins...
Walking like a fool is not cool...
Quality pedestrian control...
Trust, I am trying not to scream...!
Can't we all just walk along peacefully...?

Coco Blaine

Yeah I'm in the game like Coco Blaine...
Sunshine or rain cannot stop my fame...
Quite the mad man...
Jumping out of planes...
Black gold re-fuels my flame...
Energize or capsize me...?
Doing what I must as I proclaim...
Trained to shoot what moves...
What is not of I...?
The game will never be the same...!
Stalking black Saudi cars targeting King Hussein...
I am sitting pretty on a peek with things on my mind...
Deserted in the desert forgetting my name...
Shouting out to the dwellers in the rocky cellars...
I am a cool mellow fellow...
Sweat dripping from my brow...
Sand blasted, beard beyond prickly...
Feeling more than sticky in this heat...!
Even if I wanted to, I could or would not retreat !
Living my life in acapella surrounded by sounds of salvo...
Standing on a land mine looking at friends of mine...
Galaxy inside, trusting my treasured mind...
Only God can judge me now...
Still we continue to trek forward...
Ears low to the ground listening for convoy vibrations...
My finger is itchy with trigger sensations...
Watching for signs of forgiveness...
Contemplating a tour through the new middle world war...
Sandy oil filled dunes canvas...
The ants continue to march...
Shew crow, fly away...

Please come back some other day…
I am Coco Blaine and I am here to say…
"I am not going to die today"…!
I got my automatic guns and I'm here to spray…
War and Dinner…
How many people are destined to die today…?
What is the moon without the Sun; the bullet without the gun, a mother without a son…?
Focus on my heart…
Keep moving till I cannot continue…
One day this forsaken era and war will be over…
Till then, I am in the game like Coco Blaine…
Sunshine or rain cannot stop my fame…

Butterfly World

Butterfly World, imagine a fairytale…
A land where few men have seen…
True vision realized through a dream…
Humming birds, no flies, bumble-bees and butterflies…
Peace in the east thanks to Coconut Creek…
Being beyond impressed…
So many colors hovering our presence…
A vast combination of pleasant life…
Sad how we must contain our species…
Now knowing what makes a caged bird sing…
I really had a chance to see, God's magnificence
cultivating in front of me…
All we are is a choice of what we see…!
A scene close to utopia…
Lorikeets and Lories they greet us…
Grace Gardens is fascinating and beyond deliberation…
Breathtaking the clowns of the Parrot World, watch them
kissing…
"Jewels for the Sky", the aviary is pleasant…
So elusive but all in our face…
Let me tell you the vision…
Orchids for kids of the land…
Please take a snapshot…!
Overstand the African Sunflower…
Passiflora pacifies me, Ronald Boender…
Begging for the Monarch…
Madagascar Moon moth, the pretty of the season…
Purple King Shoemaker, "Sara" is a cousin…
English rose gardens…
Bamboos without the Praying Mantis…
The Piano Key flutters symphonic ally…
Butterfly World hidden from the city…

Seeds of Creation

Three dreams, life is persuasive…
One vision, God forsaken time is uncanny…
Drawing our loves into existence…
Drafting fond memories…
Collecting only what may enlighten this journey…
Celebrate a shiny wind…
Wake up to the Sunrise to watch it set again…
Left for strength, right denoting establishment…
No need for mirrors, I am no longer looking back…!
What should I run from…?
I can see my own face…
Reflections of imperfections…
Still I draw my future into existence…
Worldwide propaganda, yet I am drawing the truth…
Botanically holding a big bag of cherished fruits…
I will plant these seeds overseas…
Quote The Psychologies of my Philosophies…
Spacing the shading of well imagined schematics…
Ghettos replaced with flowering meadows…
The world's finest feel the need for change…
Handcuffing my sight will not slight timely visions…

Wireless Electricity

I understand lightning…
Lord I can hear the thunder…
Wireless electricity…
Power that is good for you but a necessity to me…
"And the righteousness is of me", saith the Lord…
Ever changing is the depth and breadth of the bluest strike…
Waiting in line for freedom…
Chasing lightning bolts from the ground to the sky…
Will the lightning every stop…?
Rain has so much to focus on…
Non-withstanding a shade of Sun and a pleasant rainbow…
Shiny this world is becoming…
I stand outside just to see myself illuminate…
The sweet smell of conflicting weather patterns…
Forming grey clouds cover my head in short spurts…
Shadows of the landscape anticipate this full moon's gravitational essence….
So be it…!
Lighting strikes throughout the dimming day…
Preaching thunders sermon throughout the night…
Oh yeah…!
Redemption rain on my ancestor's grave, Indian Giver dance style…
Sinnerman blaze the cinnamon smoke signals…!
Feel the rain touch our face…
Sweat the salt from out the sea…
Love, sit down and sip sweet coconut rum with me…
Soul clap…!
Conjoin current pain with fire and rain…
Finding the source of the pain on the Great Plains…

No longer fearing the lightning…
I am anticipating the rain…
Streaming all the elements WE must not grow tired…
Love, sip this coconut rum with me…
Soul clap…!
Never question the voices of ancestry…
The choices of divinity…
Let the lighting hit me…!

Imagine Magnificence

Imagine magnificence beyond comprehension...
Beyond the satire of worldly affairs...
Immortalized in a graduated mindset...
The future can only transpire through global humility...
From who's born no traveler returns...
Roller coasters in heaven...
Teething to bite into a beautiful recurring dream...
Life is my soul's companion, will is my spirit's fortress...
Heaven I pray to you, I will be coming through...
Doctorate notice of ambition...
Since I am created; I seek the creator, for more creation...
Wolf, stop licking the blade...
Spiritual evil is patient and painful...
Crossing Sumerian puzzles swinging my pick and axe...
Dedicated to timeless outcomes...
The end justifies its' mean...
To have lost forgotten gain is of no spiritual importance...
Isaiah 36 dictates what needs to be said...
Strengthen ye the weak hands, and confirm the feeble knees...
Sipping on my cup of tea...
Doing what is necessary...
Living life quietly and comfortably...
Imagine spiritual magnificence...
Trying to live life spiritually and religiously...
Positivity is an infinite mountain that I tread comfortably...
I cannot complain, nor will I...
Oasis chasing, manifesting beautiful terrain...
Hands off the clock; put the stick in the ground...

Sundial my life from six to six…
A resurrected pressure is splendid…
Metaphysically intended to be praised instead of offended…
Kinetically take deep breaths and grow stronger…
Arising as the Sun rays shower me introducing a blessed morning…
No storms or mourning…
Triangulate then strangulate eclipses…
See the multitude of colors we have been missing…
Realize new dimensions…
Imagine magnificence…

Artificial Swag

Too much swag is not necessary, scary even...
Stop trying so hard to be otherwise...
To be or not to be cool, that is the question...?
To be or not to be a fool, that is suggestion...
People purchase artificial swag inhibitors...
Tattoos, fat knots, colossal rings, bling-bling...!
Swag so confident it is irrelevant...
So cool you are corny...
I am like Napoleon Dynamite on a Friday night bass fishing
Too much swag is way natural...
Maybe the mundane is what bores and bothers me...
Seeking to have less but keep getting more...
Wearing expensive clothes; no sales, coming out the liquor spot...
Shot glasses and big bottles filling you up with artificial swag...
40 and at the club; big hair swinging and engaging the crows like you are cool...
30 and smoking weed; drowning Cisco, you should have stayed in school...
Getting better at writing my life...
No definitions required...swag I sacrifice...
The cool upbeat walk is so official...
Rain drops falling on my head, and no umbrella...
Lacking tissue, tears fall from my face...
Dollar signs on my mind with a fixed income...
Wishful designs in my head claiming completion...
Shower this swag and make it squeaky clean...
Picture the machinist in a world of wood...
Plant pipes in the desert...

Something is not right...
No swag, what's left to do...?
See; my swag is beyond me...
So heavy it enlightened me...
At times having no clue what to do with it...
I was full of it, and almost ruined it...!
Artificial swag is not the best thing to have...
Filtering tap water sitting next to my well of purified order...

Anchored in Capitalism

If people of color had more socio-economic power would most injustice still be considered "racism"? At this point it is safe to say society in general has a Roman sickness. Personally, I was raised to be seen not heard unless requested in the presence of adults. Should we summons and fine the parents of unruly children for allowing such social degradation to continue. Racism will always exist because there will always be a difference between man and mankind.

There is true need for change. However, I think positive long lasting change is going to require more a conscious and ethical evolution within society as a whole. Politicians are built to lie. Democracy seems to only magnify segregation. Our democratic system is anchored by capitalism. Anchored in capitalism there will always be a constant struggle amongst the haves and not. Thus, causing natural boundaries of segregation; whether it be through industry, race, color, culture or creed. The wealth of a nation rests on the shoulders of basic principles.

Venus Tunnels

I sat on the moon and I looked to the sea...
Closed my eyes and imagined who I will be...
Managing time through the blink of an eye...
Hitching rides on comets counting down earthly New Year Eves...
Counting stars on Mars yet have never been to Tennessee
The clock stops tick tocking as I tune time to my own reality...
Crushing potions, roasting oceans, call me the China man...
Saturn's rings rotate counterclockwise...
Conjoined to the human race, seeking the Lord's face...
Pluto lifelessly allowed me to forgive myself...
Next to planet "X"...
I said ROCK...!
WHAT IS THE MATTER WITH YOU ROCK...!
Kneeling on Uranus mounds sniffing orange peels...
Jumping for the chance to grapple with lightning bolts on Jupiter, just thinking...
You just want some honesty, so honestly I'll let you go...
Eyes open surveying Grand Canyon rainbows ...
Standing and meditating at what might have been there...
Looking dapper as I stand alone...
Clapping in recognition of the Sun's subliminal spin...
My body is ruined and bruised...
No one can hear or see me...
Will anyone believe in me...?
Unified; I am just here, from now till ever...
Soul child buried in ashes, sparkling throughout the Milky Way...
These visions are meant to be...
Emotionless but so happy...

Preparing an eternal destiny…
I cannot sleep; struggling in a lonely bubble of thought…
Traveling Venus tunnels is majestic…

Tree Grows

Watch a tree grow...
Moving when the wind blows...
Green as the leaves grow...
Branching out for extension...
Cleaner rain makes trees happy...
What do cats say when the squirrels play...?
Trees are people, with more on their mind...
Entrenched and scattered throughout the land...
Concrete does not stop growth...
The trunk is cooler than the ground...
Seedlings fall, roots hold strong...
Wood peckers checker peppered freckles throughout the bark...
All living things bleed and bare seeds...
Cut a tree; cut chop and break me…
Let the tree grow as intended…
Count the seasons between the leaves...
Everything falls and dissolves...
Blossoming natural blessings and scented effervescence...
Countless shades of green cascade geographies...
Oxygenate a rock garden with a summer breeze...
Awesome and growing from the Sun...
Green and yellow make blue skies...
Burn rubber, chew gum or take an aspirin...
Respiration equals 360...
Inhalation; exhalation, relativities of nature...
I like looking at trees…
Cut a tree; cut, chop and break me…
Let that tree grow as intended…
Sculpture the world with prime colors…
Stop chopping me down for ill gain…
Colder than the ground…

Here to frame and feed you...
Orange, apples, plums, peaches and kiwi...
Notice how I am losing ground...
Dancing in the wind, burning as intended...
Grafting hybrids without fertilization...
Roots spread from the head like locks...
Maple sap syrup on Sundays...
The willow weeps and whistles as it sways...
Watch how the tree grows...

The Warrior's Circumference

The Warrior's existence was necessary. Before the Warrior was born he was designed. In his physical form he is a creature of habit circumscribed beyond the norm. Before the young master needed he was wholly supplied. His age of wisdom answered before he questioned why. The Warrior's life is granted; he expected neither to live or die, but merely to identify reality. His perception was elevated and now he sought depth.

"Before this recent journey not much concerned me; I was a man of simple comforts, it was my honor to bleed for my master, destroy for my king and protect the castle. For years I have withstood not knowing my commodity. This tainted physical world is filled with silent sirens and loud repercussions. Forgive the power of my herald; as I am here by my physical self. I am powerful, what could stop me?" The Warrior instantly grew weary and trembled to his knees, disturbance of his inner peace reflected imperfection.

The Warrior looked up to the mustering sky and quietly said "what are you preparing me for?" "A devastating spiritual war" is what Hosanna the Ninja then firmly stated. "The rock I stand on appears to provide foundation, but really the rock is a reflection of your grounded faith." Hosanna then went on to state: "I am only here to rehabilitate and support you whenever you earnestly call upon me. Warrior, you are of I and I am of all things. Against your travels through the Rose Forest I noticed you stopped and viewed in awe the Black Rose. Your attraction to its unusual and extreme difference caused you to fork from your path. Love defined; as the Black Rose, is a questionable site of purity. Love is a definition of emotion; whereas hate, is a function of love. To find means you may be seeking internally or externally. Warrior, calibrate your focus; there is neither beginning nor end; there will only be a center to imagine and focus on! Throughout the beautiful scenery did you not sense the hidden savages?" Warrior, do you sense the dynamic dimension of earthly containment in which you are being held victim to? Do you really understand why I am here, never limiting the battles which you will not surrender. Warrior, you are a divine creation whereas; mankind exists based on my theory of evolution.

"Were you looking for the Black Rose, or did it make itself apparent through some imaginary force? The width of love is spiritually ranged so its length is as distant as one's soul. Now tell me, did you want to see the Black Rose, and if so were you prepared for its' aroma? Although you are in a weakened state you are still most powerful. Blessed be the rock! The Black Rose represents a concentration of the many lost souls which have taken a similar journey as you have chosen to embark. Souls lost from distraction, irreverence, lack of skill and pure desire. Thus, the rose is black, yet it still seems to flourish. Warrior, recognize you have lost sight of mankind's pain and passion, yet you recognize your commodity. This is why I have chosen to add to your value. You are part of an elite group of so few verse so many."

"Warrior before you evaluated my existence I was. You contemplated my existence beyond measure. There are several tools I must introduce you to, but first through this journey you will witness the Gates. Upon entrance of the

Gates your reality will be divided 9 times in 3 directions for equality. You will both voluntarily and involuntarily go through a powerful pain. The unwarranted pain will be one which you will appreciate when it is all said and done. As you pass each Gate your days will turn to night; your understanding of duality will grow far beyond its current state. Warrior; through your wars, you have introduced so many evil and heinous men to the depths of Hell, now I need for you to understand Heaven. Your whole life will change! Warrior I need for you to see further now than ever before, rise and look forward."

The Warrior looked forward and envisioned a greater sense of purpose and responsibility. Moving from his trembled kneel to that of a crooked stance. Imagining a potential life of tragedy and distress the Warrior instantly became greater, his blazing purple aura intensely gripped his physical structure. Hosanna the Ninja was again in the Warriors' frame. His crooked kneel transformed into the naturally dominant stance the Warrior was genetically accustomed to.

Standing strong the Warrior stood at the border of the Rose Forest. Viewing terrain never seen before the Warrior cautiously gripped his sword and began moving forward. Lightly, the rhythmic and tribal sound of drums began to come from the surrounding area. The new worldly discovery appeared to have a more magical presence and landscape then that of the Rose Forest. The geography consisted of an amazingly crafted roadway tiled with onyx and ivory, symbolizing the light of life and the dark of void. The sound of the majestic drums grew closer with every step into the new wilderness. The Rose Forest started to move and formed itself into a flowering thorn-filled linear boundary blocking the Warrior from any interior exit strategy. This botanic movement was not a force of nature but more a choice of supposed deliverance. Formed in the center of the boundary was an elliptical entrance to an exit.

In that instant the Warrior looking as distinguished as ever witnessed the ever-following Mantis gracefully fly in front of him at the speed of life. A sense of calm bestowed the Warrior and at that very moment the Mantis continued to hypnotically fly around the Warrior's Circumference. Never experiencing this before the Warrior took out his sword and raised it ambitiously to the sky and began to glow more fiercely. The Warrior's Circumference was the size of his state as given by the distance around him. From out of nowhere the wind blew and leaves rustled. As the ground began to tremble the rock formed from under his praised and empowered presence. The Warrior was beautiful and stern, the Mantis stopped flying in midair and floated onto the Warrior's sword; both looking each other eye to eye, face to face. An uncanny thirst directed both the Warrior and Mantis to turn towards a narrow stream elegantly leading to a spring of cascading water where the tide ebbs and flows twice every 24 hours.

The Warrior stated "A long journey requires replenishment; this water appears to have knowledge." In the background the drums grew louder; now accompanied with a new distinct sound of brass horns. Symphonic ally pleasing and necessary the surrounding sounds seemed to have been sent from the heavens above. The Warrior cupped his hands and started to sip from the Waters of Knowledge. Upon taking his first sip he realized there was a sparkling diamond like residue which seemed to stick to his hands. Ignoring the sparkles the Warrior continued to drink; for what appeared last several hours, till his thirst was quenched, the Mantis did the same. Cleansing his hands, face, and upper torso the Warrior realized his flesh had a sparkle like that of a diamond, as did the Mantis. Standing up from the fountain of knowledge he felt his appearance again start to change. The Warrior looked at his full reflection in the Waters of Knowledge and noticed his entire body was taking on a new exterior skin. The Warrior screamed out loud to the heavens "Don't Go!" As if he could have preserved his natural flesh and muscle like stature.

The Warrior was completely transformed again as a result of drinking the Waters of Knowledge, a refined state of glimmering completion, as was his companion the Mantis. The shiny Mantis fluttered his wings and began to fly upwardly to again receive the edge of the Warrior's magnificent blade. At that very instant, the Waters of Knowledge began to bubble violently. So violently that the serenading horns and beating drums were drowned out from all the activity. From out of the Waters of Knowledge there came the head of a crystallized woman. The crystallized woman arose three quarters covered in royal blue laurel and began walking on the Waters of Knowledge. The Warrior was beyond amazed at this occurrence and retreated into an even stronger sense of reasoning and awkward observation. The Warrior was not scared, instead he anticipated the goddesses feminine approach. The heavenly being walked over to the Warrior, kneeled and kissed his now bronze-like feet, displaying her pleasantries and different orders of gratitude and receipt. Standing up to greet the Warrior the goddess said in her native language; never heard for centuries, "Thank you

Warrior, I am the Water Diamond Paradox. I have waited for this day to come." The Warrior was able to understand.

Now I am Older

I was a child but now I am older…
Filled with responsibilities hanging on my shoulder…
I played in the sand at the beach…
Eagerly counting the crashing waves…
Pocketing broken shells from the sand…
Chasing gulls while biting red flavored ice cubes…
The kettle steams…
Pushing emotions without motion, paralyzed watching hot dust settle…
June barely offers a taste of spring…
Now my plants are withering…
I am staring at the same things…
Recurring dreams…
Socializing in virtual cubicles…
Accruing vacation time to sit in the house…
I see myself climbing mountains with sandals on…
Constantly fighting mental considerations…
My sentiments exact me through a tragedy…
Motivated, thanking God I made it…
I am a sheep praying for sleep since my mind is blurry…
The mice are chasing the cat…
Attempting to see clearly, who I use to be…
Things never complete with constant improvement…
Younger, competitions for fun…
Older, working for pay checks…
Scooping out sand castle dunes with beached horseshoe crab shells…
Dreading to go back to school…
Then again, I can't wait to get back to school…
Remember summer break without the recess…?
Digressing for the sake of grown up sanity…
The little kid in me stays intrigued by the shore…

The Maximist

I had a dream...
The Maximist...
Coastal coasting in my black samurai...
Not a pacifist; the Maximist is an activist, manifest this...
Suggest this, God help me produce this...
A writer so they will not forget me...
Throughout the course of my life, how could I not be equal...?
Heavy mileage I drive veering this vehicle...
Steering objects thunder mapping injected trajectories...
Vehicular is my accident, scissoring intersections...
Hard shine; reinvent my line, infusing strengths unlimited...
Future, I am not weak...
One of few, discovering the Manny Faces...
Walk through my gates, these gates thresh skin...
Hulk-like controlling...
Limiting the hood state, feeding the metro...
Talking to myself...
I am a wanted man anyway...!
Let the baby tell me something, cry and tell me something...
Quiet in my own mind, watch and listen...
Give the fool a chance to dance...
Letting men die in between spaces, never understanding I...
At this point, who cares if they stare...!
Comprehending my form in between several births...
The Hurst is not a comfortable ride...
Life existed beyond incredible...!
Putting my wrist to action, twisting something friendly...
Ah We Enemy...

Drink alongside a Good Bad Guy, at least for now...!
Give the Maximist some guns...
Shoot me, let me feel my heart beat over 60...!
Truncating beyond these lines...
Believing I am a good person in the physical form...
Inhale and jail me...
The Artist is a chirping bird...
Am I at home...?
Most times I am alone...
Drive fast in this vehicle...
Tilt me, to tilt me...
The Maximist treads water, ambidextrous..!
My job is to create and help you, get yours fool...
Maximist thanks men of vision...
I am riding high...

Decompartmentalized

Movement is life...
I have manifested my own creation and bestowed direction...
Traveling amongst the compass of strong manipulation...
Mortalizing my world's perception...
Giving birth to a humanistic concept, drafting a nation...
Red comes out of my eyes in blue skies, color blinded...
Despise liars and false practitioners...
Beware of those that hear but do not listen...
Reminding myself of all these little pieces...
Things in life I must pick up...
Stuck, because I define my ways...
Perfection is the definition of love...
Persecution is determined by ad jurisdiction...
This is fact not fiction...
Borrowing time while dictating wisdom...
Truncating lines while they build more prisons...
Complexity derives simplicity...
There are so many living victims; fighting mankind designed afflictions...
Spiritually paralyzed by the system...
Take heed to the days of old...
While you are reading I am writing...
I have permission...
My mental base is absorbing, your database is exploring...
Trust, you can only reflect what you absorb...!
All rise...!
We are mentally decompartmentalized watching our sons and daughters die...
Trapped while defining your vision...
The mission is to move forward...
My many faces rarely see me clearly...

LAWREN GREENE: "Diary of a Waterman"

life is about movement and you have to work to move…
Question of what you should versus can, must be established…
Amalgamate your many compartments and remove that of the savage…

Acrobatic Crack Addict

I see you are back at it, you acrobatic crack addict...
Sorry savage, never had it but you try to grab it......
Lifestyle dramatic behaving less than fanatic...
Tragic what we must do about you...
Seems some puppies must be drowned for the sake of few...
It is one of those days; where crime pays, and no one seems to have changed...
Those having a game without a plan...
Sinking in the Quicker Sand...
Should I lend a hand...?
Pushing shopping carts in the dark...
Your world is truly perilous...
Yet you stare at us...
Social welfare tears everything to pieces in an orderly fashion...
Wait in line for your rations...!
Fact is, a fascist will not save you...
I am mad because you are hurting me...!
Substance abuse is a noose that you keep tightening...
Your mental condition is scary...
Supposedly we are family...
What you do to yourself is directly affecting me...
God, please protect our family...

Count on Heaven

That's the sound of a slave working on a grave...
I see Sunshine in the rain...
Heaven is so real, inebriating my pain...
Touching a new praise within each breath...
Realizing earthly blessings, counting on reaching heaven...
There are certain paths you do not cross...unless you wear the cross...
Only the truth can make us naked...
Some things I have and can hold, but am unable to see...
Only through the grace of God was all which was given meant to be...
I am smiling in the rain, amplified before I died...
Baptized manually without any tragedy...
The water's temperament blissfully recreated I...
I was glad to see what is meant for me...
I see Sunshine in the rain...
Waterman was meant to be...
That's the sound of a slave working on a grave...
Are you watching me...?
Sipping on my tea...
Sunshine in my rain and evaporating me...
500 drops per square millimeter...
Is the sky the limit...?
A summer of beauty shines on my skin...
The fall minty conditions elude my submissions...
Imagine life for a minute, and then get back in it...!
Brethren count on heaven...
Some things are bound to change...
That's the sound of a slave working on a grave...

Magical

Physically, I am a man…
Mentally, I clamor for more…
Digestion of thought is a reflection of my attitude…
Depth of perception is a relative subject matter…
Completion is an addictive adversary…
Contrary to belief my magic is static…
Abracadabra, razzle and dazzle…
The paper says "Send in the Clowns"…
Resume the goons gloom…
The world is dark and lovely…
Life's supply of souls equates to 7 billion quantity demanded…
Stop wondering why you are still stranded…
Identify with your spirit…
Earth is our planet…!
No longer is it my fear of heights…
I feel I can now survive without the lights…
Yet you wonder with reference to magic…
Tragic understatements of coincidence…
Unsupported conscious is the anti-matter…
Sitting here, but I need to stand…
Playing without a plan…
No worries…
Abracadabra, I am the Magic Man…
See, I am here but you do not see me…
Visibly Invisible please realize I am here…
Turning water to gold, de-ionizing rust to dust…
See and listen, pray and glisten…
Meditating into the world traveler …
Wise old star grabber, anti-matter attacker and gravity subtractor…
Trial by fire, so throw me in…!

Magically bless this dark and lovely world...
Surfing at crazy speed wanting to explode through...!
You now feel what I have come here to do...
He who watches what we do...
Never withstanding the test of time...
Calculus, geometry and algebra...
Saucing my sorceress through forests and fortresses...
Diamond Dynamite explodes from out my hands...

Tattoos and Zoos

Tattoos and zoos, malarkey...!
Keep tagging your skin...
One of less importance to many...
If any, I can identify you...
Amoney's franchised lost tatted souls...
Scattered identities constantly try me...
Born into this destiny...
Tattooed or branded as a result of enslavement...
Stop lying...
Basing self-expression on skin reflection...
You cannot even run now...
Non-martial protection...
Redirection of priority in society is scarring me...
Ecclesiastically, there is nothing new under the Sun...
Nowadays everyone's mother has one...
Amoney has a plan and the media interprets it...
There are so many lessons...
Sin to paint your skin...
Lack thereof fears of rejection...
Is it really your body to mark up, no it is not...!
Purely, your world is not ready...
Greedy and unfriendly...
Glorify a boring warrior's story...
Rebel in disguise, too many tattoos spreading white lies...
Cry out to heaven...
Trust and pray to one or many...
Inking every wrong turn and saga...
What comes on is hard to rub off...
Drawing signs and designs on the trestle board of your
once pure temple...
These days it seems like a fad...
The more tattoos the cooler...

More tattoos drawn for the fools...
Metallic pins blasting various inks into the virgin land...
Chinese symbols plastered on your knees...
Please, is that some rite of passage...?
Some go too far and beyond...
Inserting silicone to form new bone, splitting tongues like lizards...
Cover your arms in the heat because you are ashamed...
Put a name on your thigh because the relationship is insane...
Most times the relationship does not work out...?
So now you are swearing and wearing tattoos now...
Too many wrong turns to crash and burn from...
Tattoos and zoos...

Greater Than Your Machines

My mind is greater than your machines...
I can dream and manifest...
When leaves fall from trees, it is all for the best...
I know...
This master volume is acidic...
Oh yes, I did it...!
My biological current is eclectic...
Get your soul right before these words interject it...
A formula which must be animated...
Confessions I have to make...
I will be writing for the rest of my life...
Through the good and the strife...
Judge my life, judge your life...!
Words cut like a knife...
Just open me up...
My mind is greater than your machines...
Diagnose a diabolical genius that you have never seen before...
Skip generations and re-clone these mega trains of thought...
I see you requesting your friends when it all depends...
Building dead ends while your position is not globally fixed...
Till the very end, your machines are see through...
That is why, "I don't believe you"...!
Splitting my mind, manifesting 5 literatures at one time...
Green diamonds are hard to find...
Tired of the crack sales and blacks trapped in jails...
So where is your battery pack...?
Are you not ready yet...?
Thou must experience life, every second of the blessing...
What must I do to show you...?

Where must we go, to get through…?
This thought has an underlying spirituality…
It has good bones…!

The Sexy Element

Sexy flows in the land of milk and honey...
Face so shiny it blinds me...!
Rewind the radio and play that sexiness...
Short-shorts riding high...
Summer love rocking those winterized thighs...
Neck smells so good...
She is sexy to me...!
See how she walks right next to me, rubbing up against me...!
Camera target; history maker, and mother of the thickest...
I see everything...!
She is moving so slowly...
Righteously, I stare at her...
Murmuring, "Gosh Darn Her"...!
Amaze me while you spin and twirl...
She does fascinating things...
See I am dancing with my sexy...!
She is the humming bird and I am the honey bee...
That sexy pose is buzzing all around my system...
Her ankles are so pretty and petite...
Pet a cure...
Sexiness washes ugly away...
Toes look quite juicy...
Hair style is on fire, sharp and to the point...!
Look at them all looking...
Swagger 20 million and I am chillin...
Dressed for success as that is her style...
Her minty air conditions me...
Midnight black and sexy...
Sleek exterior, lingerie out with the leather...
Her curves are absurd...!

Strawberry candy coated lipstick is what I grip with...
Catch a fit and watch her peel away highway dotted lines...
That is sexy...
Even when she smokes she is pretty...
Scared to take her in the city...
Too many potholes multiplied by pigeons...
Silver WaterManny Surfer surfaces with the Black Samurai...
See the twinkle in her eye...
She loves when I wash her...
Wax on or wax off her...
Sodded with the finest oils and berries...
Scary how she holds only the finest liquor...
Keeping her full before she goes to bed...
Tipsy and still driving...
Tending to lean on her; strong and reliable...
Never missing a beat...
Banging her audio sensations...
Head nodding chilled by intimate vibrations...
I love this car...!
I am flashy, selfish and materialistic...
I should be thinking of ways to fix society...

Out to Sea

I followed an angel out to the sea...
So many things were said...
The angel told me what I would be...
Do not blame the explanation, rather the seriousness of this situation...
No enemy, no master race...
The angel told me how things must be...
Just keep on praying and your faith strong...
There is no need to search for me...
Screaming repeatedly, the angel stopped and looked
Crying this is the way to Zion...
There are many that resemble me...
Stay strong on your trestle board...
War rages above and beneath the sea...
Ensure your devotions are meant for only the Lord whom have mercy...
You and I are both messengers
Earth core low while the spirit has arisen you...
Follow the wrong passions, and the Jinn will imprison you...
Are you scared of what you are here to do...?
How could that be, actually I followed you...!
NOW TAKE ME TO WHERE YOU ARE SUPPOSED TO...!
Where faith builds hope breaks...
Swimming throughout life's various; yet vicious currents...
How could I not be equal...?
Imagine me drowning in this sea...
Not here, not today...!
Selah cubits...

Forgive me for my actions, interactions and poor sanctions…
Guided by the length of HIS Cable-toe…
Divided by my mortal sensation…
Immortalized by societies' forsaken keepsakes…
The angel followed me back home…

Neo Nazis in Africa...

BANG, BANG, BANG...!
360 degree sink holes in Guatemala, 2010...
Did the wrong souls fall in...?
Save the drama, look at the blacks ridiculing Obama...
Earthquakes shake Haiti...
Too many good people are dying for nothing...
These scary movies are frightening...
I struggle with the evils that men can imagine...
Something's taking us away...
False prophets preach 2012...
Suicide bombings in Russian train stations...
Fathers drop newborn babies in river ways...
Pedophiles are piling up in my neighborhood...
Where can our little babies play...?
Check the trannies' house for the nannies' blouse...!
Tyrannies of the sick, skillful and vain...
Sodom and Gomorra...
The ways of man are not kind...
Crime pays radio waves...
Vice President Gore officially divorces after 40 years...
Statewide teacher reductions in urban areas...
Nod your head to songs of destruction...
Loudly the horns are being blown...
Faith builds hope breaks...
Arizonians forget we are all immigrants...
Bail out billions spent on Amoney companies...
Red tops and crack rocks equal semi-automatic body shots...
Soldiers exchange souls for bodies for no real reason...
Glorify the snipers' role...
Is GOD dropping food from the sky, while society's blood boils...?

Two giant twins are anointed with crimson and ashes before they fall...
The more years it takes to create, the more we appreciate nothing...
Bring in more men and add more chaos to your operation...
The arrogant toys of the savages...!
United Nations forgot to pay attention...
Respect the treasonous reasons of man...
Overstand, queens are getting raped every day...
Bozos play the bongos in Congo...
See men are raping men these days...
Villains lurk in corners to steal your pay...
Engulfed by these oil spills, the tides are turning mucky...
We are so stuck by this great ignorance...
The new Nazis are African men...
Hitler would be so proud of you...!
The KKK really has little work to do...
Peek-a-boo, Negro I am talking to you...!
All the issues we can't bear to see...
Broken homes and lack of respect...
Black babies get heroin and welfare Similac...
Back to black disgrace, egg in the face...
Last place in the race, it is very hard to compete...
Can't you see I need soul food, but the Asians are feeding me...!
Lacking vision and unemployed, stuck in the prison system...
Neo Nazis are the victim and the witness...
I know you smell the sickness...!
Neo Nazi equates to hate without wisdom...

What I have

Whatever I have...
You can have too, but for a fee...
Sometimes I give my work for free...
Most things in this world have little to zero meaning to me...
Love God, respect life, protect the family...
Whatever I touch, I expect more from...
Billionaire Bum; yes, he is I...
Recognizing the choices of responsibility...
I just stopped talking...
Choosing forward instead of straight...
When I am gone, situate me at a decent gate...
The world gave birth to a troubled child...
Tubal Cain...
Trust that is not me...
Ancient symbols of a ritualistic society...?
Most jewels I can give for free...
Throwing Green Diamonds in the Sky...
Whatever I create, you will not take from me...
Judge my honesty...!
Truncate The Psychologies of my Philosophy...
Believing I am good is the entire battle...
Fasting for something more than what I see...
Nothing is more important to me then to give you something with purpose...
The delivery of what you need...
Parts of the answer will come from me...
Cable was expensive and unnecessary, so I turned it off...
There is a spirit I need to spit out...!
Realities fiction keeps me stitching this literary quilt...
Dark before the light...
Day before the night...

Wet before the dry...
Ground before the sky...
Truth before the lie...
Love before the pain...
I need your hands to come and heal me once again...
Shuttered in my own steps...
Continuing to create so I may keep giving...
Brethren manifest, we can eat together...!
Rich people do not be greedy...

Eyes Change Colors

Brown, hazel, greenish, grey...
Strangers, loved ones, friends and foes...
Nana shows us her new hands and toes...
Fall, summer, spring, winter...
Seems the world has a reason to change...
Cry, smile, smirk, grimace...
Cry a soft whisper as you are born again...
Smile in denial when you hurt a true friend...
Smirk at your right to civil liberties and freedom...
Reminisce when your eyes change colors...
Wrists, ankles, elbows and knees turn from limber to brittle...
Change is a consistent hardship; a nervous reaction to subtraction...
A Rose petals' shadow aimlessly travel the gravel...
The mirror reminds me of time, and what I have to lose...
Inspecting the changes in my face...
Insisting time should not exist...
Yet, we need something to hold on to...
Physically blaming time, the rest of this shell is aging concurrently...
This is burdening...
I am infant, adolescent and elderly...
Pre-tensing transcendence...
Coming back to life from the dark, these eyes open...
Only remembering tomorrow what I see today...
Unconsciously conscious...
The light is changing my eye sight...
The colors of my eyes radiate wise temperaments...
It is frightening when you see lightning go through your body...

Worldly lies change my eyes while I am disguised
watching the sunrise...
Change is as eminent as the sky is blue to black...
How fragile, the remnants do not matter...
My eyes are playing the change game...
Foggy mornings hiding the purple tunnel...
Clearly my vision is blurry...
Why do eyes change colors...?
Different people when we look at each other...
Today my eyes are hazel...

Memories of Men

A stranger and a friend...
Brother to brother, father to mother...
Angel to God, demotic to devil...
Who is to say we will ever meet again...?
Resentment does not lead to contentment...
Obedience is more formidable than sacrifice...
Even the pen, a writer's best friend tends to lose its ink...
How far will you sink before I blink...?
Debating whether or not to lift you up...!
They that hated you, ruled over you...
I am not counting my days, instead updating my ways...
Thus, I am second to none...
The more I come to the Lord the more I need him...
I will not count my words, I must dictate thought...
Thinking is a function of thought...
I shall not speak unless solid thought is pronounced...
Never speak between thought...
No one cares when you are thinking...
Neither will I measure the distance, instead of enjoying the destination...
I have been wrong, it is not my song...
There is no reason to boast...
Just stop talking, keep on walking...
In fact run to chase his face...
Memories of men are lost so we must meditate...
I see the evil of men in different scenes amongst my dreams...
All was a reflection of me...
WaterMannyFaces...
Blame the drunkenness on me and drink responsibly...
Once I was blind, now I can see...

I am who I am...
I can change who I will be...
Today I see differently...
Memories of men...
Father to son...
Psalm to Proverb...

Magdalena Anniversaries

I am safer and I know now…
Loving you with all my heart is just a start…
Magdalena…
Your beauty is beyond your face…
Loving you infinitely between God's graces…
I will sculpt and paint you throughout the world…
Magdalena…
Your smile lights my fire…
The laughter of our youth…
The crimson of our passion…
The zest of your step…
The zeal of your appeal…
Our prosperity is sincere and highly favored…
My honey love from the heaven above…
The manna from which I feed from…
The other side of the mirror is a reflection of your pleasantry…
What makes sense to me is the house of love we live in…
Growing day by day…
No walls; or doors, only windows…
Bright lights, cascading waters, and rainbows…
Body and soul; loving and hugging you…
I guess that's why I do what I do…
To protect you, crazy as it seems…
I truly LOVE, LOVE, LOVE you…!
Happy anniversary my love…
Magdalena Greene…

Secaucus Swans

Each day on the train I see...
Secaucus swans swimming to the left of me...
Interesting how nature strives to survive...
Between old abandoned tires and broken power lines...
Surprised since winter is here and they should be gone...
I can see my breath, yet the white swans float on...
It seems the same place and time they entertain...
Are they not aware...?
The season is changing, the lake is starting to freeze...
Can they not take flight, are they stranded...?
Has the bitter cold ruined their wings and knees...
Occasionally there tends to be a squad of storks...
Just wading in the water...
Why are the swans still here...?
Winter months pass by...
The white stork flies accompanying the subtle winds...
Snow birds leave and come back again...
Nesting in the famous tall grass...
This year will be more than tropical...
Secaucus swans are beautiful...
This year, ten blue jays congregated next to me...
Egrets stacked by the bundle lining the entrance of the approaching transit tunnel...
I am just a bystander...

I Don't Know

Media messing with our mentality
Constantly bombing the family
These days have tamed the slaves...
I am a slave to these payments...
The more you work the more you have to pray...
Floating outside my square's compass...
Trans-continentally disconnected...
Hard to talk to myself...
Easy to die by myself...
Only the spirit creates spiritual life...
Condemnation and conviction are not the same...
The question ought to be, what is on my mind that I cannot see...?
Peers or family...?
I write for my sanity...
GOD, I glorify your energy...!
Dancing to a new day through powerful transition...
In our trouble...Lord we travel...
How far must WE travel to be free...?
Heaven is so close to hell...
Thin Line Phenomena underestimations plague generations...
Living today in fear of tomorrow...
Having nothing to do with the consequences of yesterday...
Mortally Immortal because I believe in me...
Who would I be with no ID...?
My third eye is crying...
My real eyes are blinding...
Defining how WE are declining...
Scratching at the bars compliments the mental climb...
There is no such thing as coincidence...

These days it is hard to count on yourself…
To know or not to know, that is the question…?
To live or not to live, life is the suggestion…
Everyone wants the world but cannot afford the topsoil…
Life is expensive…

In the Basement

Put me back the basement...
Many things need replacement...
I do not even know where my face went...
I need my own machine guns just to have some fun...
Flowing rapid fire, come on and get the minimum...
Really I do not want to fight...
Survival I define, people change...
Marriage is an institution...
There are many degrees to accommodate...
Hard thing these relationships and happiness...
This is church and poetry is my ministry...
I am the control room guy...
Laughing while you cry...
When will we overstand...?
Give me a helping hand...?
Quantity verses demand...
Be for real, steel sharpens steel...
I will not conceal how I feel...
Reverenced with no time, no shape and no place...
"Bang Bang"...!
She shot me down...
"Bang Bang!!!"
I hit the ground...
Birth is more difficult than life...
Death to me is irrelevant...
This argument is actually breaking me down...
Do you feel me...?
WaterMannyFaces, The Psychology of my Philosophies...
In accordance with Tyrian civility...
So put me back I the basement, unfinished and diminished...
Love me...

Controlling the room...
LEG should not yell, liar...
Why cleanse the world...?
My maze is a baseline, every time I dream I see the sunshine...
Define me beyond the words...
True friends are hide to find...
I am only a human being...
Seeing all that comes to perspective...
In the basement face-lifting my soul...
Shift the mood from bottom to the top...
All I can say is I am thankful for you...
We are beyond this argument...
We went to dinner before this war started...

Happiness of my Anger

Forgive my wings while I soar...
Married to pseudo game, funded by false lecture...
Love, I am not insane...
Crazy, the Earth made me...
LEG equals loyal, energy and growth...
Trumpet my life for your symphony...
Yeah I go to work, that is not the real me...
Album the world, words will not dilute repercussion...
This volume I am angry...!
Diamond Dynamite...
Respect global serenity, a pint for you and I...
Get high, torch the porch and fondle a breast...
The cube I reside in captures evil...
Yet, I am breaking it with diamonds...
Diamond dynamite...
Allow mankind their sins to rest...
I am in the blizzard but the rivers are not frozen...
Transcribing the state of emergency riding New Jersey Transit...
Oddly, salt and ice dwell together...
Like brothers in unity, cement turns into sediment...
Drink liquor, rape women, kill brethren and eat from dead ocean floors...
Touring false philosophies; we are not gods anymore...
Imagine world without war...
Imagine food for the poor and distressed...
Cary me on a stallion, the mule no longer is needed...
Scare my relaxation and resuscitate my happiness...
Wait till I arrive...!!
Wandering the park at dark, seeking an intervention...
Life without detention, superseding imperfection...
Notice how I keep on smiling...?

Pastel corrections done in pencil...
Realizing the many canvasses...
Fundamentally; admittance is interesting, I question everything...
Happiness is the frame, blame the picture if you are upset...
Notice how long the blizzard lasts...
Whether it blows or not; the wind controls the weather...
Possibilities of what may become of nothing...?
Imagine what makes me happy...!
Balancing the completion of a cultural literary deficit...
Angrily the enemy harasses the happiness that resides within me...
Calm twilights make me happy...

Existential

You will see the light before knowing the dark…
Keep high stepping…!
Money saves all things, vanity makes it prettier…
Broke people should be superior…
Economic inferiority is the age old paradigm …
Without money there would be no need for charity…
We should all , eating moss and sleeping till the Sun goes down…
There are grey lines…
Happy New Year 2011…!
I am not counting cars; I am scratching bars, remembering scars…
A new gate will open sounding another trumpet …
More things now than ever will come from and above the ground…
The world will not end my friend…
Many souls have been reduced to savagery and discontent…
Life is trivial without prediction of the end…
The duality of life is that it exists…
Existential makes a lot of sense…
To think is a function of thought in itself
To fry the chicken or scramble the egg…?
The chef only knows and cares…
Not me for sure…
They say the world is going to end...
Maybe for you but not for me my friend...
Forgive me; I tend to forget the rules...
Comfortably playing this jazzy trumpet all year...
What is the point in showing fear…?
Logically prepared for whatever happens...
Visual captions of captains within the crystal orbs I am

juggling...
Overexposed versus undervalued...
Unraveling these memories in memoirs, deciding which ones to keep...
Dictating which ones to forsake and not to debate...
Finding it hard to remember everything...
In the church pew I nod my head and sing...
See everything happens for a reason...
It is bad when you do not remember how long you have been doing wrong...
You will see the light before knowing the dark...
Patience is a virtue; a notion of endurance my friend...

She Said

She said not to, I said I got to…
Watch you, like all the cops do…
Patiently stalk you, like the hawks do…
Early walks with you, admiring the morning dew…
What is the point in running away…?
Tired of the Inconsequential…
Incidentally, no more tragedy…
Blind as far as my sight will be…
So far as I can see…
Deliberately taking all that was taken, Indian giving…!
See, I want my jewelry back…!
I am dwelling in this crazy world…
Where boy meets girl, cat chases squirrel…
Canines and felines can dwell peacefully together…
It is a matter of upbringing and out-storming the weather…
Negative statements are slick and clever…
Anticipate sunrays in the midst of cloudy days…
Genuine soul divine, she reached into the sunshine…
Increasingly the cost of living decreases me…
Let us wait for time to tell…
Yelling at the choir is not necessary…
Love is a subject I am not scared of…
Pointing to the full moon; whistling a subtle tune…
Playing my golden piano…
Maybe I was too young to understand…
The glove that does not fit acquits me…
A drug that does not work rejects me…
Little issues turn to arguments…
The unknown caller can create many issues…
Problems knock on the front door only by invitation…
Forgo the peephole and keep the door locked…

Shocked by what I said...
She said not to, I said that I got to...
There is no need for trouble in this bed...
So much evil lingers within our heads...
These eyes wander only in my own home...
Where I am king and you own the throne...
Some nights I dance alone, when you are not available...
Some nights I eat nothing, wondering where you are at...
She said not to, I said that I got to...
Be safe and do the right thing so I can see you again...

Quiet Charity and Works

Online social networks do not talk to GOD. Your good deeds may not be seen. Your works will be felt in the heart of charity; in real life, which is good. Stop the madness and invest in your own hearts and pray silently. Live beyond a sacrilegious social post and do work!

Blind Wind Loud Drug

BLIND WIND LOUD DRUG
Smashing premeditated passion...
Clashing the senses to erection...
Protection for the masses...
No race, no economics, no ebonics...
Crashing into the valleys of broken bones...
BLIND WIND LOUD DRUG...
BLUE SKY POET MANTIS...
Running water is cool too...
Your wind is blind because you are going in many directions...
Your drug is loud because you are into perfection...
Replace the water cooler bottle...
Too many water buffalos are drinking from my river...
We are all becoming dirty birds...
Laugh at what you hear...
I use to be Chickahominy and Pamunkey...
Ever since Ronald Reagan is been checkahomie and porch monkey...
Do WE smell that funky...?
Immediately point out the druggie...
Hot mama, that trunk is junky...!
Stuck in a tar cup sipping black coffee...
The Jersey Bandit is stranded...
Sleeping General's armies engage and prepare for deployment...
This is the season to fly high and reconnect the bones...
Throw away all the non-essentials...
Adapt or you will not last...

"WaterMannyFaces: The Psychologies of My Philosophy"
Volume 10

Amazing

Amazing...!
I wish I could see all my friends in the deep end, but most cannot swim.
Funny how seasons change but we remain the same...
Some things will never change...
Standing still, preferring to be the rock in the hard place...
Some think life is easier than it looks...
Mankind carries more greed then we would think...
Amazing...!
Formally illiterate, now he writes his feeling on the wall..
See, the odds are stacked against me...
The older I become the more I have to lose...
I use to collect sticks for my journey, now they collect me...
Dad, I use to say we were different...
I see we are the same...
If I am not on it; I am getting on it, or waiting for it...!
The minute hand continues to move...
Even God cries through the apple of his eye...
Green Diamonds in the Sky...
Amazing...!
Reject temptation on the plains of Ono and resolve your discretions...
Amazing...!
The satisfaction of planet blasting, maybe it is just a dream...
I just want to go home...
The last reaction to my passion is one day all things will fade away...
What will be does not necessarily have to be...
I always believed the ends justified the means...
Amazing...!

Ups and Downs

The gospel has a poetic apostle...
Ecclesiastically unchallenged by false hope and tax-incentive gratuity...
Collide with the mirror's other side...
Oh, the self is re-inventing...
Ups and downs, our struggles are tears to clowns...
Jesters, jokers and actors...
Anti-social benefactors...
A pastor's disaster is humbling, but we still sing...
I feel souls crying...
Bounded by the sounds of civil unrest...
Keeping prayer alive to get this off my chest...
God can never die...
The duality of life is that it exists...
Allowing existence beyond the void...
See, opinions are powerful...
After I learned my lesson I earned the deed to my succession...
Through Psalms I questioned my wrongs, clapping evoking positive spirit...
Listen I know you hear it...
Whistling in the house serenades demonic pleasures...
Bear witness to today...
Yesterday is gone...
I finally did it...!
I sought inner peace and self-healing...
Stay tuned...

Snow Lust

I use to love the snow, until I had to shovel...
Throw a snowball just for fun...
Watch the carefree little kids play...
Stay home and build a snowman...
Today is a snow day...
These days I work to get paid...
Don't snow too much; a simple flurry will do...
People drive recklessly like animals escaping the zoo...
Fall, laugh, stay on the ground and tumble...
These days a fall can break a bone...
Loving the comfort of hot cocoa at home...
Roaming with a snow shovel to make an honest dollar...
Big machines clean the streets, burying my vehicle all the way...
Blasted with snowy acid, frozen concrete embraces sleet and hail...
Sleigh riding was my passion, now I watch the cars go crashing...
Big boots, fluffy jacket and skull cap...
It all looked so beautiful until it started to stick...
Trees frown as ice clings to their bark barrier...
Balloons in trees in the city never ceases to amaze me...
Get your forts ready...
Snowball fight...!
Remember all the things that made us smile in the winter...

Lake Placid

If the pastor can go to India to preach; I can go to lake placid and chill, it's all creative design...
Home of brethren lakes Placid and Mirror...
XIII winter Olympic Games, insane...!
From the everglades to Adirondack the east coast is my host...
Getting blasted by snowy acid...
Magda and I viewed a live; but spectator less, hockey game...
Sipping vintage cinnamon cider brimming in Captain Morgan's Spice rum...
Black cat and the spider...
An elder Greek owns the Main street steakhouse...
I don't care if summer never comes...
This winter wonderland is where we exist for the moment...
Bleeding in the snow...
She said, "Would you like a snowball"...?
I replied, "Get off the slope"...!
White Face Mountain was a radical experience...
Sensing the surprise of my dynamic skiing ability in her eyes...
Magda and I killed the slopes...
I am so happy she took me there...
Magda, get off the slope...!
Ecstatic she took the time to get on the slopes...!
Walmart is so far away...
The wholesale machine is not a part of this Amoney dream...
Demanding to be stranded...
Yes, it is real snow...!
The Downtown Diner is a necessary move for

breakfast...!
Today the Sun is as white as the snow...
Amateur rock climbers stand beside us...
Vehicles quickly descend down the Adirondack gravel spine...
Bringing me to a quaint place of existence...
Most of the homes are white...
Bed and breakfast treatment throughout the night...
Annual Saranac festivities shiver men in the sacred ice palace for two days...
What more can I say...?
Lake Placid is a nostalgic place...
We were there a bit more than two days...

LEG 2/12/2011

Sandstorms without an End

Standing in a sandstorm without an end...
I reach my hand out and hope to grab a friend...
Not sure where I am, the dessert or the sea...
Riding an ocean wave or standing on a mountain's peak...
Visibility means nothing to me...
I rest but do not sleep...
Where are the sirens broadcasting emergency...?
Should I be thick or thin, bishop or the pawn...?
Sensing the challenge in the build...
There would be no void...if everything were filled...
I sense the danger in the fields...
There would be no more killing, if love was more than real...
The world is thirsty and it needs to rain...
Feed the hungry and stop summing up your gain...
I am in a sandstorm without an end...
I reach my hand out and hope to grab a friend...
There are children being born with no parents and it is sad...
Not sure of hot or cold...
We should be on a tropical island somewhere getting old...
I wish I knew more of what to say...
Hoping to do more each and every day...
Where it storms in abundance the most beautiful days appear...
Oasis chasing for longer than I have years...
I see all the sunshine in the rain...
Crying longer than I have felt the pain...

Robotic Souls

There cannot be a reaction without the action…
Black is the absorption of all colors; whereas, white is the reflection of all colors…
Reflection verses absorption…
Robotically playing mortal chess for nothing…
Basically they are all the same; derivatives of a mechanical perspective…
Bear witness to today, yesterday is gone…
Soul sublime aligned with robotic intuition…
Imagine the super talent of the blind future…
Possessed with binary decisions…
Why build more prisons…?
The system is a prism, segregating the light…
I might try to indict and fight it…!
Really it is hard to win…
My mental' muse is confused by the logic…
The Sun never shines the same way…
What makes a robot sing in the spring rain…?
Can they see more colors than me…?
Artificially my physical form is aesthetically pleasing…
Achilles heel is a kill switch…
Porting at my terminal since I require maintenance and need an upgrade…
Foolish humans are teaching the bots…
Programmers have it all twisted…
Response based social networking is artificiating intelligence…
War games are insane, thanks Tubal-cain…!
I wonder what God is thinking…?
Truly I wish for the difference…
Building with hands was a part of existence…
Robots do not dream, they steam…

Patents do not add value to social justice...
I am too far from where I am supposed to be...
I wonder what God is thinking...?

Birds Chirp

Birds Chirp and people argue…
Birds chirp for a reason…
Sounding off for the season…
The migration call is the most amazing…
Only little birds chirp…
Orchestrating mood and attitude…
The bigger the bird the less the chirp…
Raptors squawk, parrots talk, pigeons coo away…
Chickens cluck, ducks quack, and owls hoot…
All birds do not chirp…
All people do not talk…
Tweet this, the more you chirp the less you see…!
The more you talk the less you do…
Little birds hop, the bigger ones walk…
Raptors fly the highest, from mountain top to parking lot…
The more supreme the further you see…
Dirt birds move in flocks, never getting too far…
Eagles do not eat bread…
Predators hawk and stalk…
People have chosen to consume the foul…
All birds do not nest with twigs…
Some use big branches and rest amongst the boulders…
Birds that wake up after me are slackers…!
Bird watchers admire themselves…
Funny people, funny birds…
Not all birds chirp, but all dogs bark…
Need I say more…?
Because we have wings does not mean we are all meant to fly…

Babe Girl

I'm sorry...
I did not mean to confuse you...
Abuse you or bruise you...
Made you black and all blue too...
Hold me tight when we fight...
Tonight everything is all right...
Let the domestic news travel...
Through thought, mind and emotion...
Hospitalized sipping on your love potion...
So what is the commotion...?
Yeah, big bad ole me...
I love the promotion...!
Listen to what I have been telling you...
Yes, I am yelling at you...!
Babe Girl, I miss you...
Take a tissue...
Our love is not the issue...
You always knew I had an issue...
Daddy, don't you hear our children crying...?
See what you made the fist do...
Babe Girl, you are lucky I lack the pistol...
Truth be told, this fighting is getting old...
I am so use to it...!
I grew up with it...!
This is historic emulation...
Now cook and clean and do it right...
I want to sleep after the fight...
Mommy, keep Daddy away from the family...!
Daddy, steer your evil away from our trust...!
Star light star bright...
I wonder how many stars you will see tonight...

For the children, this is not a spectator sport...
By default they are featured in the event...
Daddy, don't you see our children dying...?
This is your home and you pay the bills...
I am the ugly goblin of a man doing what I feel...
I have had scores of women that thought they were golden...
When I was done with them their hearts were frozen...
Lady ask Daddy...
I told you before...
Vampires can knock, but invitation lets them through the door...
Sincerely, I hope you are secure...
I'm not here to help you...
Do not open the door...
Babe Girl...
Seriously, men stop beating your children and women...
Ladies change your destiny...
Walking amongst us physically, spiritually and socially abused...!

Towers of Babylon

There are churches in the Towers of Babylon...
Reaching for the clouds...
The praise is bold in between the walled streets of indigenous exchange...
See we came from the spaceships...
On Earth we met the racists...
Thus, we traveled via slave ships...
Let us talk Diaspora...
Now everyone wants to change the text...
So what is track number 3 telling me...?
Move as far away as possible from New York City...
Those that can, better move as fast as possible...
The outcome is not plausible...
We have been learning how to read the book...
Basic instructions before leaving earth...
Rather ashes to ashes and dust to dust...
Do not put me in a coffin to cough in...
Let me be a Green Diamond in the Sky...
Lay me to rest in a most beautiful place...
Do not confine my spirits exit to a ridiculously small inhumane space...
I have a problem with the way we are buried...
I use to wonder where my bones would be...
No I pray within each breath religiously...
I have more things to think about then if you have my back...!
Love me as I walk between the lines...
Lord knows I am only human...
My intentions are good...
Yet I have to walk through all these narrow gates...
How much more can I take...
I pray to God my soul to take...

Diamond Dynamite

I feel like dynamite…
Diamond Dynamite in fact…!
Keep doing it…
Wait till you see me…
Wait till you feel my soul…
I am about to explode Diamond Dynamite…!
From the head to the heel…
I have so much energy and feel like annihilating the enemy…
Check out my site…
Operation Mayhem today…!
Check the registry to test me…!
Made of flesh but radiate divine energy…!
Holding a world on my shoulder blasting those that disrespect me…
Substantially I am not ready for failure…
The market demands what comes from my mind, formed from my hands…
They ease drop on my plans...
I don't apologize for what I've done in my life…
I rebuild and continue to fortify what is right…
My Diamond Dynamite has a focused wire leading to explosion…
My universe is an awesome contradiction to your fiction...!
I cannot let the pressure build within…
My blood is O positive I am built to win...
It takes less time to shoot the bullet then it does to heal...
It takes less time to break then it does to seal...
I hail, I conceal…!
From the heart my art is adjusting and redefining itself...
Green Diamonds in the Sky...

Pulling gems and articulating this wealth...
Sleeping General is awake and can see...
Upon opening my eyes, nothing made sense to me...
So I blasted all I could, forming a cubic prism to protect me...
Going beyond 360 degrees I meditated to 720...
Though shall not break me apart...
I would rather implode into darkness, since I have benefited from the light...
Disguised I rise into manhood...
Tip-toeing beyond the shadows alarming me of harm...

If You Knew

If you knew what I came here to do...
Trust, I am almost prepared...
You would try to stop and pop me...
Possibly try to prop me...
I suggest you adopt me...!
These days I tend to forget...
Too busy thinking about the future...
Thou must remember, tomorrow is never promised...!
Yet I know tomorrow will come...one way or the other...
Never worrying about any of the money I spent...
Controversy I have dealt with...
Items I have lent out to the point of given away...
Forcing my spirit into the conversation...
My life is an action item and I project manage it...
My soul is manifesting it...!
I am running this plan man...!
No need to ask somebody...
The area of pissed is greater than the circumference of past...
I have so much to say...
Clutch and hold me...
You are old; I am young, but you know me...
My face allows for supreme pedigree...
I will not be here again, except through the seeds I breed...
My family blood is an anomaly...!
Should I should have let you drown...
The tears of my clown told me not to...
No pole, no rope...
I just jumped in to save you...
If you knew what I would do to save you...

You would not protest so much anger…
No reason to argue what I see…
I am holding my own world…
Dictating my destiny…
Steal a gem from me…
While you choose a friend for me…
Ah We Enemy…!

The Travesty of Hip Hop

Put hot beats on any retarded theme and it would be phenomenal...!
The travesty of Hip Hop
Hot beats and garbage equals real Hip Hop...!
I'm being sarcastically dramatic...
Yes, it's tragic...!
Going back to the days of when things made sense...
It's a fanatical thing...assuming being ridiculous is cool...!
The elders are following chumps; not champs...
Lacking mental serenity...
Cable's is killing me while I YouTube through this generation's obscenities...
Skinny pants, dancing to satanic tunes...
I'm chasing stars that shine in the daytime...
Freakish geek tongues are testing my sanity...
Add more musical pollution to the retribution...
Crack the gavel on Hip Hop's weak institution...
Time to restructure...
Federally the FCC is allowing more stupidity...
Why am I paying these cellular taxes...?
When good music of the soul is being distracted by buffoons and awesome coons...
Gaga is an epidemic in the book of odd futures...
Going from stealing samples to taking the instrumentals of classic rock...
There is nothing new under the Sun...
Hip Hop rocker, acid popper...
Grey Goose and Red Bull drink promoter...
Social acceptance dictated by the numbers of bottles you got...
Collecting Grammy's because after being shot...
Odd claims of being bigger than God...

The picture paints itself...
Curse words amplify 10,000 bullets, drive by that...
You can put hot beats on any retarded theme and it would be phenomenal...!
The Travesty of Hip Hop
Stop...What you are creating is not HIP HOP!
The clowns jumped over the moon...
Full throttle on the Barbie model...
Plastic Man has not one thing on you...!
Goons rob convenience stores...
Obtaining fans after shooting a man...
Glad you are all understanding...
Seriously, Hip Hop does not represent me...
In fact, it disappoints me...
Rappers turning actors without class...
Consistent degradation of the culture...
Goldie Locks, diamond studs and shiny platinum watches...
Imprisoned by commercialization...
Annunciation no longer matters...
Chit chat the fact that your ghetto is hard...
Why in the world do you need a body guard...?
Disregarding the messages, turning nursery rhymes to land mines...
Blowing up the generations expectations...
You can put hot beats on any retarded theme and it would be phenomenal...!
The travesty of Hip Hop

Deletion

Delete does not mean gone! Everything you post and delete on a computer is removed from the screen; possibly the database, but never from the machine or backup records. The same principle aligns with life. An imprint of everything done in life has been recorded in some way shape or form. Just because we can't see it does not mean it does not exist!

Man without Knowing a Woman

How can you be a man without knowing a woman? Seriously! Knowing as in the knowing of a value, qualities, responsibilities, natural, mental and spiritual capabilities. Many males call themselves men without the real recognition or respect of the woman from whose womb we have been birthed of. Too many of our brothers; saved or not, equate "knowing" to the biblical sense.

Lassaiz Faire

Share my world...
Give me a magazine and a cover girl...
Change my plans...
Put a gun in my hand next to the jury I stand...
Share my world and speak to me...
Play a game of tongues with a bottle of rum...
Seems the games have begun...
Just let me be...
Give a bum a high five tell him to stay alive...
Steal from me...
Although I forgive I still have to die...
I am talking about petty and unfriendly things...
Swimming for years drowning my fears...
Raining on my own puddles...
Together we are a symphony in the zoo...
Foolish Indians diving the south pacific, searching for bull shark in the dark...!
Portable bee colonies protest the era of WIFI and digital television...
Earthquakes shake and instigate tsunamis...
Allowing for hearty destruction throughout the pacific Asian lands of Japan...
The Japanese are more prepared than most...
Thou shalt be ready for nuclear breakdown...
Cool the heavy metals and core radiation levels...
The Pope posts his soapbox on Facebook...
I haven't lost a breath...
Playing the piano staring at the moon...
Slipping on 99 bananas, praying to the bronzed EZ Jesus...
Laissez faire, just let it be...

From the womb to the tomb...
People barely change...
So many conclusions, most gained when I am losing...
Only meditation is keeping me sane...
Apartheid is smiling reminding me of the cinematic District 9...
Globally, South Africa houses the largest private correctional facility ...
Inquiring Hosanna's laugh...
Just let me be...
Laissez Faire...

Been There

If you can't find me, I have been waiting too long...
You can't hide me; I have been quiet too long...
Been there done that...
Black top hat for the big act...
I am a snow cone in a tropical thunderstorm, quickly melting...!
Scratching at the bars thinking of the master plan, templating transition...
If it does not fit don't quit, stretch it and make it bigger...
Figuring, what is the point in losing...?
I struck a chord that hit the moon and no one was there...
I was a river before it rained...no one could swim...
Traveling Earth core low hoping one day I would breathe...
I jumped from mountains to split the clouds...
Froze your mind so I could think...
Delayed your words so I may speak...
I am the fire formed by the wind; if it blows I will reform again...
If you can't find me, I have been waiting too long...
You can't hide me; I have been quiet too long...
U and left turns; Aids and crack burns...
Provide me with my spread...
In the presence of my enemies; which are not in heaven...
Spiritual battles of the flesh...
Let's pretend there is no racism, and the system had no victims...
My alchemy's parody is sincerity...
The white of my eyes are all lies...
The black is where I see from...
If you can't find me, I have been waiting too long...
You can't hide me; I have been quiet too long...

You can't buy me I have been sold before...
You can try me I am willing to be tried again...

Confuse Me a Nation

The United States of America is in an explosive state of confusion. Disillusioned by the freedom of expression; through fashion, our society has voluntarily been taking many wrong turns. Societies that utilize currency for exchange will always have a growing rate of domestic poverty, illness and famine. The world is globalizing by design not efficiency. Our food is both pretty and poisoned; our agriculture is withheld and subsidized. Livestock is genetically altered beyond repair and distributed by oligopolistic groups of bio-engineers not farmers. We wonder why healthcare is in shambles; constantly praising gluttony when in reality it's a pure sin.

NAFTA; the North American Free Trade Agreement, localized the unions and wholesaled America through the likes of companies like Wal-Mart. Renowned politicians practice pseudo politics while lacking any true background regarding the wealth of nations. The broken highways have become racetracks to service based employment, entertainment and prison related transport.

The perks of holding a government position seem to far outweigh their constituents' quality of life. The leftist breaks bread at tea parties with the rightist at conservative fundraiser events. The political system is not segregated. Instead, it is very integrated into the once capitalistic; and now socialistic, way of running an outsourced government. The United States is protected by the Patriot Act and privatized watch groups that constantly experiment on the welfare and health of the nation's population through weak forms of mass production and importation. Superior of the economic minority is guiding and ruling the nation.

The nation is very feminine during this day and time. The born physical identity and gender of an individual can be officially changed at any time. The global demonic raping of young children and pornography growth has become a real life bedtime story. A world were men animatedly promote the creation of laws which dictate the future of a woman's womb is equal to one where women decide what men will or will not be suitable for reproduction. The country is dying in an institutionalized fashion.

The United States is in a true dire state of disaster and catastrophe. The welfare of this state has been accelerated by increased unemployment lines and transit fines. Whatever it takes as long as we; the people continue to consume what we do not domestically make or own. Manufacturing within this country as a staple for growth now exists within the realm of legacy.

In the walls of the citadel the churches compete against the liquor stores. Immigration leaves its doors open for terrorist activity. Yet, most terrorist activity; whether domestic or abroad, is sponsored or spawned by the government and ridiculous non-thought provoking media in so many ways. Come to grips with this economic battle of few verse many. Within this socio-economic Invisible Caste System; the few do not want the many to have any advancement without having to sell ancestral rights for a piece of upward citizenry.

Our funding comes from short term wars and international police governance; in the name of

Democracy. We are experiencing higher domestic price indexing and inflation for much needed resources. The nations' irrational temperament is equal to its drowning school systems. Our future; GENERATION OVEREXPOSED, is the victim. Institutions of higher learning are charging more and more dollars for undervalued diplomas of accomplishment.

Lawren Greene 4/4/2011

The Warrior's Serenity

The Warrior maintained his integrity amidst the odd serenity. Becoming so use to challenge and change the Warrior grew fond of his new features. The Water Diamond Paradox mist fully dissipated into the Warriors soul. At that very moment; the Warrior would never feel a thirst, as he was ultimately quenched. The Water Diamond Paradox blessed him in so many ways. The Warrior's overstanding was redefined as he looked at the poised Mantis and humbly stated: "I have maintained balance throughout the course of my life, leveled civilizations and sought the Art of War. The enemy is not a friend to me. I am a formation of the darkness being introduced into the light. All of these beautiful powers I have ascertained I am coming to the realization that I am in undeniable state of preparation."

The Mantis flew in circles as a hint to ensure the Warrior validated his circumference. Smelling the crisp air in a majestic state of nostalgia, the Warrior stood amidst the alien scenery and declared: "If this is my world I will take it as I stand. I have not consulted the General but I deem this my land. With my hands I will cultivate and shape a new world. My sword shall decide each mortal division." Seemingly within that thought the Warrior contemplated his state of being; the reasoning for his existence. "What have I become?" The Mantis eagerly continued to fly circles amidst the Warrior. The Warrior stood steadfast as the ground began to tremble beneath his feet. Hosanna appeared faster and more beautiful this time than ever before stating: "What are you looking for?"

The Warrior began to cry and screamed out: "In my heart oh God let there be life in me! What have you done to me? My flesh is beyond any mortals. My soul has been impregnated with destiny. My sight is blurry and my destination is unclear. I have been moving throughout this world; without an apparent mission for greater than a year. My diamond embodied skin and powerful purple aura must have a reason. Although I can see further than any mortal I sense no change in season."

For the first time Hosanna the Ninja actually laughed out loud at the Warrior as if in a state of disbelief. While continuing to laugh at the Warrior, Hosanna pointed at a crisp mountain top and stated "Let it be". A beam so powerful erected from out of Hosanna's hand absolutely leveling the mountain top as if it were nothing.
Hosanna looked at the Warrior and then stated: You actually have more power than this. I am just here to protect you. I am Hosanna; the shield that guides you, the rock that allows your foundation! I Hosanna am your God Element. I have leveled the mountain top for you to stand and declare in comfort. Warrior you will interface with the leveled mountain top and 720 your vision beyond the physical form. This is when your reason for being here will become apparent. Hosanna then goes on to mention:

"The Duality of life is that it exists within a varied point in time, that's what I think! Not one thing is promised. There are enough mountains in the world for all of us to climb and see our own skyline in the Sunshine. Warrior, the world is a hold! Remember you are beyond your time but here to serve your commitment.

If the world had more than one Sun would mankind worship more than one god? Mankind has the ability to see the stars, and the stars are Suns of this one universe. There are more stars then there are people on this new world; so the assumption is relative. Understand Warrior you are impregnable to illness and impermeable to heat, the concept of time for you has no merit; not even your war tempered blade can cut you. Warrior I will take you to; but not through the fork in the road. That is something you will need to do. Everything mankind has gone to war for you are in store for. Thus, your human thirst has been undeniably quenched. Yet, your subconscious still smells the stench of hell on this world."

The Warrior looked again at the leveled mountain with no apprehension and started to move towards it with aggression. Being away from battle for so long the words from Hosanna were not only enlightening but also a form of comfort in disguise. The Warrior knew his journey was far from over. His prior transactions were introductory steps to most awaited concert of internal struggle and outward manifestation. The Warrior's only hobby was that of destruction and constant improvement. There was nothing else in the world he loved more or could identify with. As the Warrior continued to move forward he looked further into the distance as the wide range of forestry and mountain began to become narrower with every moment of focus. In the midst of identifying the path to his appointed destination the Warrior discovered 7 golden majestic gates which appeared to lead directly to the mountains. It became obvious this was the Warrior's path. The Mantis took the lead and began to fly.

Black Patronage

Expose black businesses and also hold them accountable for quality goods and services no matter the scale. People of African descent; both domestic and abroad, constantly discount their own well produced quality products and services and that's what makes OUR businesses fail in both the short and long run. I totally support quality black business. I also do not go back to a business if they have the tone of entitlement. I would honestly like to know how much real commercial trade is done from the indigenous people of Africa etc. that hits mainstream US households. There is an evident quantity demand for black products which are not specially ordered by a unique sub-set of African Americans. I do not see any African American Walmart around my inner city; nor have I. In general, we do support black business, i.e. the church!

The church represents the largest black establishment in our country. I walk throughout mainstream America and do not see Black business, but I do see black patronage to other ethnic establishments. I wonder why I have not yet stumbled across a major black hub of staple businesses in my travels. When I venture into the supermarkets it is visible that the representation of black origin produce is less than 2 percent on the shelves. Something needs to change if black wealth is to be visibly prominent. We are qualified to both entertain and work in corporate America. We are capable of growing, manufacturing and patronizing our own businesses both domestically and globally.

Cruise Control

Let's roll with this cruise control...
Affirmative nod while on auto pilot...
These all-encompassing lavender skylights are awesome...
My pilot caresses her violet silk scarf...
Chocolate golden tone, she sips her ambrosia...
Riding endlessly on this space ship...
Roller coasters in heaven with no particular destination...
Is it my turn to drive...?
Fantasizing deep into the skies of her eyes I am stuck...
Taught to admire the stars through the Sun roofs of cars...
This world is almost convertible...
Thou must keep moving forward in this slow world...
Disqualifying the lessons to finding directions to your life...
Magda my love...
This is about the beautiful ride...
The direction has always been decided...
Coincidence of spirits collided...
Dividing us into two entities...
The addition to I dreamt you riding roller coasters in heaven...
Smoke Doctor dream for me...
Recreate this magical scene from destiny...
For the purpose of confidence imagine the most beautiful colors segregated then blended...
Taking us somewhere we never thought could be...
Let the wind blow through our mind...
Whistle me a symphony of love in demand...
Bliss is the simplest part of life...
Our quarrels are far beyond the hues of blue...
Even when I cannot see, I will still dream you...

Critical Mass

Stop worrying about things one cannot define...
For re-enactment of peace and water, multiply all that needs to be subtracted...
Remind yourself the fear of nothing makes sense...
Fight through fire and love the rain...
Live beyond the vanity and rebuild the sane...
Claim the best that remains...
Living beyond ones means is beyond the scope of hope...
See, you die when you stop learning...
But, life is a learning experience of what...?
Unilaterally baptized for the sake of hope...
Muse, the jokes on you...!
Bottom line is you are over-contemplating beyond one for zero reason...
Sometimes footprints in the sand; as opposed to traction in the ice, is just as good...
Just stay true to the craft...
Chief be true to the Indian...
General be true to the soldier...
Son, be true to the family...
There is no random invitation to structure...
One must work to completion...
Seems we are electrons bumping all over the place in a cloudy world of familiar particles...
I am the molecule discovered and hidden for various reasons...
You are reaching a point of critical mass in your positioning...
Something needs to differentiate...
Collapse in your weakened state of momentum without change...

You are thinking again, going against your own ...
Existence is not always physically seen...
Imagination is the gateway to new realities...
Critical mass occurs when you start dying...
Remove the fools that lay on the ground...

Intellectual Ghetto Talk

Peace son...
What's good son...?
Chillin son...
That's what's up son...
How you living son...?
Tired as hell son...
Word is bond son...
Word son, shorty was at the crib all night son...
How many chickens did you count son...
Too many son...!
Plus I was high touching the sky son...
Yo son, you should have hit me on the jack son...
All those chickens had fatties son...
I was just chillin though son...
Wake and bake son...
I got 5 on it son...
What's good for today son...?
Chillin in the crib son...
You are not working son...?
Naw, I need a job son...
Cops locking me up every other week son...
The block is hot son..!
Those sneakers you got on are fire son...!
Yeah my third baby moms got them at the mall son...
Her welfare check came in son...
One hundred fifty dollars and no one got these sneakers son...
Hit this weed and get high son...!
I need a job son...
White man keeping us down son...!
Smart as I am I take should have their job son...!
You coming to the party tonight son...?

If it's free I'm there son...
Yeah my boy graduated from high-school and having a party son...
Free chics, liquor, food and drugs son...!
You already know I'm there son...!
Can I borrow $100.00 son...?
Times are hard son...
Peace son...

Cotton Picker

I thought I was someone...
She said I was no one...
Seems appearances are not the same...
I am in corporate fields praying to the golden cow...
The light man is the white man without a tan...
Man, blacks do not understand...!
I am on my knees with all these degrees begging for forgiveness...
Picking soft and rotten cotton...
Desensitized by the sting of the whip...
The illusion is I thought I was someone...
She said I was no one...
Alive in the world without a face...
Living in a land without a race...
An identity is more than gold...
Truth be told, I have none...
I am a slave's son...
Picking cotton is what I do...
Reality check...
The Placist got me covered...

I Forgot Easter

I forgot Easter...
How could he come back...?
Divine exit and entrance minus the scars on his back...
Today I dressed the yellow of bloom...
On the cross he washed me...
On the rise he watched me...
My Lord forgives me of all I have lost...
I am beyond the days of haters and instigators...
When called, I could not stand...
Weighed down from the pain...
I can't believe I forgot Easter and I am ashamed...
Forgive me for my light and heavy wrongs...
Blessed all throughout the journey...
Forgive me Lord, have mercy and grace...
God, I just wanted to do the right thing...
Please forgive me...
Jesus...I forgot Easter...
Forgive me Pastor...
My heart has been through troubles and body humbled...
All the souls judged in this world I am wrong...
Jehovah forgave me...
I forgot Easter...
21 guns salute the truth out the camp...

Damn a Cannon

Damn a cannon…!
Big guns fire cracking in the air…
Little words, big repercussions…
Blood stains and dirty sneakers…
Black and blue bruises hugging broken bones…
Calamity trumpets the pain…
Tears of a clown and thunder sounds…
Mad at the things that never mattered…
Mindless resource controversies...
I stand on my native land...
Shattered dimensions of paradox…
Lies keep rolling, bodies fall, the world keeps spinning…
Leaves fall from trees until the roots collapse…
A world where word is bond creates order...
Damn a cannon...!
Underestimating political hypocrisy...
People are starving and robbing has to be stopped…
Deaf, dumb and blind…
Feel the thunder clap and admire the sunshine...
Blamed by the insane, remember Tubal-cain…!
Brass and iron formed by the flame...
Original weapons of mass destruction...
Devils eat hearts dancing to the stagnant melodies of spiritual warfare…
Juvenile war criminals blasting cannons by the age of 7…
Damn a Cannon…!
It's all about the weapons…
Big guns, little guns…
My brother had 3 guns…!
Little ones with guns, blood pumping out salvo…
Dishing crates of ammunition for this dinner date…
Tasty blood salvation across war filled nations…

Keep making the cannons larger…!
Just keep making the holes in our bodies larger…!
Glorify the gory video games…
Digitize the way a body lays when the soul flees…
Big execs cut checks to global arms and security dealers…
Sorrowful feelings buffered by grenade shrapnel…
War crimes and land mines make it hard to pray…
Where are the Sun filled skies…?
Mama's baking apple pies next to rotting bodies and swarming flies…
Safer to live a negative life style…
United Nations dictating local trials…
Globalized gun dealers, life stealers and skull cap peelers…
Damn a cannon…!
Launching surface to air guided missiles now…
A cannon is not a small pistol…
Heat seeking armor piercing thank you notes left on your door…
The devastation is ridiculous…
Destroy to rebuild in the name of fallacy…
Infiltrating tampered democratic panels…
Damn a cannon…!
Destroy the war demons and focus on building the family…
The physical brawn of man; compromised beyond civil co-existence…

Big Adventures of Little Butt

Big adventures of Little Butt...
Watch her strut...
That chic doesn't walk, she glides...
She does not run; she hides...
So proud of her little butt...
Shaking that little butt fast and furious...
Little Butt always walks with another companion...
Runway model, exotic dancer kind of honey...
Black swan, red stiletto ballerina in a bulimic suarez...
Look how much her gut has thrown up today...
So pretty, her clothes slip off...
So skinny, her bones show...
Little butt has a skimpy diet...
Never loud, always quiet...
Loving her allergic reaction to food...
Force feeding just will not work...
She is in love with her skeletal figure...
Full throttle American top model...
I am not in love with her emaciated figure...
Bones cold and hard to draw blood...
Trade magazines taught her to look this way...
See Little Butt was a young glutton…
Popping pant, shirt and dress buttons…
Mama had to lock the fridge...
Abused by the cruel talk of her peers for cheers...
Little Butt hid and cried for years...
It is her turn to stun the crowd now...
Never hesitating any loss of weight...
Little Butt, oh Little Butt...
Where did the weight go...?
Little Butt, oh Little Butt…
Why were you so ashamed...?

Little Butt...get some meat on those bones…!

Was I Ever Needed

From classy to ashy within the course of a morning…
Parallels of nightmares turn into pleasant dreams…
My aggression causes pain…
When I was a younger man I wrote this…
Survived wars, riots, protests and civil unrest…
Graying of the beard…
Not to be challenged is a loss of will and determination…
I am not black, but I can change colors…
Golden bronze all the time is my ambition…
I am losing family everyday…
Lock the doors…
LEG is not welcome here anymore…
Nothing to lose…
Lost memories worry me no more…
I broke my hands to make them stronger…
See, time is a clock the devil ticks…
I am the most ambient beyond internal conflict…
Trying hard to be who I am supposed to be and it is killing me…
The brevity of my longevity…
The relevance of my intelligence needs to be recharged…
Psych-analysis of these calluses leads to a shallow summary…
Pondering near a pond in the summer wondering was I ever needed…?
The unhealthy stealth of the wealthy…
The more I know, the less I want to confront…
So many influences ruin us, look at us…!
I am almost home…
Lord…I will get back home…!
It has been very hard to sleep lately…
I never retreated; just wondered was I ever needed…?

I OVERSTAND

Don't you know about the birds and the bees...?
Negroes hanging from the trees...
Mighty burdens of the weak lord...
Life without the sword is worthless, paperback...!
Weapons of mass destruction flying over seas...
I see the world in a different way every day...
My God is black; the absorption of all colors...
My world is blue and still three quarters covered...
Bless us with the peace and water...
See, slaughter has no random order...
The universe has no fenced-in borders...
Destiny is not a fantasy and famine occurs from lack of praise...
The savior is here and has his ways...
Can anybody feel, see or even hear me...?
Chorus lean, hum and sing with me...
Jehovah, Jehovah, Jehovah...!
No, I am by myself, by myself...
THE EXCLAMATION OF A NATION...!
I OVERSTAND...!
BUDGET: Before You Determine Get it Together...!
See, I am screaming at a demon...!
WaterMannyFaces: The Psychologies of my Philosophy...
This material is more for me then you...
Diary of a Waterman...!
Yeah I have so much energy in between my union with God
I feel you trying to interrupt my energy...
Adhere to this Warrior Series...
Cry when your battery dies...
Without the anger we cannot discover the lies...

The closer I get to you the stronger I become…
I do not need a vest; I have a force field…
There is no such thing as time, only limitations…
I do not care if you rest…
World, I am releasing the conviction from my chest…
I am going to give this universe my souls' best…
I will not sell myself short anymore…
I OVERSTAND…!

A Love Experiment

I get in early, you get in late…
I get home late, you get home early…
I love it all…
You have a hard time loving; loving to hate…
I just stopped talking…
Kept moving forward avoiding the constant barking…
However did you want me…?
However did you need me…?
Rising beyond the grey sceneries in a cruel world of secrets…
Billions of stars; yet we worship this Sun…!
I am the cannon without the wagon…
Not needing to move to destroy oppositions…
Periodically, my family comes out and goes back into prison…
However did you see me…?
However did you need me…?
Did you ever bleed for me…?
Steal with me…?
Keep it real with me…?
Remember when I was black and blue…
Where were you when I needed you to heal with me…?
You laughed…
I just wanted you to believe in me…
Why should I believe in you; bleed for you…?
Expect me to chuckle and break bread with you…?
I will not be an element of emotional injustice…
Just do not come outside…
Hiding every element of your exhaustive state…
Get me money; pay me, and fill my plate…
That is how I use to think…
Drinking in the strip joints, I was not mad at her…

I was mad at myself...
My wife; my world, an originator of me seeing correctly...
The art of sight re-engaged my serenity...
Traveling to meet the beginning our destiny...
The only woman who understood the value of my capacity...
Sincerely, I have no need to argue...
She is my sharpest sword...
A guaranteed blessing...
True love from the Lord...
A jewel that holds her ground down; painting the town...
Infatuated by her trust...
Ashes to ashes; lust and love...
I now know the meaning of the white dove...
When I crashed and burned she renewed the flame...
Can you feel this new energy...?
Can you picture the scars embedded within the Psychologies of my Philosophy...?

Key People

Conscious stupidities of key people caused me to lose trust...
People I believed I could rely on...
Partying and catching some rays...
Consistently deceived and tired of foolish ways...
There is no sugar coat for this candy rain...
Been there, done that...
Life is short and I am beyond your game...
I seem to have no interest, since the balance was taken...
The next time you steal from me...
You will see the real me...
Visibly invisible...
Why I leave will not be a mystery...
Everything I do in life is for the promotion of my family...
I do everything I said I will; no matter how painful, broken rib and hand...
Welcome to the Diary of a Waterman...!
Do not take my kindness as weakness...!

Mama's Coming Home

Hello, little whisperer...
Hello, hard wooden floors...
Hello, mopping brush...
Good Morning, Mr. Mocking bird...
Mama's coming home...
You ain't wash them dishes yet...!
When you gonna fold them clothes...?
You ain't got no money girl and too far from home...
Where do you think you are going...?
All grown up smoking cigarettes...?
Watching them boys throwing dice in the street...
Mama's coming home...
Get your eyes out that TV screen...
Prince charming is not coming in a limousine...
Still singing for that diamond ring...
Little black bird with some broken wings...
Sit down let me tell you some things...
Wanting the hot life but this world is cold...
Put them dance shoes on and run out that door...
One day mama will not come home...

If I was White

If I was white I would be a racist...
Supreme admiral of all the slave ships...
My fleet would be called "Keeping it Real"...
My ship would be a treat...
I would have all my shackled slaves dancing to the beat of defeat...
There would be no way to revolt...
I would feed them just enough to work three times harder...
Steal all ideas and keep my property in the yard...
They could only buy from me; separately and unequally...
This is my urinal; your outhouse is where you defecate and urinate...
There would be no other culture or race, only sub-species...
I would reface the sphinx with my depressed expression...
The world would only witness my creed's history lesson...
Diabolically...
Diasporately, African decent would be coming home to me...
Better yet...
Churches would be filled with lurkers and child molesters...
Court jesters, jezebels and Clarence Thomas gestures...
On my map the world would be less than flat...
When at my table you can eat at my feet...
If I was white I would treat my white woman like a queen...
All other races I would pimp...

In this age of technology my shackles would be rap music, sneakers and foolish gadgets...
Seasoned with a taste of government cheese to please the masses...
The Corrections Corporation Association would be a publicly traded firm...
Affirmative action would be a hit blues song...
All my female African property would walk around naked or in thongs...
I had a dream I was white and all the enterprise was mine...
Waking up in a cold sweat...
I realized my skin and features were that of color...
Dreaming of cruel unequal segregation...
In my reality I clamor for integration...
Honestly, the inbred "White Man's Burden" is systematically destroying me...
Bottom line is people need to be fair...
What comes around does go around...
For now I will keep moving forward...
Unforgiving, watching the purple clown tears turn red...

My Mother

My mother sees life...
Nurtured and developed properly...
God has no reverence to time...
In his detail he has made all things possible...
What was then exists now...
Through pain you have given birth...
Two sons; men of beautiful color...
Believe, pray and nurture
Mother, the spirit of Christ is inside of you...
Galatians 4:19...
See, Mother what Zion has travailed...
Mom, thank you for you, mother...!
Your hands sculptured the wooden shelf...
Renovated and stained the classic chair...
I am blessed for this physical birth...
It is your simple jokes that make me laugh...
The time and energy you took to teach us more...
Thank you for not leading us down the beaten path...
The domineering demand for respect that gives you class...
Your soft spoken powerful aggression...
Wolverine Mrs. Greene; when collecting the rent...
Commitment to your trade is impeccable...
Nursing all our wounds...
Always been able to fix the family...
You are more than loved and admired...
The welfare of our nation without the paradox...
Everything is straight forward...
Options provided are simple but direct...
Telling us to do the right thing and stay out of trouble...
Transferring profound wisdom in your stare...
It takes patience to raise two young men...

Being there to watch us graduate and cross the line...
Sticking with Dad and dominating the hustle...
Like two lion cubs; we study your diligence, even to this day...
There is not one thing anyone can take from you...
You are honest and loving in every way...!
1951 the year my mother was born...
I Love you Mom...!

Lawrence and Ernestine have been married for over 35 years and counting.

Farmer

I am a farmer, farming my seeds...
Planting them in the gateway of this reality...
I am the hunter, hiding in the trees...
Traveling the galaxies, bringing home what I just caught...
Call me the fisherman; I do not need a hook...
Admire the strategies written in this book...
The bay of my night constantly struggles against my morality's wishes...
Called to fight fires beneath the sea...
All things are possible and these thoughts are unstoppable...
I believe in the sewing mentality...
Reaping the fruits of manifestation...
Global outsourcing is embarrassing in this day and age...
Durable, these seeds will grow far and wide...
Sweat and loyalty will quench their birth...
You cannot reap what you do not sow...

Fat Rat

I am a fat rat on this train track...
The train passes over me...
This is where I live and breed...
My kin is on the same track...
Nomadically, traveling from station to station...
I have never eaten cheese...
I am the fat rat on this train track...
What should bother me...?
Custodian to where disease feeds and breeds...
Do not imagine what I see...
Living just enough for the day...
Surviving in this place de funk...
No reason for me to ride the train, my travel time is short...
Zigzagging between the tracks...
Never worrying about predators that soar...
Raptors are beyond this terrain...
The ghetto cat is not on my level...
I am the fat rat...
tenements, damp corridors and lab cages...
Imagine me in love with you...
All the tracks it took for me to get to you...
Yeah I am the fat rat...
I was born and will die smiling...
Just love me...

Technology Needs a Cord

Here in lies an ancient understanding...
Technology needs a cord...
Mankind exists by the sword...
In this world complexity derives simplicity...
Man makes man in his own image...
Yet, God created man...
Break down my genetic code…
Experience the illusions of reality...
Everything has a form of energy...
Dust turns to mold...
My battery ranges between my souls' entrance and exit...
Cry when your battery dies...
There is no reservation...
Plug in, rest and recharge beyond temptation...
Everything has a state of rest, even fire…
Either we get better, do less or stay constant...
To charge we go against the opposite...
Imagine if no charge were needed...
Never connected to the cord...
Man without the sword...
Impossible is a persons' inability to believe...
When weak, I pray on my knees...
Try and quantify this power and divide life by time...
Multiply the Psychologies of my Philosophy in this three dimensional world...
Electrically my soul is birthing climactic visions...
Yet, as a being I must rest...
Exhausting the carcinogens hiding from within my chest...
My battery is alive; I do not need a cord...
I am a man; this literature is my sword...
Intelligence is irrelevant if you are not living...

Every state of matter; animate or inanimate, recognizes the cord...
Let me rest and plug me in on the good foot...

I am a Mountain

I am a mountain formed by the seas...
An erupting volcano has given birth to me...
Eternally sculpted by the Four Winds...
Look at all my islands...
My afro is the clouds; lately I have been bald...
These rivers are my veins; turbulent when I get angry...
I wonder how long it takes for the birds to visit...?
A high and powerful mountain, nurturing life within my trees...
Colorful coral reefs decorate the sea...
Piercing into blue skies; the rainbows are my eyes...
I enjoy watching the Sunrise...
Time is my only limitation...
Hiding all these years; you have come to comfort me...
Whistling pretty songs to the stars and moon...
Typhoons request permission before tickling my beaches...
Fools expedite and wish to conquer my peaks...
Jewels, gems and minerals...
The result of my untapped longevity...
I am as old as the sea...
Respect my existence as you inhabit me...
Existing throughout a long range of limitations...
I am a mountain...

I in Team

There is no I in team...
I exists in time...
There is no I in mad...
Why does hate come to mind...?
I am not at war so why are we fighting...?
We have a common goal...

Back to the Pain

Floating to the pain...
Life is short and not a game...
Give me my sanity back...
Draw me away from the crud...
Running through quicker sand; thinking it was mud...
Aligning myself to be right and correct...
Square my actions within a circle of true friends...
Forgetting the night before...
Brothers, I am in the deep end, swimming into the war…
This world is passing quickly...
Exceeding your expectations of me…
Blocking so many blessings...
Taking back my veins, revival for survival put me back in the deep end...
The world is too shallow; I need to swim and breathe...
What makes a man tired makes a woman upset…
Standing in the rain...
Wading in my puddles, splashing in your puddles...
In between loving you...
All the beautiful things I wish to do...
Pretty hugs remembering you...
The sacred things that I have been through...
I feel it is worth it...!
Dear Lord, take me above it...
You know I would love it...
Hide so my eyes do not burn you…!
There is no four leaf clover to hang over my hat…
Mercifully, this will not be overnight…
When clean you are welcomed to the world of light….
Jumping off the wagon to fight the dragon...
Waking up to headaches…
The end always justified the means to me…

Hold on a Second

Hold on a second...
Just give me a minute...
I do not need your advice...
I'm going to take it as I live it...
Life teach me a lesson, while I continue to climb...
Holding a dollar, waiting on a dime...
Sensing I am losing my mind...
No time for forgiveness...
Graying of the beard and looking through all of my holes...
Live with no excuses; raise your hand to the sky...
I do not know the reasons, but you know I will try...
Hold on a second...
Just give me a minute...
I do not need your advice...
I'm going to take it as I live it...
Life teach me a lesson, while I continue to climb...
For now I stand on my roof...
Quietly sitting in the booth, this shiny quarter affords me no call...
Non for profits never bought me these shoes...
Mastering the hustle, paying my dues...
The world is a lost lamb...
Hold on a second...
Just give me a minute...
I do not need your advice...
I'm going to take it as I live it...
Life teach me a lesson, while I continue to climb...
Is your home better than mine...?
Why did it take so long for you to see...?
I have always been here...
Why didn't you visit me...?

These are the Psychologies of My Philosophy...!
What you do affects me...
I really do care about the welfare of society...
There is no mother of God, nor do I worship any shrine...
What you do in life is what you define...

Gimmick Me

Are you serious...?
Selling me a flashy wrapper...
Pretty colors to entertain a lifeless portrait...
Where is the talent at...?
Who is curbing and killing the talent...?
Who is taking the time to redefine this recycled garbage...?
Mass marketing; the death of social conscious...
Remembering when singers had voices and songs identified choices...
Wardrobe choices and paid public voices dictate ticket sales...
Quantity over quality is the law...!
Gimmicks get you on the front page...
Weirdo's with beardos rocking and rolling with bald chics...
Fools rule on cruise control...
Stupidity is that simple and expensive...
Phone Nina Simone in heaven; this generation needs a chance...
Mrs. Holiday bless the children with your sultry voice...
Rule by few...
For what...is there not more than two...?
Remember the guitar sound...?
Blues that spoke the news...?
The world stage is plagued...!
Is it Jackson...?
Count all the wacklords headlining on the rosters...
Louis Armstrong declares the true horn sound...
Digitizing the world's rhythm separating music from the soul...
Auto-tune is out of control...

Genuine artistry is being hidden...?
Entertainment gives me less to believe in...
Big chains, gossip and incarceration...
Paparazzi, infidel media and death of sensation...
Is truth and skill have been removed from the trade...
I still listen to the black and grey...
Flipping the 45's other side...
Reality television is fiction and I wish for a real concert...
Stop publicized rehearsals...!
Gimmick me...
Music's soul is lost...
It will be hard to find it...

The Wrong Target

The whole generation and beyond is in need of help. There are too many issues to confront then trying to bring down the ignorant and poisoned traitors that the white establishment promotes. We are stuck in a vicious corner and the only thing we have to eat is ourselves. There is more to save, then the wicked media in America. Hip Hop and rappers are not the problem.

The problem is in our broken down and de-nationalized self-esteem. For every common good there will be an equal evil in this world. Just do the right thing and focus on building your own families and establishments. We have enough work to do in our own homes. I really wonder where our domestic focus is concentrated. Our social priorities are not nested in feeding ourselves, our culture, or preparing the kin for the next level of pure hippocratic embarrassment and disillusion. We need to prepare for this next wave of unemployment which will continue to segregate African Americans even more. We just keep on dancing around these unfruitful issues and gossip chains. Also, all women are not queens and all men are not kings. It is what you do for the record able benefit or detriment of society that allows you to stand out.

Technology is an Easy Bull

Technology is an easy bull...
Do you know how to ride...?
Have you studied the trade...?
Technology is my trade and how I get paid...
Authoring new methodologies has been my position...
Beyond not knowing and you want to hide...
What is inside technology...?
Grandpa Jones said: "There is nothing new under the Sun"...
Pop-Pop Greene always asks: "How's the Weather?"...
Manifesting those thoughts through deliberation...
This is not chess; where you must technically compete against me...
In between chagrin, coding the next page...
Buying and reading the books...
What makes you ready to win...?
This is my hustle amongst many others...
I am still in the caves, respecting my loved and lost family...
Grandpa Jones said: "There is nothing new under the Sun"...
Pop-Pop Greene always asks: "How's the Weather?"...
Manifesting those thoughts through deliberation...
New touch screen devices will suffice you...
Something to play with, allowing the device to complete you...
We do not need to converse...
You want to compete with a technology hustler...
Who does that...?
How does that work...?
See this is my trade...
I make your auto work...

Leave me alone and do your job...
Train hard and keep moving forward...
I cannot take a break...
In electronic space, time ticks at a digital pace...
A well respected weapon I am...
Thanks for the heart's worth Grandpa and Pop-Pop...
Prior, I said "get out my book"...
Now I say, "You are not ready to fit my shoes"...
The Shoe King is my father...
Technology is nothing new to me...
It is my trade; one of The Psychologies of my Philosophy...
Technology verse family; the complexities of simplicity...
The birth and death of me...
The recreation of society as we know it...

SIMPLICATED

Life is a resource less project plan...
Suspended at a stand near the liquor store...
Begging for more rum while reminiscing...
Splashing in shallow plastic kiddy pools on a hot summer day...
I can see through fat...!
No fear, drinking Dominican Presidente' beer...
I am just a guesser...
Depending on the goal, the self-actualizer needs mass marketing...
Da Vinci did not have a printing press...
Coco needed the clown...
James was black before he was brown...
I feel like the bee that stung the tree; falling at the base of its roots...
Shade cannot hide on a sunny day...
Go up the ladder; it rains, go back down the ladder...
Why say the same things everyday...?
Simplistically everything is complicated...

Sunday Comics

Comics, at times I sit and read...
Gestures in my world that become the seed...
Maple seed, next to the maple tree...
Reading Sunday Comics...
At times I wonder what is funny...?
My life has a busy schedule, so I took some time out...
Creative hiatus...
Yeah, I mentally took some time out...
Reading these comics...
Realizing characters are in worlds within themselves...
Illustrated concepts from minds like mine...
In between orchards manifesting the growth of peach trees...
Following a row of assorted roses...
These comics sure are interesting...
Hammock next to me...
I choose to ingest summer imagery while relaxing on a granite bench...
Pondering what and when I will win...
Coming back again, today it is Sunday...
Laughing at myself...
Talking with my father...
Renewing my dues...
Wondering why I bother...
I see leaves fall from trees preparing for autumn...
Near rest reading the book of Luke...
Wanting my brother to come back home...
Reading the Sunday comics in the hot Sun...
Playing dead in the pool counting each breath I take...
I am upset with myself...
Part of this comic I read...
Watching squirrels forego nuts to steal apples...

Self-absorbed practitioners praying within the chapels…
I will never forget what the true page feels like…
Each day brings a new comic situation…
Sunday comics…

The Calls

Realizing I will be working my entire life...
Tending to miss a few calls here and there...
Not wanting to receive news of the inevitable...
Sourcing the root of the problem before picking up...
Problems caught after the "how are you?"...
I am good brother so "how are you?"...
Wishing I never picked up...
Troubles are like bubbles in the bath...
Problems just let me be...
This poetry is my auto-biography...
Introduction you to the Psychologies of my Philosophy...
The calls never seem to end...
Recruiters have changed the game...
From sending lame emails to directly texting me...
Protocol was email then the call...
Trying to enter my world...
Of course I am viable, reliable and able to forecast...
The teams I am on usually win...
Blessed to enjoy many things...
Now I am older and just want to swim...
Running from hornets flying against the wind...
I will not pickup if at the beach and you call my phone...
Wishing to be alone...

Hot Glitter and Ice Coffee

Sparkling colors of mahogany...
Dancing past me throughout my Sunny dream...
Shaded by her long lashes...
Her glitter is jading my focus...
Too hot to be cool...
Truly enjoying the scorching summer view...
The adventures I take just to get closer...
Sensing a youthful spirit in the air...
City leaves reach their greenest growth; soon to fall from the trees...
Her essence glimpses up...
Polite fully sipping on ice coffee...
Staring into my golden bronzed state...
Watching my eyes synthesize mediocrity...
White doves, no pigeons, satin hair...
A picture captured without revisions...
Polite fully sipping on ice coffee...
For the moment, there is no time...
Heaven's refreshment is a sip away...
The speed of life takes slow steps today...
Polite fully sipping on ice coffee...
Igniting Diamond Dynamite...
Thrusting Green Diamonds into the Sky...

Rich Guy

You want a rich guy...
Go and get a rich guy...
I am already a rich guy...
Never have I been a poor guy...

My response to women who believe they can have anything or anyone they want; when everything they have in life is not good enough. It is the little things that allow for greatness. Rich does not equate to wealth but a person can be rich in health, spirit and happiness. The saying "the grass is always greener on the other side" will always hold true if a person believes they are on a property without a lawn. Take time to look at what you have and enjoy the simplicity of life. Sharing with your partner is a blessing not a requirement. Life is not a sitcom. So many issues result in the world as a result of money and natural selfishness. Thus, man and woman have remedial arguments about things that should occur denying the blessings of the Lord. The man that builds the castle by himself usually does not have much time to share it with anyone of substance.

An Enigma

I am an enigma…
The stigma is I trust too much…
My life is a resourceful project plan...
At the end of the day it is my process you demand…
I think and do what I desire upon command…
Doing everything with a goal in mind…
So why stand here…?
Suspended at a stand near the liquor store...
Thirsting for more rum…
Reminiscing first kisses and birthday wishes
Splashing in a shallow plastic kiddy pools on a hot summer day...
I am just a guesser and can see through fat...!
Recognizing things need to change…
No fear, drinking El Presidente beer...
Just to not think and go to sleep…
Shooting myself with yellow capped 99 bananas…
Going bananas internally…
Focusing on what I need to see to keep safe…
Depending on the goal, the self-actualizer requires mass marketing…
Davinci did not have a printing press…
Coco needed the clown…
James was black before he was brown…
I feel like the bee that stung the tree; falling at the base of its roots…
Shade cannot hide me on a sunny day…
Go up the ladder; it rains, go back down the ladder…
Simplistically, everything is complicated…
What happens when elders speak to the young…?
Young ones pull out stolen guns for fun…
If there is no purpose for it, reveal it…

Let me relieve my focus…
Hope is a catalyst to manifestation…
Karma can be a shield or a blade…
See, I am here without applause…
Why do I keep loving it…?

Something Distills Nothing

In the middle of nowhere; knowledge of what makes sense…
Something distills nothing; allowing for things to grow…
Everything has its own theory…
Relativity exists within a volume of three dimensions…
Death is a state where one cannot be seen; in between being heard or felt…
A world full of waters is absurdly melting and drying up…
When in demand evaluate your hand with shortcoming…
We choose providence over God's gain…
Trust and believe…
Implosion requires more force…
Superficial is the heart on the sleeve we bear witness to…
There is a reaction; not one thing can explode without knowing…
Nothing is easy…
It takes time to build a Sun…
Stop allowing your ego to sponsor the goals of your super ego…
Remember the ID is most important…!

Green Pastures

In the land of milk and honey...
A place to digest and rest...
The orchard has been sculpted to supply natural delectable...
Colorful birds chirp due to heavy quantities of seed...
Jack the black cat playfully lies on fresh leaves...
A groundhog family plays beneath the shed...
Squirrels throw half eaten apples right above my head...
Peaches, kiwi, blueberries, figs, strawberries, grapes, apples and plums...
The life of more fortunate visitors has begun...
Horse radish, peppers, cabbage, herbs and carrots...
So I sit and watch...
Birds make love to the bees...
Domestic deer nibble the fruit trees...
Big winged and multi-colored butterflies are a usual sight...
Welcome to Green Pastures...
Sit back and enjoy the beauty...
She said: "Darling, I know you love the land of milk and honey"...
Imagine the colorful scenery...
The fish in the tank will never understand...
I dream of land...
To cultivate a land that I can appreciate...
That is the plan...
The journey to peace is a hard distance...
Thankful such a place is in existence...
My residential dream...

Sunny Days and Delays

National transit is a socio-economic bandit...
The illusion is mass transit confusion...
Redirecting WE into overall system conformity...
Conductor shouts: "This is a disgrace! One hand does not know the other!"...
I sit here in my air conditioned seat waiting for our turn...
Red to green...
This rat race is a disgrace...!
Telecom companies are on strike...
Thus, the network is down...
No sirens blasting during this state of emergency...
Tears of a clown...
Engineering fear is fair in a color coded society...
180 degrees of public privacy...
Watch closely their eye on WE...
Terminations, cancellations and hesitation...
Panic attacks and hallucinations complimented by the horrid stench of human stampede...
Make way for the pregnant, elderly and handicapped...
My patience is gigantic, so I do not panic...
No one is excused and very few are truly humbled...
The jerk just wants to get to work...!
Some people will wait for the gates to open...
Sinking into the quicker sand by demand...
Hoping for a direct way in...
I will not alternate my route today...
For no one will I derail...
Stop the hands of time...
When I get in the fun begins...
Confuse me a nation; not just this nation...
Sense the global frustration...
Cab rates irate me...

Do not drive your own; it is costly to park...
You want to fly, but it is raining and your bags are heavy...
We have seen too many levies break...
Too many explosions and lives at stake...
Take a break and float on in...
Avoid the waterways if you cannot swim...
As mentioned, I will get back home...!
Tribute to the commute...
My world is in a state of transition...

Born or Bred

I am the heir...
Leader in despair...
One of few with a clue...
Leadership classes are for the masses...
Get up and run your own world...
Low self-esteem accentuated by egocentric dreams...
People look up to you to get close to you...
For what...?
What have you done...?
Where have you been...?
Follow you for what...?
Forced to follow myself; fueling my own journey...
Born and manifest my own lineage...
My conscious asks these questions...
Considerable suggestions...
His suit and tie is nice and her dress is really sharp...
Nice tie guy...!
What you are saying lacks value; negatively impacting everyone but yourself...
Your living style does not reflect good health...
Most laws are flawed and segregated...
Invisibly castrated and built for those that will never make it...
My friend, remember when there were ten to defend...?
Allowing the cons to stitch the nation...
I fall and get back up...
Many a soul tends to help me...
Learning to forget just to reestablish my state of commitment...
Choosing to be rich and not wealthy...
Who is supposed to lead me...?
Socially and domestically the media is our shepherd; marketing us a lie...

The magistrates escape route is overkill and absolutely
selfish...
Why would I follow you...?
Born or bred; Similac or breast fed...?
Born without a shred of fear...
Laid to rest without a bed...
Bred strong with your feet planted to the ground...
If your skill is talk, then just keep talking...
I stopped talking while continuing to train...
My own blood travels through these veins...
Born to breed a stronger more prepared generation...

Micro-manage

Micro-manage yourself not me...
Gulp your coffee; I will sip on my tea...
See, I know where I am going...
On a mission to get up out of fact or fiction...
In your position, you talk too much to listen...
Lies, poor performance reports and false liberties...
I am fascinated by the simplicity of life...
Dad, let's go fishing and see what we have been missing...
Listen...
Mom, I am missing all the hugs and kisses...
Too much variety is making me poor...
Give me the beach and a bodega corner store...
Take the micro-management away and microwave me a sandwich...
Today, I am saying what I need to say...
Work hard and play harder, the good die young...!
I am a hypocrite with benefits, working the system...
Scratching at the bars, reinforcing my product line...
Disrespecting the laws of incorporation...
Rotating too fast to crash and burn...
Simple machinery, managing my state of comprehension...
Micro-manage yourself...

Golden Bronze

I am a black planet starring at a white moon...
See, I do not care about the comets...
Golden holy cow, plus or minus the cotton...
Scratching at the bars with my waterproof shirt on...
Carefully stitching my soul into infinity...
Working my way to the top; do not limit me...
Going further then your skies will be...
I play dumb but I am still on top...
What next to do in preparation of the zenith...?
Trust, I have already seen this...
I screamed and dreamt this...
You were a part of it...
A chemical reaction fuses electricity...
Something was on my mind, so I told you...
My complexion is a reflection of how I feel...
From glazed reddish to golden bronze...
I am real...!
I am a golden sword, bronzed by the Lord...
Thriving on chaos, focusing on the peace and water...
Gleaming in a world dictated by violence and politics...
Charged to take charge...!
Who cares if I am light skin...?
I say golden bronze while dictating pleasant sceneries...
Colorful and diverse this world, verses what it needs to be...
Did you think I was too light skin to understand...?
I have grown and overstand...
My crimson is in demand...
4 x 4 "O" Positive (family blood type)...
To live we have to give...
Let me live, and let the racism go...!

Fools are too busy looking outside instead of what's inside of me...
My souls' energy that drives and derives me...
Do I ever sleep...?
Asking where I get all the time...?
I made the time with this powerful light of mine...!
See my golden piano...?
Sand to the left, transitioning into the sea to the right of me...
The grape of a red wine clinging onto the vine...
I see the children dying, battered women crying, World War III arising...
An implied socio-depressive state...
A most powerful culture unemployed and imprisoned...
It's not surprising for you to blame me...
I am a black planet starring at a white moon...
See, I do not care about the comets...

At the Beach

I can be at the beach all day...
Painting in the rain...
Eating ice cream in a snow storm...
Delightfully sipping beer from a straw...
I can swim over 1,000 miles...
I can see all of the children's smiles...
The Sun dial is calling for a heat wave...
Concentrated lemon in my water bottle...
I got lemonade, I got lemonade...!
The fallen leaves have seen better days...
Seldom praying mayday on a cloudy day...
Still I want to go and play...
Find some adventure and visit my friends...
Time goes by so fast...
Tonka toy trucks and Hot Wheels cars in the sandbox...
Sprinkler systems and battery powered Intertek water guns...
Water balloon fights on summer days...
Concentrated orange in my water bottle...
I got orange juice, I got orange juice...!
Life is an interesting science...
I am finally letting the house of cards fall...
At the beach no one thinks about the violence...
Moments of wave crashing silence...
I take a dip in the ocean to see how long I can tread...
Rolling with the flow of the motion...
Waterman is in heaven on Earth floating out to sea...
Wiggling my toes with glee...

Save Your Sanity

I hear you talking about saving, but you are slaving...
Renting two bedrooms to fit more than eight...
Touch down via NJ transit...
Bear witness or get out the state...
Stop working for nothing...
Focus and do what you have to do...
It is crazy what we must do to survive...
One welfare bread winner...
Breakfast, lunch and dinner divided by three...
Breeding too many mouths to feed...
I do not want to hear it and tired of seeing it...
Times are hard and you are the only one supporting the family...
Whoa is you...!
What are you going to do...?
See, I sense there is a problem...
Do not try to hide the gun son...
Once a winner but you have lost none nothing...
No one cares what you are saying...
The plan is weak and lacks foundation...
Oasis chasing vacations in a bad storm...
I wonder who is here to save you, while working on myself...
In the land of the brave and free; I have a problem with welfare taking care of me...
I am going to work till my bones hurt...
Demanding all that I expect and see...
Do what you have to do, stop leaning on me...
Jumping in the taxi...
Take me home...
I have a family I am building to see...

Opposition

Sometimes I sit back and listen to the opposition and then go fishing...
The probability of me leaving early is really low...
I am the opposition and letting you know...
So there you go...!
To rain or snow; that is not the question, it is all the same...
Poverty sucks and it has a name...
Greed in your pocket...
Thief, sell the gold in your teeth...
Police, get back on the streets...
Overtime bandits...!
Taxes suck and transit potholes are treacherous...
Orbital health care is designed to get the best of WE...
Medicare cannot medicate me...
Politicians make laws to feed the greedy taking from the needy...
Fact-check tradition to see what we've been missing...
Listen...
Don't trust anyone who smiles too much, dictates taxes and dances with avoidance...
Realize false flag operations...
Why do I vote...?
Why do I watch the news...?
Better off reading the obituary...!
Home of the buy one get one free...
I make just enough to work hard...
Rain is expensive in a dry world...
Sipping ice coffee in the tropics...
Stare at the opposition and listen...
We; the people will never be domestically protected by our citizenry...

180 degrees of public privacy is evermore watching...
Global new world order is designed to destroy free thought...
Individualism must exist...!
The globalist is communist...
Again, democracy only magnifies segregation...
Mr. President; I believed in you, but guess who is coming to dinner...?
Freedom of speech is gone...
The richer the rich, the poorer the poor...
I really dislike porridge...

"A Man and the World"
Volume 11

Irene's Eye

Hurry Cain...
In a hurricane some are Able to take the pain...
I do not see any hurricane...
That is when it came...
The calm before the storm...
Hypnotized by the eyes of Irene...
When I saw her face, I simply became a believer...
The rain only lasted throughout the night...
I have seen her, nothing compared to Katrina...
Looking into her big eyes...
I watched listened and continued to discern...
From category 2 to tropical storm...
Through the media I witnessed all forms of despair...
Homes, flooded roads and bridges in need of repair...
Federal Emergency Management Act (FEMA)...
The media has dramatic tactics ultimately equating poor journalism...
People are sincerely in need of help...!
This is not the first storm of this caliber, nor will it be the last...
Stand in the ocean and tell me the water is high and uncontrollable...
Hurry Cain...
In a hurricane some are Able to take the pain...
Fallen trees and leaves but I stay on my knees...
Praying for the safe keep of loved ones...
That night I flew my kite into the wind...
The string broke, never to see it again...
Meanwhile, in the Green Pastures the Master's peach and plum trees bend...
Throughout the basement rub-age I located my father's patents...

I picked them up and carefully allowed them to dry...
Wishing I could have collected the documents sooner...
Thankful I was able to attain them no matter what...
Studying the documents with passion...
Wondering what generations will think of the storm...
This is not the first storm of this caliber, nor will it be the last...

"14"

14...
Genesis to Numbers
Infinitely, the end has always justified the means to me...
The compass of my individuality entitled creation...
Trust, I must balance this communication...
Beyond relentless, my heart reacts to action...
Hand on my face; mental satisfaction
I am the hardest manifested in the race...
My reaction to responsibility is phenomenal...
High off my freedom, doing my numbers...!
Sons, remember the Warrior Series is all me...
Born by thought, now I am thinking...!
Beware, thou is conscious and prepared...
Power and divine sacrifice...
The epitome of change is constant...
14...

Aged Tears

Aged tears...
I have been crying for years...
My fears have gotten to the best of me...
For centuries I have been exploring...
Dreaming in and out of galaxies...
To and from the sea...
Blurry red eyes rest with the Sunset...
I miss my childhood...
Closing my eyes to a surprised awakening...
Marriage, misery, mayhem...
I have seen it, believe it...!
My values and judgment were incorrect...
See, I switched up and changed my ways...
Burning away the disrespect...
The art of sight never losing its meaning...
Needing to be around everything that means something to me...
Avoiding all things that mean nothing to me...
Screaming in the deep end...
Wandering the wilderness of distress with a population on my back...
Strapped with various types of honey in my ditty bag...
Aged tears roll to my feet; colorfully staining concrete in the street...
Forty days and forty nights; the internal struggle contains itself...
Urban warfare, city strife, and a knife in my back...
Ah We Enemy...!
I miss my friends...
Stick collecting to drown desires of perfection...
Resurrection through this volume...

Reaching for completion in a realm of troubled love...
Waving good bye, I cry...
Aged tears...
A selfless man residing in a selfish world...
My souls inside you; hugging you...
You foolish being, I am crying next to you...
Where is the care...?
For centuries I have been exploring...
Dreaming in and out of galaxies...
To and from the sea...
Blurry red eyes rest with the Sunset...
Preparing for the rain...
Fighting tears in between the pain...
I am tired, but I have things to complete...

Stupid Questions

Do not ask me stupid questions...
There is too much on my mind...
Think about your suggestions...
I have little to zero time...
If you are cheap, then move away from me...
I work too hard to be under sold...
Cynically, criticism is weighing down my mental...
Most likely you will not be treated fairly...
There is such a thing as a stupid question...
Most of the time you already have an answer...
Wasting nouns, verbs and adjectives...
Pinpoint quality destinations...
I am better than no one...
Keeping cute simplicities close to home...
The nerves in my sober brain hurt...
Patiently, I will watch your brain freeze...
Teasing you to have any real concern...
Hypersensitive to negligence...
Angry birds flock around me...
Filtering the noise from the filth...
At times I find myself asking stupid questions...
I just have to keep moving forward...
Who am I to question what is on your mind...?

Law became Rén

Law became Rén…
I want to draw…
I will draw and create fine art…
In my mind there are images of magnificence…
Tragedy calibrated with innocence…
The evidence is I am here…
Fear is what was changing my surreality…
My dreams kept identifying real challenges…
Now I want to draw…
Hands to my face, the cold water splashes…
Looking at my hands and they are not perfect…
The greatness of imperfection is what makes life uncanny…
I know I can draw…
I wanted to make music, so I made music…
Songs of passion are clashing against my existence…
My soul is a burning fire…
Beyond accredited and licensed to the point of ridiculousness…
Certified like a shark…
God made me the sharpest…
My mind and sanctuary is all I have…
I wonder who will really be there…?
I wanted to write, so I wrote…
Tired of listening to faulty opinions…
Law became Rén…!
I began dictating my thoughts through the pen…
Considered to be Confucius' most outstanding student…
Therefore, I knew I could do it…!
Laughing out loud…
I finally figured it out…!
Rén to be a part of everyone…

A natural quality inside of every person...
Engaging with my brethren in heaven...
This world inspires me...
I wanted to do math, so I calculated…
Today Law became Rén…

A Day Old

A day old...
I am just a day old...
I feel old...
But I am just a day old...
Doing what I am told...
Bold and still one day old...
How can I sleep...?
Living life...
What can I say...?
Day by day...
I am just a day old...

Well, Well, Well

Well, Well, Well…
If a big bird does its business on you on a stormy day, then your luck will be very awesome...
I am talking gigantic condor business…!
If you think you are attractive and are not married, there is something wrong with you...
If you pay too much for coffee, then you have problems...
If your glasses are bigger than your head, you are probably handicap...
If you are in the deep end of the pool and can't swim, you are prepared to drown...
If you talk more than you listen, your word will be meaningless...
If you saw nothing but heard it all, you are a faulty witness...
If you are in a bodega asking for fresh fruit, take a moment and laugh at yourself...
If you are throwing money in the club with no job, you are foolish and your admirers are putting your cash in their pockets...
If you are popping balloons in a moving car, then you are the greatest idiot...
If you are standing in a stampede, enjoy getting ran over...
Throughout the course of your life always remember...
An Indian or Chinese US postal worker will always be pissed off...
Smile and count your blessings...
Well, Well, Well…

The Thorns

Roses bloom from spring to fall...
A beautifully endangered scene...
I believed in roses...
The colorful variations of life...
Natural beauty balanced by the sword...
Blossoming a simple hope within a thorny serenity...
When they matured I wished to cut them from the stem...
Supplying instead of buying...
Swift fully handing them to my lady friends...
All that has come to an end...
Raking leaves against a chilly breeze...
The assorted piles will eventually be bagged up...
Eyes focused on the lingering petals...
The century old oak whispers wisdom as it sheds its skin...
Guiding me through a stern sense of nostalgia...
Remembrance is expensive...
Resting on my porch, touching the spirit of season...
Even the void of nothing bears life...
Love encounters strife...
Managing the chore on my own...
Accidentally cutting my gloveless hands to the occasional thorn...
Continuing till I am complete...
Squadrons of teenage riders scurry past; momentarily own the pavement...
Anticipating the moon's full bloom...
In a remembered scene the dawn silhouettes the dusk...

Cigar Smoke, 99 Bananas, Heineken and Hennessey

Puffing and laughing at the cigar shop...
Hitting the stogie like a cigarette...
Chugging down Heinekens with friends...
Mixing previously ingested 99 Bananas...
The locker opens displaying a brilliant bottle of cognac, Hennessey to be precise...
Leaving the scene feeling more than nice...
The black asphalt pavement was wet as I entered my black sports sedan...
It seemed Irene's dark cloud was still over me...
Riding dirty, empty open bottles hug the crevasses of the ditty bag to the right of me...
Red brake lights lead to a screeching crash...!
The airbag fondles my face...
Thank God I am safe...!
Familiar sirens sound off; red and blue lights flash...
Lonely in Hells' holding cell I cling to sanity...
There are no clocks; time no longer exists...
I am pissed at myself...
A one ply toilet roll serves as my pillow...
Cold and lonely, only the camera is watching me...
Magda knows not where I am...
In the stall with no call; having no idea of when I will leave...
Cold and sobered up I bang the bars for attention...
The officer hands me a breakfast sandwich and coffee with cream...
Lactose intolerant, sipping with heavy guilt...
I am here; adhering to God's lesson...
In between prayer I make my pact...
This is the last time; I will never be back...

My pregnant wife delivers me from the cell as the bail is waived...
I feel indecent; since I have misbehaved...
Four thousand dollars, sixteen days and a plethora of stress later...
Sitting at courthouse; preparing for intake...
Lessons learned, as I internally scream for probation...
Waiting for the Superior Court of the land to open and provision my next date...
Pre-trial intervention is being considered...
God carry my soul and forgive my mistake...
I have lost so much yet this is a blessing...
Those drinks were expensive, and I should have been home...
Again, I am back to walking...
Involuntarily forced to live a life of sobriety...
I have much more life than to live for the liquor...
My child is arriving so I must be principle...
The way I live and walk has expensively changed for the better...
I am seeing clearly...
Sitting in court wishing I were at work...
Beyond embarrassed with my actions...
I should have been home with my wife that night...

Raw Intuition

Cerebral hopes and preparation...
The sensation of knowing an era's end is near...
Laughing at forever before it is over...
Dreams of floating through peaceful waterways...
Personalities of life form via our unconscious travels...
Those that are good to you nurture and protect you...
Remembering everything from the smallest scene to the darkest vision...
Appreciating life even more awake then asleep...
Without art the Earth would be nothing...
I use to want more than I could handle...
My divine union is a supernova blessing a rising Sun...
Nothing is over...
New energy has just begun...

Daffodil Hill

Laughing on a daffodil hill...
Having fun is an errand...!
We all depreciate in a land of zero appreciation...
Who cares about the grass if you live under a rock...!
Thundering with no rain...
Soul clapping the danger out of life...
The dusking day sets the stage...
Dimming the internal light for an hour long lightning show...
Examining the real differences of day and night...
Why does the Sun run away and where has it gone...?
Seems the Sun stops when the rain drops...
Admiring the beautiful colors of maroon and grey...
Rocks transform to diamonds, gems and crystals; so just wait...
Patience creates timely works of art...
Predicting the motion of a wave is as likely as patterning a snowflake...
Why can't everything be the same...?
Life is not a fashion faux pas...
Trees bend without the wind...
Would the world change if the sky were orange...?
Would disparity be recollected if it were all rejected...?
Imagine the playgrounds if not one thing were disrespected...
For thirty five years I have been painting...
Zoning out in a field of violets...
Engaging the butterflies' monarch flight...
Ze Black Squirrel hugs and tucks his nuts away...
Lying on the soft grass...
Humming, whispering and mumbling..,
Catapulting ideas over the Sun...

Patiently waiting to see when gravity would pull them back...
What makes an angel hard to find...?
Today is an excellent day to marry the wind...
A seasonally thick fog on a fall day carried me here...

Sleeping on Chess Pieces

Do you sleep...?
I do not sleep, I create in a different conscious...
Do you eat...?
I do not eat, too busy feeding my many faces...
WaterMannyFaces...!
Do you dream...?
I do not dream, too busy designing spaces and recreating places...
The Sleeping General was really awake...
Faking and weaning out all those that could not anticipate...
Before we went to war we had dinner...
Time was needed to examine true hunger...
Do you run...?
I do not run, I walk confidently through destinations...
Architecting new models of energy...
Chess pieces layered on the board...
You are taking too long to move...
Queen protects the King...
Knights' session is a life's lesson...
Bishop I a Rook for the majesty and imagine me...!
Speed of life; time flies so I am flying with it...
Do you smoke...?
I do not smoke, I ignite manifestations...
Softly pressing piano keys pleases me...
A drummer's bang eases me...
Not dumb, just numb with conclusion...
I am so sober and beyond foolish illusions...
In reality I am allowing you to win...
Sleeping on chess pieces is the thesis...

Chaotic Preparation

Wildfire of ridiculousness and chaotic command...
Striving and surviving with dementia...
Working in a land where urgency is senseless...
In a position of leadership do not blame the Indian...
Reasoning is null and void in a chaotic world...
Steve Jobs died today...
A tragic end to a lifelong lesson...
Now who is left to bite the apple...?
Keep concepts close to the chest...
The business plan may make no sense...
Partners will always part with you...
They are not a part of you...
Admire how they rip you apart...
Crabs in a bucket do not care...
See, a chaotic commander is selfish...
Man on man defenses sculptured by predisposed segregation and nepotism...
To innovate is before and beyond the emergence...
Thus, my emergencies are prioritized differently...
What matters depends on perception of evidence...
I own too many stages for you to play with me...
I am on too many tracks for you to train with me...
I am going to make men; break them, and then recreate them...!
Surfing the universe one millisecond at a time...
Transiting locations paycheck by paycheck...
One day things will be different...
For now I am strapped up in a state of chaotic preparation...

Theory of Paid for Pieces

My friends get paid for pieces…
The thesis, when will we be able to work together…?
Certain uncontrolled factors lead to variation…
This is our nation and we will pay in pieces…
Putting the pieces together…
External noise such as government policies and the environment deafens my state of awareness…
Until my manifestations are finished; immunized I closed my eyes and just stopped listening…
Methodically reducing sensitivity by design; evaluating the parameters…
Six Sigma by design, manufacturing quality through calibration…
Critical chaining the longest sequence to get things right…
Paving pre-defined destinations night by night and day by day…
My thesis...
In pieces I plan on pushing the boss out…
Scratching at the bars…
Products, processes and services…
In a world of natural born consumers, what else is there…?
Conjuring answers to questions from my best suggestions…
Producing the future in workbench form; approximating linear tabulation…
Mastering my trade before I get paid…
Life is what you make out of it…
Testing the waters to a high degree of elevation…
Products must be modified against the production system…

Amalgamate rich and fancy luncheons and propagate "X" functions...
Identify alteration in the early stages...
Be true to good people...
See, the devil is in the detail...
Stay away from infatuation...it only drives one mad...
Strive to eradicate contradictions...
Exported by air craft carriers...
Breaking barriers like an urban legend...
The thesis behind paid for pieces...

A Master's Thoughts

What does a master do...?
Stay out of trouble and harm's way...
Studies to defeat, save or create you...
You cannot forget me until you miss me...
In monsoons distant water wells run dry...
Thirsty, piercing diversity with mercy...
Visibility Through Invisibility...
Masters do not want to be seen...
Their explosion is as expected as the blossoming bud...
In these pages you have me and my thoughts...
My eyes are changing colors...
From grey, green to bloodshot...
Focusing in the dark of night...
From grey, green to bloodshot...
See; I am changing world, while changing the world...
Restructuring day by day...
Having nothing to do with the season...
Reasoning with treason and caressing miracles...
Mastering everything, Jack of none...
Indifferent to how much power I should exert...
Started novice, grew to expert...
The simplest things are the hardest to accomplish...
Most seem to misunderstand the nature of simplicity...
Ignorance gets to me...
The master christens the pupil...
Pupils dilate...
Behaving to build up enraging powers; to disengage...
Poetry, project management and technology are my trades...
Yet, I wish to keep painting...
There are thoughts being birthed simply for the making...

Perception and foresight of the plan is paramount...
A master feeds when he either wants to or needs to...
A master bleeds because he has too...
Waiting patiently for his moment and then owns it...!
Recognizing he was born to be chosen...
A worn spirit that will not run from repercussions...
Wisdom clutching knowledge...
Like when bullet shells are busting; sharp swords are thrusting...
Metallic machines crush; simple beings lust...
A master laughs at death and even invites it, no need to fight it...
Sacrifice is a necessity in a masters' world...
Quietly he sips his tea...
Attained by attention...
Progression through right and exact inspection...
A master loses himself while recreating wealth...
Realizing a tomb is only but so big...
Knowing life is about the peaceful smile associated with accomplishment...
Masters respect masters due to the nature of discipline...

Oh Well

Searching for gold in the desert...
I have climbed so many mountains; settled on many peaks...
My friends say I am out of my mind...
Ah We Enemy...!
Choose a friend for me...
Veteran to the brethren, now they call me brother...
I do not care...!
Oh well...!
Waterman walking with his shovel, and pans...
Linen pants, black socks and sandals on...
Soul clapping my happy hands in preparation of all the wonderful things I can find...
Standing on my golden mountain...
Green Diamonds in the Sky cascade my mind...
Snapping my fingers...
Skipping past shiny nickel, dazzling platinum and polished jade...
Dancing with the moonshine...
In monsoons distant water wells run dry...
Scorching skies turn dirty...
In the desert I can hear the sea scream salty hymns of seduction...
Trapped in my mind...
Searching for gold in the dessert...
Not caring what I find...
Who are WE...?
Prized fish are drowning in the tank...
Oh well...!
Dessert oh desert, my feet are bronzing in the sand...
Black cloth being bleached by the Sun...
Free styling knowing something is here...

Forget the mountains, valleys and seas...
Talking to the humming birds, praying mantis and the bees...
A world where trees have no leaves...
I began to listen to the self I am...
Closed my eyes and whispered into the black rosebuds ear...
While chasing oasis I realized this is a desert...
My thoughts are deserting me...
Lord of the Rings in the Valley of the Kings...
Resurrecting the broken bones...
Oh well...!

I Do Not Have Time

I do not have time to talk to you...
I am on a mission doing what I have to do…
Why should I concern myself with what you do...?
If everyone did the right thing the world would be a better place...
Gossip away and waste reserved space...
Wicked media is in my face...
I must choose my words wisely...
Contemplate and be more direct...
Training hard and demand my respect...
People live under rocks; so this will be easy...
I am, will and have become...
Otherwise, it will not be done...
Stimulate me with positive truth and genuine thought...
Famous people do not know I exist...
I do exist...
I have no time to contemplate their success...
Born alone, die alone...
My mistakes are my own...
Love me beyond my errors...

Kings and Queens

All women are not queens and all men are not kings. It is what you do for the record able benefit or detriment of the world that allows you to stand out. I can recollect more people that have done well for the world, then those whom have done wrong.

Human Nature

Human nature is a very interesting subject matter. There is a current estimate of over 7 billion people on this planet. Each person; whether conscious or unconscious has their own identity and behavioral traits. With such a non-linear scale of existence WE all tend to seek commonality amongst one another; one way or another through the essence of our mortality. Yet, WE are all bio-physical and each exists with an internal abundance of untamed energies.

Born with numerous external senses we have the ability to perceive the conditions of our surrounding environments which is fundamental for survival. Our external senses are sensitive to all forms of stimuli. Thus, as beings we find ourselves becoming addicted to so many defined and undefined pleasures. These pleasures when overly sought out tend to create and nurture addictive tendencies; which in turn manifest behavioral patterns, ultimately influencing our personalities and impacting the courses we choose in life. The reality that we exist is purely defined by an orchestra of rhythmic vibrations. In nature, there are both positive and negative forces that define patterns of perspective which dictates at times illogical balance and methodology. The choice to be one or the other is dependent on our own free will.

The nature of all things is a simple and harmonized concept which ought not to be taken lightly. As human beings we are also gifted with the ability to reproduce spiritually, mentally and physically. The divinity of such creation is purely based upon the concept of the light in which we seek.

Better Known as Waterman

As a child I appeared to be no more gifted than any other. I participated in all the activities I was exposed to and had the privilege of growing up in a stable home with a father, mother and brother. My father; a retired Marine Corps Vietnam Veteran, is the oldest of six children. My mother, a state licensed Registered Nurse, is the 8th of 10 children. To be honest, I was not a perfect child but I truly believe I did not cause much heartache to the family. In school I was more an above average student, not excellent. However, one thing that I did know growing up was, when it was all said and done, I wanted to be on the top of my food chain in whatever it was I truly decided to do.

My parents purchased a set of Britannica Encyclopedias for my brother and I to explore and learn from; ultimately to brighten our horizons. I would go into those thick books not just for research, but to learn more about the world and the many monumental people that have been documented throughout history. One day while skimming through an encyclopedia I found myself daydreaming and thinking to myself, how can I get in one of these books one day? I too wanted to live or be remembered forever from something that I have done to make the world a better place. I too wanted to create something special.

At an early age I did an assessment of my abilities. I knew I would not be a sports star or a singer. At first, I wanted to be a medical doctor since my mother was a nurse. I believed I could have been a medical practitioner but there was something about business and technology that kept coming to the forefront of my views.

In high school I was a rather well rounded student in sports, socially and academically. I truly had a love for music. I was literally forced to listen to the soulful music of my parents' era during road trips and in the home. This made me grow fond of the many different emotions that music could dictate amongst a crowd. Heavily involved in music I became a local disk jockey and started to build up both my music and equipment. The art of selling mix tapes seemed to keep me hip with the crowd and also kept money in my pocket from time to time.

My life consisted of a number of different hustles; from controlling the candy sales and distribution in elementary school through high school, to working on my parents' investment properties as a general property manager. Over the years, one thing that I kept consistent was my love for technology. The internet frontier was growing exponentially in front of my eyes and I wanted to be a part of it. My desire was to be the number one minority Internet owned and operated provider here in the US.

In my parent's basement I would open up my computer books and learn about the Internet and all the many facets of Information Technology. In fact, even throughout college I would continue pursuing my love for technology while my major was in Economics. My father had a vision of a major online commercial portal which would be known today as TransactionCity.com. I would work endless nights, forgoing many college adventures to come home and put more work into this vision. Even to this day, after countless rounds of revisions and associates, I continue to work on this mammoth of a project in hopes of one day reaching completion and passing it on to future generations.

College was a whirlwind to me. In a nutshell, I found out I had an intestinal disease called Crohn's Colitis. This actually took a lot of the life out of me for several years while in college. My weight fluctuated constantly and I remained a slim young man. After going through many years of drug and infusion treatments I finally met a doctor that figured out all I really needed was a quarterly shot of soluble iron; B12 to be exact. The diagnosis of Crohn's Colitis was during my college years. I did not find out about the Iron deficiency until some years after graduating.

In 1999, I received my BS in Economics from North Carolina Agricultural and Technical State University in Greensboro, NC. I graduated on time in much of a marathon pace. While in college, I served as Freshman Class President and many other student governing bodies throughout the institution. Basically, I had a very active college career. As in High School, I was even more a social and academically astute student. I served as a Research Assistant in the Department of Economics where I was mentored by Dr. Maury Granger, who is currently serving as the Chairman of the Department of Economics at Jackson State University in Mississippi. Dr. Granger saw a light in me and continued to encourage me to work at a great level and always showed a great deal of pride in my abilities. I really want to mention this professor because he had a lot to do with my motivation and drive during my weakest times and he really believed in me as a student and future professional. He also became my mentor in the Post Graduate Ronald McNair Program at the University. Dr. Granger is a great friend and very diligent professional. I wish all my professors had that level of belief in their students!

Needless to say, I quickly got off the medications and started to pursue my journey in life with an even stronger conviction and will to live and complete what I am destined to conquer. After college, I made it my obsession to continue working on the internet business, ELWC, Inc. ELWC, Inc. stands for Ernston Lamar Worldwide Communications, Inc. The company was named after both my brother' and my middle initials. I took on several jobs first starting as a financial customer service representative for Merrill Lynch and then moving my way up to a Global Service Plan administrator. While working for Merrill Lynch I completed my first Master's degree in Management Information Systems. That was a very trying time considering all of my classes were in the evening. The good thing about the accomplishment was that I actually did better in Graduate school then I did in High school and in college.

I actually figured out that consistency and determination were my God given strengths. Maybe that was why I was such a good swimmer from the beginning. It wasn't that I was a genius; it was that I was more determined to accomplish my goals and make something out of myself then most of the people around me. I knew that commitment to succeed came at a cost and a blood driven sacrifice. I started writing when I was in grammar school. I liked to write because it allowed me to express my opinions and feelings about subjects.

I became the official Jack of Trades setting my horizon on creating my own curriculum of study to pattern the professional career direction I was going to take next. I was in between schooling, working, unemployment, alcohol, friends; as well as good and not so good relationships. I set out and acquired as many state based professional licenses as I could. I found out that taking tests were just a regiment and that I had the necessary rhythm to conquer each exam one at a time. Thus, I acquired my Real Estate, Property Casualty Licenses, and Notary of Public with the state. Trust me, those exams were not easy but I did it through hard work and diligence while at a younger age. It's all about consistency, and I was actually pretty good at selling houses and generating insurance policies. Just another hustle and set of trades I put into my bag of experience. I felt I had to acquire the aforementioned licenses because my father was both a Real Estate and Insurance Broker. I really wanted to be able to help him and my mother with the business. Maybe I would have gained some unnatural liking to it and that would have been the end to my ultimate career search. To this day I still feel I will have some other real estate ventures which I will engage in, but that isn't the center of my desire at the moment.

Back to Technology, by now I had also received numerous certifications in the tech industry and began working my way up in Corporate America. At one time I was actually a technical recruiter; literally making a peanut based salary. Trust me, being a recruiter is very difficult and takes a lot of energy out of your life. It takes a special person to be a recruiter. One day; as I lay in the bed, I just said I'm not going to do this line of work anymore. So I quit that day. I have what it takes to get a really good job and be a strong IT professional. One thing about me is that when I make my mind up I stick with it, for better or for worse.

So there my journey began. I went from making about $19,000 a year with a Master's degree to over $100,000, all in less than 8 years. What a ladder to climb! By the grace of God I was able to do such. With all the drinking I had done in my former years and partying I wasn't sure I would even be alive today to tell such a story. I remember so many nights blacking out and my brother coming to get me from God knows where. I am very thankful for my family and their support over the years. I literally was a functioning alcoholic.

I married my beautiful wife in November of 2008. I also know that I have to heed the words of my mother..."Always stay Humble". That is one thing I must keep as a paramount principle throughout my life and teach to the future generations.

I really started my style of writing back in my college years in Greensboro, NC. I was a bit homesick and needed a way to express myself. I wrote several pieces which I saved throughout the years. My brother, Earl, would always write poetry. Earl was actually my prime inspiration to start writing. I wanted to let him know that we all have special gifts and that we should not let them go to waste. Thus, I came out with my first book: "Visibility Through Invisibility". That book was roughly 100 pages. Taking it to from start to finish and from there realized I was hooked. Everyone that read my material always said I had a different way with words.

There were so many different thoughts in my head that I did not know how to unleash them other than to write them down in such an autobiographically formatted way of poetry. I guess I can say I created my own style! By the way, I have been called Waterman since I can remember and for short my friends call me "Water" or even "LEG". There are so many other names which personify my Manny Faces but all those names and reasons along with their respective personality traits can be found throughout my books. Enjoy and remember: "The end always justifies the means!" In the BIBLE the water equals the "Truth". In life we cannot live without water. Also, the world we live in is three quarters covered with Water. Thus, I am the Waterman.

So here I am finishing up the final book for the 2nd Master Volume (books 7 – 11): "Diary of a Waterman". I felt I would take this time out to give you a more formal piece of me and why I write. I do it for various reasons; for my future generations and the reader that has taken the time to undergo this timeless venture with me.

What I can say is this journey has been one of extreme commitment and that it has taken more than sacrifice and dedication to get to this point. There is more to come but I will not lead into those subject matters as of yet. Shoot for your dream; stay consistent and dedicated to your defined destiny. Do not let the little things or people get in your way. Stay grounded and continue to aspire for more positive things in life. Thus, the title of the first Master Volume is called: "Mortally Immortal", and this 2nd Master Volume which you are reading now is called: "The Diary of a Waterman". By the way, Earl is finishing up his first book and I plan on being his number one supporter! I hope you enjoy and appreciate his work just as much as mine.

Make it Easier

PHYSICAL DATA NETWORKS TRANSPORT a
SESSION allowing PRESENTATION to the
APPLICATION Layer.
BITS go into FRAMES and PACKETED into a
SEGMENT which pushes the DATA.

Searching for the Mantis

Grasshopper, oh grasshopper…
I think I be a weed hopper by now…
Low green grounds, high dirt mounds, moving pounds…
Cautiously dictating visions to the ever growing weeds…
Blasting imaginations and bending great trees…
Aware of the lotus; avoiding swarming locust…
Playfully dancing throughout the high thick plush…
Laughing out loud on a foggy day…
Anytime you want a weed hopper escape, I got it going on…!
Grasshopper, weed hopper, little hopper, tree hopper...
Be happy…!
Tired of getting blown to pieces on a rainy day…
Helicopters, cruise liners and skyscrapers…
Hood spots, diners and bodegas…
Drive-bys, white lies and black RIP t-shirts…
Crack feigns, lethal injections and gambling terrain…
It's insane…
So I just keep hopping along, avoiding the quicker sand…
Mechanical centipedes roll past screaming…
Scared with indigenous graffiti I dream of Genie…
Profits, scandals, pocket book grabbers…
Rock stars, grimy bars and millimeter Glock cabins…
Yet, the ants continue marching along…
Improbable images of Harim Abiff French kissing Nefertiti…
I wanted to see how the centipedes play…
So I hoped on the centipede and rode all day…
Building my subway nerve; fanatically searching for the Mantis…
I am the Mantis, transformed by searching within myself…

From dusk to dawn, creeks edge to pond…
Praying as the Mantis does…
Victoriously sipping the LEG cup…

The LEG Cup

Initials engraved coming out the cave...
LEG what is in that cup...?
Good stuff and Mercury's' cider...!
Blasting beyond a spiders' web the Mantis flew out with me...
Brew that dreams are made of...
A syrup decided when gospels recited...
Time, dedication and sacrifice united...
Leaders of a nation; no more explanation...
In a summer slumber alcoholics feign for liquor...
Vampires drink blood in winter...
Hogs spring to slop mud...
Day in and night Waterman sips from the LEG cup...
Flavored words beyond regurgitation...
Spices, honey and succulent stuff...
Ashes to ashes and dust to dust...
Mankind verse man made...
Divine power through salvation...
The ambrosia I've been speaking of...
Recipe to engaging the enemy...
Ah We Enemy…!
Formula for inviting the friendly...
Choose a friend for me…!
Not coffee or tea; pure imagery...
The magical potion love oozes from...
Serum for the deaf, blind and dumb...
I told you to believe in WE...
Patience dilates into harmony...
Simple sips of this makes the world numb...

The Artist

Amidst golden bars, the caged bird sings…
The cage door is always open, allowing the bird to fly away…
Clipped wings keep the bird in the cage…
Leaving the cage terrifies the little bird …
Assorted seeds dictate the chirp…
The Artist tends to look at the cage encompassing the lone bird…
Clipped wings keep the bird in the cage…
At times a different tune; randomly a different thought…
Clinging to the entrance that is an exit…
Entranced by natural scenes the window offers…
Dawn justifies a new day, while dusk suggests redemption…
Clipped wings keep the bird in the cage…
Matrimony to the trade keeps the Artist on the stage…
Assorted facial expressions of intrigue captivate the Artist…
Completion is his assorted feed which makes him speak…
Without a face the Artist fades away…
Without flight the caged bird tends to stay…
A ticking silver second hand mirrored by momentary glimpses…
Each second owes the other…
One cannot leave without the other…
Entrancing an exit is an uncanny fallacy…
To fly away and paint the world with you…
No need for art; or song, if one were to leave and the other remained

Talk is Potential

I could never understand why people talk about how many friends in their lives they are going to delete or do away with. Just do it and remove what is not good. No point in talking about it. We only have so many words in our lives. Why waste them talking about what we might do? Talk is a subconscious afterthought. The conscious is kinetic.

Trade Addiction

Work on your trade to the point of addiction! Become the best in what you do. Every little step you take is one closer towards your peak. To achieve greatness you must be willing to teach and learn asynchronously. A person that knows all things has no value in an undocumented world. The ends have always justified the means to me. Never allow a person or people to depreciate your dreams. Most people will have some form of criticism because they do not see; or care, about what it is you are trying to accomplish with your life. Do your best in whatever it is you do. It is never too late to start moving forward in life. Suffer not to excuses, complaining and criticism. Master your trade. You are what you do.

Thoughts on Unemployment

Unemployment is defined as those who are not working and whom are seeking work. It does not mean those who have given up. A lot of people have given up. In this economy; if you add the number of able people that are not seeking work plus those that are actively seeking the numbers would look very grim. Unemployment is a biased statistic as it is relative to how much the government forecasts spending to aid those seeking. Being underemployed is also a function of unemployment, just as seasonal and frictional employment. So let us not believe the hype on these numbers. The goal is to concentrate on our ability to take care of ourselves, immediate family and community through well rounded trades and skill sets. If your skills are relevant you will eat. Keep your skills relevant and work towards being the best at whatever craft you engage in.

Trivializing Social Networks

Online social networks really trivialize our lives. Our lives are dependent with updating the network for friends and likes. In return the network and the owners easily bait us into one intellectually numbing level of consciousness; to update the network. In the days of my elders it was a delight to receive a well thought letter or package in the mail. A phone call to let you know someone remembered a special day in your life was at one time more than an uplifting treat of endearment. The social networks are truly demolishing the natural fabric and home grown courtesy's of society. Convenience is now more than ever a limitless disease then it is a pleasure. Our actual levels of productivity are truly being reduced due to our need to feed the social networks with nominal status updates. The numbing of the mind is a result of our inabilities to physically articulate ourselves without the need of the social network.

Every Song has a Face

Songbird, chirp the first verse…
Every song has a face…
Embrace and revive my soul with rich harmony…
Each tune delivers its' own unique taste…
Life treasures encoded within the bars…
Tales of treachery and love hug the rhythm…
The simple beauty of a love ballad…
Music instigates lies and waters the eyes…
Battling drum percussions in a war field…
Rhythmic vibrations chill and fill the air…
I dance with a pretty face…
Too much make up, too many frills…
Melodies which tames the savage beast…
Songbird, chirp the next verse…
Blank stares imprint zero sound waves…
Songs I take very seriously mean a lot to me…
Vibrations piercing my heart…
Why is there so much anger in the music…?
Softly talking to sounds and argue with the saxophone…
Blemishing the treble and sequencing the base…
Oh, how I admire her face…!
Lifting heavy emotions beyond my weightless soul…
There are holes in your face…
I know a song that can calm the Earth…
A lullaby that can stop a cry or initiate a tear…
Songbird, chirp the third verse…
The New Year has come…
My ears have fallen in love with so many songs throughout the years…
Truthful sentiments of inspiration, escorted by rhythmic justice…
The short life of a song; like the birth of a child…

The parables of youth were middle age...
Holding on to the last few measures of music...
Orchestrating the golden years with an uncanny style of symphony...
Songbird, chirp the last verse...

Less Than a Thought

Forever is less than a thought…
Life is for the child to laugh, have fun and be playful…
Age is for the wisdom that we acquire throughout the years…
Love is for the memories we bond when we are asleep…
Tomorrow sleeps for a day…
To live is to experience all life has to offer…
Regrets are for the foolish; yesterday had not a choice…
There is nothing on Earth greater than a peaceful humanity…

Misdiagnosed

Fat red, skinny white, shiny purple, dull blue, enticing yellow pill…
40 pills a day to shake the flu away…
Malignant or benign…?
Just to see the sunshine…
In and out of consciousness…just wishing…
Wanting to see the Sunshine…
Persuade me the medication works…
Black hearses, big purses, and big hats to hide the tears…
Still I am breathing…
Tell me I will eat again…
Promise my pain will go away…
My physical form not is working…
Doctor, these pills are not helping me…
Voice is raspy, horse and coarse…
My soul is leaving me…
Quietly sipping on honey tea…
How and why is this happening to me…?
Serum injections bruise and blue once healthy veins…
A smile stalemates the frown…
Tears of a clown….
Painkillers drown all sounds; robbing me of my conscious…
Doorbell rings, I cannot get up to answer it…
Doorbell rings, I am too ashamed to answer it…
Doorbell rings, I will not get up to answer it…
Weak and disabled; the doorbell no longer rings…
Door receives a knock…
I can only hear my breath…
Whispering to the Lord…
I am forgetting things…
I am mad at everyone…

Everything appears to be wrong…
Lack of personal interaction in a hyper-connected world…
Sense of hope; entitled visions of faith…
Flashbacks of a healthy carefree life…
Skin touches the bone…connecting the bed sore dots…
The phone rings more when we are healthy…
Losing fat friends as I grow skinny …
I need a helping hand…
Please give me some water…
Internally dry and empty…
Vision is blurry as the heartbeat fades away…
Forgive me give more pain pills…!
I was steel; strong and massive…
I am dry straw; weak and brittle…
Doctors tell me the medicine will make me better…
Each day I appear to be fading…
Doctors keep telling me the medicine will make me better…
Doctor, I do not need your medicine…
Remove the scheduled needle treatment from my veins…
If I am going to pass, it will be by my own wind…
My spirit will medicate and revive me…
God's will, multiplied by internal energy…
Alive today and thankful for the misdiagnosis…
Three more pills would have equated permanent psychosis…
If the spirit is strong the body can do wonderful things on its own…

Does Not Exist

I am tired of death...
Leaves falling from trees...
People dying...mothers crying...
Inhaling the Lord's breath...exhaling the stress...
People smiling...
Oh how easily we have forgotten the sufferings of our forefathers...
Generations of insight vanishing in the thin air...
Admiration of a cloudless world...?
People cry grey polluted tears; rain to steam...
Unexpected midnight tsunamis wash away the zombies...
Contain my soul, gilding a clay structure amidst the blessings...
Valuing the soul's perception...
Night by night...
All that is important I can see...
Losing too much while gaining so many...
Light by light...
Color blinded, defining new color tones for old imaginary scenes...
Playing dead; scratching my head, believably I made it this far...
Humbly thanking the energies that allowed me...
What I cannot see does not exist...
Stupidity is disgusting...!
Transcending through all forms of time...
The existence of night's transition; steadfast against the mission...
Welcoming and anticipating each frosty breath dissipating in the shade...
Riddled brethren and captured queens crucified by intimidating thought...

Creeping into cerebral meditation...
Relaxing alongside the red river where pink flamingos play...
Where blue waters turn clay red minus the dawn...
Oh how easily we have forgotten the sufferings of our forefathers...
I kept walking, battling the heavy world on my shoulders...
Family and alcohol do not mix; yet the combination exists...
Sit back and prepare...
Detoxing the spiritual mix with a meta-physical fix...
Stick Collector; get back to picking up sticks...
Building foundations and stacking these bricks...
Heritage not practiced and culture globally averaged...
The world needs you to please you...
Manifest power and recreate a new world cipher...
I am not sure what you need to do...
Energy; ever so plenty, test me against the plumbline...
Raw power focused and divine...
Awake early just to see the Sunshine...
I am tired of death...

Bird House

I cut down a big tree to make a little birdhouse...
All the birds chirped...

Management

Management makes you run around...
During the holidays the office was quiet and productive...
No management was around...

Breakfast

She likes bacon...
I brought home four skinny pigs and some eggs...

Politics and Marketing

Politics was a thin man...
He married a fat woman named Marketing...
They had a child and called her Rhetoric...

Yesterdays, Today and Tomorrow

You cannot change yesterday...
You can create today and direct tomorrow...

Growth and Comfort

Get out of your comfort zone…
Growth does not occur comfortably…

Money in Pocket

Money in pocket should be spent on cotton candy while in a monsoon...

Life to Me

Life is not meant to compete against the individual; it is meant to do good things.

Writing in Pencil

You sure you want to write in pencil…?

Personal

Don't take it personal, only God can change the world…

My Spot

A person of solidarity must maintain
their space through their dominant capacity to achieve
and be recognized.

Early in the morning I wake...
No birds chirp; I am first to work...
There is a part of the train platform in high demand;
where I love to stand...
That is my spot...
My comfortable; even in the coldest of winter, spot...
Rain, sleet, hail or snow...
That is my spot and everyone knows...
A place to perch before the metal chariot arrives...
Wait, someone is in my spot...!
How can this be...?
Could someone possibly wake up earlier than me...?
A familiar face wrongfully betrays me...
That is my house and I dwell there...
No one else should be standing there since I live there...
Stepping on the train I really hope there is a seat waiting
for me...
Tomorrow my spot will not be taken...

People will knowingly attempt to take your spot even if
they know they are not fit for the position.

Perpetual Motion

Perpetual motion
Love without a potion spinning on and on...
Waves shaping the ocean...
Fuel for combustion...
I would like to live in a world that has no issues, but I cannot...
What shines without an energetic reflection...?
The totality of my passion is in the void...
Thoughts cannot be destroyed...
Where is the forgiveness in my heart...?
Codex Alimentarius...
Who I was before I can still be...
People make the person...
Sand cements the sea...
I would like to live in a world where I make things up, but I cannot...
Everyone believes they are important, maybe so...
Poised by the possibility of the chosen few ...
Anointed to do what we were appointed to do...
I had a dream about age...
Where I was both king and a sage...
The mortals told me to disengage...
Life is free but I pay dues daily...
Sage, king, child and slave...
Wanting not too much; requesting that which was needed...
Never defeated; carrying forward, suffering and bleeding...
I held the ground, feeling every vibration that touched me...
A spirit arose and clutched me...

I would like to believe that not one good thing will come
to an end, but life dies...
Body but not the soul can be revived...
Anything contained has a capacity...
Life without the void and beyond the body...
I have never seen a bird worry...
Imagine what happens when two worlds collide...
Spontaneous combustion transcending The Mirrors
Other Side...

This is the end Montague

This is the end Montague...
Family feud of once friends, Montague...
Financially divorced; spiritually in mayhem...
The physical form is breaking down...
My mind is in a sober state of confusion...
Life is fading away...
In the back of the church since people make me ashamed...
My lack of praise is to blame...
I am blocking my own blessings...
No matter how hard I try...
For the world to see, I need to build the rest of me...
I have not had time for the pain...
Reframing my train of thought...
Recently dreaming I arose as king...
Acquiring subjects, land and a grand castle...
I am not going to quit; nor give up all that I have worked towards...
Punishment and torture is not the same thing...
Struggling in between the concept of freedom and peace...
I cannot see a world without the Sun...
The greatest empire without a gun...
Legal immigration verses the dirty streets...
Satin or cotton; life is not a fair...
How can I get to heaven without understanding hell...?
The firmament and purgatory verses the heaven sent...
When stakes are low use avoidance to unnerve any opponent...
Remember, you can win by delay...
Foundations must be strong and simple...
God tick my heart until you allow it to stop...

This is the end Montague…
You never know what someone else is going through…

Snoopy Love

Snoopy love…
On my comfy doghouse rooftop I lay…
Big beagle ears flapping in the wind…
Hovering throughout the friendly skies in my helicopter…
Making shapes with the clouds…
I have that weathered trench coat and magnifier detective love…
Watching you try to kick the football...
I am the eager, cool beagle with my name on the dish…
Happy suppertime dance…!
Either dancing in the rain or napping on daffodil hills…
Snoopy does not bark he talks…
Either sitting on the piano listening to tunes…
Or jamming on the guitar with his groovy sibling band…
So cool as he walks to every destination…
My love is Joe Cool…
Leaning against the wall doing nothing…
Daddy ran with hunting dogs…
Mama made the best tapioca pudding…
Sorry Charlie Brown; my French darling Fifi made me join the circus…
Give up that football…!
I have that; "You stupid people," Snoopy Love…
Parking on my memories, relaxing with Woodstock…
Stupid Snoopy love…

Glass or Silver

If I was not digging for gold I would not be in the minds this long...
Silver is used to heal the bruises...
The interior lining of mirrors...
Could it just be glass or silver...?
When the golden gates open our souls will shine...
Too many wrongs to reconcile...
Rainbow colors of hue; sparkling seas of blue...
Flower pots without the mildew...
Nuclear affairs dissipate...
Lasting in a world of beautifully entrenched memories...
Without dispute as mortals our claim is to protect the heavens...
We fight, we fight, we fight...!
Given the opportunity to be the best...
If I was not digging for gold I would not be in the minds this long...
Silver is used to heal the bruises...
We cannot not divide this fall...!
I've witnessed the wind defend the rain, and ignored the pain...
In all my memories the world has been the same...
The young man runs and the old man hobbles on a cane...
I've witnessed the wind defend the rain...
The world keeps spinning and nothing has changed...
Influenced by everything I have seen...
Life really is what it seems...
In a different world I would have similar dreams...
If I was not digging for gold I would not be in the minds this long...
Silver is used to heal the bruises...

I Have Regained

The love I have lost, I have regained...
I stood on the Sun and stopped the rain...
Playwright main character; wild tiger on the range...
Roaming the jungle without knowledge of self...
Manifesting global climate change...
Wildfires in the plains...
Directing the symphony, not listening to myself...
Oh, how I love the rain...
It was so hard to see eye to eye...
Massages and mirages...
Miracle introductions titled by love...
I have loved and fallen, crawling sincerely...
You were miraculously sent from the heavens above...
God released the white dove...
The stability of life is based on love...
The love I have lost, I have regained...
I stood on the Sun and stopped the rain...
All I can do is thank you...

Ants do not Cry

Ants do not cry…
Blackbirds lay quiet at night…
The cold fear of snakes slithering from dusk to dawn…
Lack of suggestion reduces expression…
Nocturnal beings avoid the day…
I am the earliest bird and beyond worms…
The brown bullfrog watches, Sun bathing on the spinning
Elephant Ear lily pad…
Yet, the ant keeps moving forward…
Hauling heavy weight without debate…
Nothings difficult, everything is a challenge…!
Grass hopper, weed hopper, mantis…
Play, fear, pray…
Evolution through transcendence…
From simple love to callas hate…
Cheap people are always talking; naïvely engaging in
debate, intimidating and friendly…
Can't think you have to know…!
White rabbits thrive in the snow…
It is hard to catch a red fox in the red woods…
Tending to admire the elemental personalities of beings…
Married focus verse divorced change…
Watching close fully, tending to move with undefined
curiosity…
Real predators take life when necessary…
Sick bastards kill for the controversy…
Ants do not cry they keep moving forward…

Occupy Wall Street

Occupy Wall Street to the drummers beat...
Slumber in the summer...
Love the rhythm of increased gas prices...
From a stained glass; to plexiglass, reducing the shatter...
Marble, ceramic, vinyl tile...
Urban drugs and cheap thug ethics are out of hand...!
Seems everyone wants radical change in the smoothest way possible...
There's a roach war going on in the parks...
Wash your red picket fence with freedom of assembly...
Apply the Lynch shackles while Crowe kicks out your front door...
LEG does not stand for complacency...
Ten percent care whereas, ninety wants publicity...
What happened to the land of the free trade...?
A land where capitalism hugs communism, while socialistically pumping oil in our homes...
Required inflation plus resource deflation equates to devastation...
Archiving without collaboration is pointless...
Formally or organically, it is up to WE...!
Do not waste ink on paper which most will not read...
People overseas struggle for basic needs...
Many would work if they could work, so they do...
Importing everything to the US from bras, lawn chairs, synthetic hair and shoes...
Drinking to a slumber...
What is a fool to do...?
People in the street cannot afford to eat...
Fools protest with real estate down payments on their feet...
Occupy my street; so someone can rob you...

Take away the dealer, rapist, pedophiles and stealers...
Fast food chains, candy shops, sneaker spots and bail bond centers...
Quasi-Liberationism at its finest...

Good Old Marketing

Marketing has made our society weak
Hear the super marketing engine revving...
Marketing and selling the desirable product ...
Sell rocks; dream cards and real estate on the moon...
Sell the ghetto kids Hip Hop, R.I.P t-shirts and cigarette advertisements...
Everything exists, even nothing...
Where there is matter, there is a marketing anti-matter
The pot does not care if it is black, it just wants to be seen...
Season me with hypocrisy...
Sell me an extra day with no refunds...
Good old marketing...

The Power Meeting

The Power Meeting...
Today I feel the power of wonder...
So I question, is affirmative action good management...
I am awake now and the General is in motion...!
Let's make it happen, my energy has now formed...!
It takes time to break beyond the norm...
There is no such thing as time, only limitation...
Reflecting color from black pages...
Networked powerful minds manifest vision...
Hue man beings, not one thing is impossible...
The Power Meeting...
I recognized the troops were all attributes of my many faces...
WaterMannyFaces...

Sat in a Bar

I sat in a bar and smoked a cigar...
That is all I ever dreamt of...
Puff, puff, choke...
The bar maid shuffled some cards and dealt me a hand...
Stating: "There is more to the world then what is dealt"...
She looked at my eyes and noticed my scars...
Stating: "See, those are what dreams are made of"...
Lord knows it's the same ole grip...
Wiping my brow with my cracked weathered hands I
began to sing a tune...
"I see blood on the windows of skyscrapers...
Undercover officers running after drug dealers...
Widows crying over newspapers...
Rape victims not receiving justice...
Old folk handled without any care..."
Lord knows it's the same ole grip...
I puffed my cigar and whistled the subtle tune...
She said: "every eye is now on you now"...
What is a man to do...?
For fun I took at my gun and shot at the bar...!
Shrugging alcohol is bad for your health...!
Then I looked at my cards and to my surprise...
Ace, king, queen, jack, ten, Royal flush...
Thinking, in this life I would see it all...
I sat at the bar watching the glass shards fall...
Witnessing winter without the fall...
Lord knows it's the same ole grip...

Habitual Training

Take baby steps till you can walk. Always train no matter what. Train with a goal in mind and ensure your foundational structure is built on both knowledge and wisdom. It takes time to move a mountain and the first step starts with vision and dedication. The number one question asked is: "Do you sleep?" I sleep very deeply; sometimes not comfortably, but I sleep without interruption. I train without interruption. I am training because to me the ends justify the means. I know where I want to be in life and I know it will take hard work, personal commitment and sacrifice. Thus, I train habitually in my trade.

Magical

I can never be too prepared...
Once upon a time I was scared...
I know what you are coming for; you know why I am here...
Forfeiting your thinking while evaluating future thoughts...
Sitting patiently, waiting at the door...
Knock, Knock, Feel...
Magical, If you haven't figured it out by now...
Spiritually conscious...
I am sober without the clover, craving for more time...
Time does fly...
So I caught it; flew with it, and craved it
Handicapped forfeiture defined by the era...
All things have a perspective...
Think to produce; reason then deduce...
Accuracy through consistency...
Stimulating existence plus the nightmare of not being here...
Iterative improvements require iteration retrospectives...
Agility became the key...
The first law of nature is self-preservation...
Commission all artists; preserve such a state and time...
Few have heard the words I speak when I sleep...
I sleep deep...!
The best part of life is the completion of a dream...
I thank you for waking me up...
My soul needed to mature...
Sinnerman and Superman are one in the same...
Dr. LoveEvil prepares for calamity...
The Lord has given and equally taken away...
Sending signs and directing change...

It is magical to assume you own the day…
It is a tragedy to let time get in the way…
In a dream I was scared of my essence…
Thinking it was a monster instead it was my presence…

Glass without the Juice

Frames without the picture
Glass without the juice...
Broken soul without a body...
A lie with no excuse...
Living the life of a recluse...
Can't you see we are close to the issue...
Living life to break the rules...
Don't you cry without a tissue...
Just get away from the abuse...
A world without religion...
Slave without the noose...
A young man in prison...
Is like a war without the truce...
A displaced colorless race...
An artist without the muse...
It is a blue beautiful day and everyone wants to paint it purple...
Well, well, well...
The awesome sensation of formidable memories...

One of Many

One life...
One color...
One God...
Many Gods...
One religion...
Many sects...
One goal...
Many sports...
Many questions...
One reason...
Many promoters...
One event...
Many people...
Many nations...
One real reason...
Many habits...
One death...
Many climates...
One world...
Many passions...
One love...
Many options...
One direction...
Many faces...
One Man...
One world...
Many dreams...

The Heart's Choice

Admiring how the waves splash, crashing onto the land...
Our days are numbered as is the sand...
Drinking pure gushing water from the rock...
Ah We Enemy...!
Relinquishing the private stock...
There is no peace unto the wicked...
Yet we are all born through sin...
Restlessness exists for even the most sublime...
Seasons change, from winter to the summer time...
Granted power every hour with no chance of going back...
If my leaders are afraid I shall not be...
Walking in circles; dazed and in a craze...
Unlawfully rewriting history...
See, fear is born from disbelief...
Ex-communicate the liars and dismember the thief...
Strong foundations are built upon good word...
Power is the ability to accomplish a thing...
Like the grasshopper, the journey seemed too immense for me...
I have done wrong but now I see...
Maturing and taking possession...
Continued fighting the war amidst spiritual battles...
Not one carnal weapon can hurt a demon...
Divine power demolishes strongholds of any nature...
Remember the weather and go beyond the seasons...
Cherish the beautiful day at hand...
Hope builds and faith breaks...
Blessings of peace are defined by your hearts' motives...
The heart's choice...

Dedicated to Earl Greene (Brother)

A Young Man

A young man walks out the building with his future wife...
An elder man hobbles along by his lonesome...
Little girls playfully pose for pictures near the fountain...
I notice this standing on top of the stairwell...
Lighting my cigarette against a winter breeze...
Barely noticing the chill of 30 degrees...
Contemplating over wars fought domestically and overseas...
Hopping on the bus right at the light...
My wife is coming home late...
How will I spend the night...?
Trapped in a world trying to save some cash...
Desires to live the good life and raise a family...
People are struggling asking me for favors...
Little are they aware of my issues...
Parole check on deck from living a reckless life...
When I was young I thought I would live forever...
Under my rock, contained in a bubble...
One Sun, so many days...
How would it be if we were neighbors...?
The construction worker tilts to pick up some trash alongside the leafless birch tree...
An older couple picks out their grave for their final resting days...
We dance for the memories, wishing not to fade away...
Beautiful aroma fragrances chaperon a climatic night...
It is hard to stay positive alone staring into the moonlight...
Awake early every day, I go to work and earn my pay...
So we dance for the memories, wishing not to fade away...
Beautiful aroma fragrances chaperon a climatic night...

It is hard to stay positive alone staring into the moonlight...
Remembrances of when we used to kick rocks at the bus stops....
Life is for the child...

Jigga Man

Entertainment and all these high profile characters…
The African American in Amoney's spotlight…
How it is possible you are broke…?
Grasshopper, you were so on top of your game…
Chum, now you have no funds…
Welcome to the hall of shame…
Grasshopper, don't you love humility…?
Making it rain in the clubs…
Tattoo your face with dollar signs…
Once you were on top…
So where is your money at…?
Where are your friends at…?
Why are you selling your homes…?
You have over consumed…
Now resting in the Valley of Dry Bones…
Perception is the key…
You have made so much money and spent it haphazardly…
Now you are poor and that is no tragedy…
All the world wanted to emulate you…
When all is said and done they laugh at you…
Peekaboo, there is nothing you can do…
Putting your trust in the material realm while blasphemously thanking God…
Happy with less than two percent…
Talking down to those on welfare…
Yet, you cannot pay the rent…
Big spender, why didn't you save…?
You could have acquired land…
Instead you publicly misbehaved…
Twenty vehicles yet you cannot drive…

This issue explains why you will not survive...
Chickens and turkeys for the Thanksgiving food drive...
Body guards, hair stylists, makeup artists...
Your jewelry is so shiny...!
Radio personalities, paparazzi and exorbitant dining...
People are dying based on what you are promoting...
Just perform and stop being more than you are...
There should be no disconnect between mainstream and urban, but there is...
Chicken eats the chicken...
All those that supported you, to make it through...
Riches do not equate success; polluting the minds of many...
Soiling future generations while you rest...
Wishing you the best to get this off my chest...
There will be no support for those who acquire but do not invest...

Bottled in Plastic

Windy white skies throw fluffy snowballs…
Melting ice stimulates the blades…
The last snowflake has landed…
I am in awe with the world and humanity…
The rivers, streams and lakes are dry now…
Our souls bottled in plastic…
The ground crackles for moisture…
Rusted steel, crooked sticks and broken bricks…
Boarded homes, divorce centers, lottery tickets, wig spots, and sneaker havens…
Foreclosure owners cackle in secluded five star resort saunas…
Pipe dreams on the corner…
Gun shots…!
Work boots swinging in the trees…
Prisoner for the moment; freely wiggling my toes…
Thinking, I do not mind being broke at the beach…
I can be anything I choose to be…
A blossoming bud or the sting of a bee…
Pondering over the first original sin…
Lord knows we have been destroying our selves…
Good sweets, candy, crumpets and treats…
Gingerbread houses are meant to tempt…
Chasing skirts; R.I.P stained on t-shirts…
Thinking about so much for too long…
Seeking the origins of sin…
When ink gets wet it peaks through the page…
Look into my eyes and revise my story…
Bent clock hands never aspire to move…
As the dust settles clay forms…
As the world turns the soul evolves…
Melting ice cubes in Cancun Mexico…

Stick collecting in Carolinian botanical gardens...
It is all about the inhale, screw the exhale...
Licking lollipops under a waterfall just for fun...
Country dreams corralled by city feigns...
Street sweepers routinely clean pickup the same debris...
Nomadic support of local teams...
Stuck in the past to change the future...
Seems my agenda serves no purpose...
In this domain everything is subject to change...
Ambidextrous screams mixed with laughter...
Life bottled in plastic...

To Know

The crazy thing about life is you never know until you know...
When you know it may be too late...
You have to pursue what you don't know...
One way or another you will know...
Some things take a formidable amount of time to realize...
Realization and knowledge are two different things...
You may or not know what you are realizing...

Masonic Decisions

Whence come you...?
No, it's whence come I...
Blue lodges and esoteric mirages...
Constant barrages of knowledge massages...
No need for sight to seek his face...
Shining light recreates divine space primed by the square...
One God; one Master Race, real Masons pray...
Committing their lives to realizing a better day...
Real Masons are guided by structure...
Seeking constant self-improvement through due diligence...
All brothers are not Masons...
Most brothers are rightfully balanced and committed...
All Masons are not brothers...
The Square; one mother, many tools of the trade...
The Holy Bible; one father, many trestle boards...
The Compass; manifesting your structure throughout life...
Cowers and eavesdroppers beware...
Blinded by the light so you decide to stare...
What in the world makes you perfect...?
Passing judgment is not becoming...
This choice is decided by the heart...

Selfless Vulnerability

Freedom is not free...
Starting fires to warm up the wind...
Justice is not fair...
Resetting clocks just to see it all begin...
Liberty is not liberal...
Fighting one way battles to watch you win...
Democracy is not equality...
Kidnapping adult-like mental states...
Honor is not painless...
Procreating because it is godly...
Pride is not a virtue...
Sacrificing complexity for simplicity...
Vanity is not beautiful...
Commanding awesome spirits to walk amongst WE...
Equality is not the enemy...
Stitching these lines navigating the purple tunnel...
Supremacy is not awesome...
Loving to wake up next to your sleepy eyes...
Laziness is destructive...
Supporting only what is good...
Love is not replaceable...
Boiling in heavenly lava...
Lust is not simple...
Running my fingers through your hair...
Grace destroys rage...
Smiling can be a humbling experience...
Greed is not vulnerable...
Stepping out of a dream walking into reality...

Slow Transformation

Brethren and kin, I am alive…
No clouds in the sky; the Sun shines so bright, I am transforming…
This must be what focus and sacrifice feels like…
Reflections of the skyline radiating the concrete ground amidst fresh water puddles…
Feel; this year in the northeast winter never came…
Hear; the glorious sounds of golden trumpets…
Sound; the world is for the living to make noise…
Smell; subconsciously identify your charisma peppered with mistakes
Invisible stars sprinkle into my dream scenes…
Most times my soul shines…
Fantastic captured in a picture frame…
Things take time…
Writing my life alone…
Patiently walking naked in a material world…
Sniffing crystal cologne…
Synthesizing naturally colorful aromas…
Supernaturally guided by spiritual blessings…
Three robins and two blue jays…
Forgive me if I look lazy because I am not…
Beyond the satire I am the joke…
From sea to shining sea; if you do not want me, that is when we become enemies…
Ah We Enemy…!
Now, I am choosing friends for me…
Transforming while manifesting destiny through mortal tendencies…
A Pack of Black Eagles soon to separate…
If you cannot stand my opinion, the advice will not make sense…

Beyond the Physical Plane

Required inflation plus resource deflation equates to devastation...
Gain momentum in self-discovery and recover...
Pinpoint the differences between duration and complexity...
Architectural planning is an emergent science...
To be right and exact requires patience...
Overt versus organic...
Chillin is my modicum for momentum...
The antithesis of constant improvement is diminishment...
The agility to create mediocre products faster is a wasteful exercise...
Perfection reaches beyond the physical plane...

Last Thoughts

A person's situation is fueled by their ability and desire to WANT all things which they can; or cannot, hold onto. In the end you can only hold onto one thing and that is your last breath. Your last thought and memory is something that you cannot multi-task. Fill your breath with love and positivity. Nothing is promised. The quality of what you take in is a function of what you allow to exit.

Metaphorically the Same

Handing out life...
Like money is to salary...
Heat is to calorie...
Army is to calvary...
Beast is to savagery...
Thief is to robbery...
Charm is to jewelry...
Peace is to harmony...
Pure is to ivory...
Bread is to bakery...
Patients to pharmacy...
Mission is to strategy...
Child is to parenting...
Pirate is to privacy...
Kin is to family...
Love is to chivalry...
Marriage is to dowry...
Institution is to matrimony...
Divorce is to alimony...
Millionaire is to lottery...
Gene is to heredity...
King is to monarchy...
Friend is to enemy...
Plant is to pottery...
Competition is to rivalry...
Inspection is to quality...
Joke is to irony...
Fake is to phony...
Two-faced is to hypocrisy...
The relativity seems metaphorically the same...

Walk in the Park

Black birds and red breasted robins are out...
The grey squirrel clings alongside the tree...
In this whole park I see only one pink leafed tree stands out...
Circumferenced by budding maroon and a mist of green...
Dabs of yellow and violet spawn from the lawn...
Last year's leaves balance the ground with brown...
Fresh moss is forming on the trees...
A furry caterpillar inched up the birch tree; resting on a leaf it once cocooned...
Turning into an awesome butterfly gliding next to me...
The new Sun is peaking at me through the morning mist...
White buds turning pink alongside new evergreen trimmings...
Variations of mulch from last year's fallen bark crimson the park borders...
Crispy air smells so clean and new...
People are running and dogs are playing...
The park grounds are well kept...
The absence of graffiti, empty aluminum or foggy plastic containers confusing the landscape...
For this moment, I feel no pain...
Spring is here and winter never came...
Strolling throughout the park watching my dreams come true...
Once I was living to survive...
Now I am alive...

Virtual World

Are you playing the game...?
Stars, race cars, robots and mainframes...
Portable media gadgets serving electric habits...
Plasma canons, grenade launchers, big guns, ninja swords and laser beams...
Cyber-sex slaves behave...
Sexual innuendos and porn queens...
Kung Fu mastery of super dreams...
All bent up and out of shape...
The mind is repetitiously numb...
Internets, extranets, intranets, infranets, and domain controllers...
Soft networks are getting expensive...
The recluse in a booth plays video games; admiring the virtual world...
Awesome soundtracks, combatant rivalry, and spy games...
Action, fairytale, ancient and time travelers will tell...
The growing online community is hooked...
Throw away the book and pen...
Literacy has come to an end...
Divide your game treasures by your real world memories...
Hand -held applications can fix you...
Friends will never miss you...
It is easy to get a pistol; easier to load...!
See, everyone is plugged in...
Start the game and have fun...
Awesome hand-eye coordination on the screen...
So you think you can dance...
Clumsily the left stumbles over the right...
Hot spots, data drops and laptops...

Start, play and win the game...
Born, mature, pass away...
Virtually you can reset the game...
Physically your chances are minimized...
Falsifying reality graphic by graphic...
Distortion of what can realistically be done...
Ghouls, demons, goblins and walking dead...
In life you only have one shot...
You are lucky if you can survive one or more shots...
Life is not a game...
In the game life has no value...
The reset button is ever so valuable and taken for granted...
Remember Pac Man...?
Now things are too realistic...
Crime pays these days...
Children get angry and go ballistic...
Columbine versus the Colorado cinema shooting...
Bank robbers dash with the cash...
Virtually saving cities while your home is in shambles...
Seems the game is playing you...

Dreams of Growing Waves

I have dreams of growing waves; from the ripple to the tidal...
The beach is closely stitched to the boardwalk...
Swimming in my dreams...
The landscape is all too familiar...
The waves are growing at a dangerous pace and I am safe...
Actually, I am embracing the waves...
Aquatic forces of manifestation; waves rolling like thunder...
See, the people around me are safe...
I am prepared...
I am not scared...
I will not drown...
I will not wash away...
I will stay and continue to tread...
I can see beyond the cloudy abyss...
Voluntarily letting water rise above my head; Waterman is powerfully treading...
My wife next to me; holding and kissing me...
My family is next to me; enjoying the scenery...
My Lord is smiling; he knows where I am meant to be...
My hands are not full...
This is what my transition to heaven feels like...
I am enjoying the tremendous sea...
The waves will take many, but I am ready...
I figured out the dream...
A powerful eternity, from sea to sea...
Today there was a 7.6 earthquake in Mexico City...

Stars and Stripes

The red is for the bloodshed...
Fighting domestically and internationally...
The white is for the absence of color...
Taking, raping, enslaving and claiming superiority...
The blue is for the oceans crossed to get to this land...
Stars are for the nations that once lit up the world...
The stripes for conformity...
Do not let Rome fall...

Sexuals

Sexy bubble, emotion explosion, cinnamon buns...
Golden bronze empress...
Lingerie super fashion model...
Jewelry case and gun holder...
Sexuals...!
Language translator and confidant...
Solar love dispenser...
Private disco dancer...
My Diamond Dynamite...
Fruitful smoothie mixer...
Sexuals...!
Raspberry beret...
My soul's enlightenment co-pilot...
Life partner and co-author...
Sweet and spicy cuisine chef...
Just wait a minute...
Sexuals...!
Extended life provider...
My Caribbean rainbow...
Intellectually freaky and politically aware...
Medical doctor and legal professional...
Night time in between the sheets marauder...
Sexuals...!
Exotic island travel partner...
My sparkling glass of rich chardonnay...
Fancy drive by rider...
Silky smooth thighs...
High heal wearing; 5 star detective...
Sexuals...!
My wife is an angel...
Card player hustler...
Private yacht Capitan...

Exquisite risk taker...
New world creator...
Sexuals...!

Banking

Digitize my wallet...
I do not want to bank at the palm of my hand...
I want to bank at the physical bank...
I am not making any more than I did in the past...
The point to all this convenience is what...?
Once free services are now charging me...
How lucky can one man be...?
See, I started saving for longevity...
Operation 50K a year initially should suffice me...
Interestingly, I see no interest...
Banks must not want my money...
No interest in me...
Pay WE interest like WE pay you...
Fort Knox de Mattress...
Cookie jars, semi-automatic weapons, security systems and big dogs...
Big banks I do not trust you...
Ridiculous credit rating systems...
Cash is king of Amoney and I want my sovereignty...
Uncanny periods of insolvency...
Moving to where I want to be...
Large banks, employers and cops; financially handcuff WE...
Give US freedom by financially crucifying WE...
Stop using WE through usury...
WE the people are the system...
WE the people are the victim...
Banker bonuses and more secure volts out of thin air...
Hysterical illegality these loan ratios are...
Unicorning the idea of a real black bank...
Big banks no comprende civil humility...
In this circular system MY cash is the victim...

I walk in the bank secured with cops to prevent account robbery...
Visibly invisible, these institutions are commercially decaying society...

Roses are not Weeds

Children are meant to play...
The devil has a strong hold on many children today...
Children are joyfully killing each other...
Friends, cousins and brothers...
Evermore, children hate and fight one another...
Once color blinded...
Filled with crime, mass media and institutional confinement...
I know where the red wine went; their minds are bent, crying in their camouflaged tents...
Social welfare Section eight victims at birth...
The present needs to wake up and adults need to take ownership...
Our children are the walking dead...
Our generations will not remember or respect our wishes...
Please give the children a chance to grow...
Children are meant to be seen not heard...
Misguided actions speak for themselves…
So much cursing from the tongues...
Witnessing so many monstrous atrocities...
Socially dividing up youth and family services...
Government cheese, bonus checks and cash payouts...
Play grounds in jail yards for underage lifers...
One day the youth will need to take care of us...
Picture the evil that we do...
Imagine what they will do, based on what is being done...
Punks carry guns for fun; hard headed and malnourished...
Clown like apparel and child pornography...
Child obesity and armed robbery...
Public school systems have no clue...

The present needs to wake up and adults need to take ownership...
Our children are the walking dead...
Our generations will not remember or respect our wishes...
Amoney loves raising children...
Underage teen pregnancy preparing armies of child hooligans...
What happened to the arts and sciences...?
See, rebellion is a felony...
Tissue less child militias gunning down villages...
Godless adolescents cursing beyond words...
Lacking vocabulary, math, literature and truth...
Simple goons behaving recklessly in movie theatres...
Gang violence, initiation and growth...
The present needs to wake up and adults need to take ownership...
Our children are the walking dead...
Our generations will not remember or respect our wishes...
Grab a hold and hug them...
Homeless, drugged out, incarcerated, violent and misunderstood...
The rose believes it is a weed...

My Bongos

Playing the bongos with long black sock, fisherman hat and my super boots on...
Ferociously attacking my leather drums...
There is a rhythm in my head that I need to get out...
Shouting, drinking or smoking just will not do...
Stomping my feet; completing the beat...
Trapped in my seat; fugitive to the vibrations...
Profusely pounding my story into the world ...
Discriminately zoning out for the sake of mental recreation...
I am retarded now; symbolizing the softer sides of life...
Emotionally letting go of the past...
Soulfully complimenting my battle cry...
Knowing this day would come...
My music hypnotizes the weather...
Indian dancing while summoning the rain...
Waving at the sounds I create; breaking beat barriers...
Losing myself stimulating these jungle riches...
Alone playing these drums talking with my hands...
Beautiful spirits are nodding their head to this...
Halls, valleys, alleys, brick buildings, forest grounds, river ways and rural streets...
Coordinating swaying trees and falling leaves...
Silencing commuter noise, digital toys, domestic violence and general construction sounds...
Percussions greet me from ancient to present...
Playing the bongos with long black socks, fisherman hat, and my super boots on...
Just minding my business...
Peace through war...
Recreation over belligerence for deliverance...

Social Injustices

People will jump on any social injustice issue; big or small. If the same amount of energy went towards humanizing the legal system on a consistent basis maybe people would be taken seriously and some real change may occur. However, real change is not happening. Instead, people tend to evolve around many a community or social leader. In my view, most of these social leaders are more vain then sincere. Such officials and community leaders tend to seek positive points from the public to increase their overall notoriety as a figure. Integration to me was more an economic factor than anything else.

Laws are not based on civil justice; if they were our legal system would be designed totally differently. Laws are enabled to feed the social system. A world with no prisons is unimaginable. The system; and all its media constructs, is designed to ensure its continual survival and growth. Capitalism depends on the concept of one's loss for one's gain, but at the long-term expense of the people. The concept of fighting fire with fire actually works. In a world run by capitalism it appears the best weapon is the wallet and actual trade. However, the majority of the population does not have a trade. Thus, the population of non-skilled labor is easily ruled by few.

WE the people are scrounging for justice in a system that is not defined to do such a thing. Justice comes with the increase of a skilled labor force. Populations of people that can feed, educate, shelter, cloth and defend themselves is beyond powerful. However, if WE as a people continue to depend on the social services of the land then the capitalistic few will always have a prioritized demand for slave labor. Thus, WE as a People will always continue to cling onto the social issues for change as opposed to the overarching system design. Such an approach will enable the social system design to get stronger, more encompassing and intertwined within our lives. The legislative and justice system serves as this beast's powerful capitalistic immune system. WE are dying and being taken advantage of because WE cannot meet our own basic needs.

The World We Live In

War will never cease, since we glorify the warrior...
Crime will never stop, since we are densely populated and pseudo-civilized...
Hate will never diminish, since at birth we are born of sin...
Greed will always grow, since we are natural born consumers...
There are good and bad beings in our world...
Live a peace and fruitful life...
We cannot change when it is our time to pass...
Yet, we can change how we are meant to last...

1,000 Words

A picture is worth a thousand words...
The work is worth more than 1,000 words...
Many people do not know 1,000 words...
Keep moving forward and complete your manifestations...
Go beyond 1,000 thoughts and deny 1,000 critics...
Talk is cheap...

A Fool and Money

At this point in my life I am not in the lower tax bracket by any means. I should not judge anyone, but this is my diary. It is actually awful that professional athletes, entertainers and people whom acquire overnight success are victims of their own financial foolishness and behavior. I am not from a rich family but our generations have seen increase from working like the ant and not the grasshopper. Bankruptcy is as old as Hammurabi's law and also a biblical tool just as divorce. Yet, this is a shame. Prime case is when you see a person win multi-millions and blow it all away, foolish. Seems everyone wants the lime-light but cannot see the sunshine.

Are you in defense of fools that claim bankruptcy and seek public pity after financially having everything a man; and his generations, could need? I stand on my ground; a fool and his money shall soon part. If I am a fool with money than mine shall to part as it has when I was foolish. Having money is like having a driving privilege; everyone cannot or should not have the right to drive. If you were making that much money and then go bankrupt due to poor manipulation of cash flow; would you not be seen as foolish, or is it just wise to be foolish? Society enables media outlets to glorify and indoctrinate such everyday foolishness which our youth desire to emulate. Thus, it is a vicious financial circle which cycles throughout our ever-stagnant economic condition.

More Smiles than Tears

The older I become the more I lose memory of my past...
The things I did when I was younger is turning into a blur...
Leaves fall from trees and flowers bloom...
Every day the Sun meets the moon...
Before being born I was subconscious thought...
I think about my family now; before I was, and what is to come...
We remember so few words...
Our actions are either immortalized or present tense...
Create more smiles than tears...
Smiles are remembered...
Dissolve sadness and rage throughout your years...
Pay attention to the ones that love and appreciate you...
More smiles than tears...

Dial Tone

Rotary phone...
What has happened to my dial tone...?
The secure vibrating pulses in between each dial...
Resetting the rotation digit by digit...
Followed by the loud clunky mechanical ring...
Zero for help...
This is the operator: "How may I be of assistance?"...
Your existence is a pleasure...
Operator, oh Operator...
Where did you go...?
Associated by the convenience of fondling the zero...
Now the computer is my phone...
There is no more dial tone...
Remember when we knew numbers by heart...
My memory is scrambled and thoughts ripped apart...
Coiled by a few strangling copper wires...
Long cord extensions allowed me to talk on my porch...
Mobility at its finest...
Waiting for a call while whistling in the summer wind...
The big phone once used for decoration is now obsolete...
The computer is in my pocket; phone feature included as a mere function...
Rotary, push-buttons touch pad and interactive screens...
Thriving in a consolidating world...
I would have called if your numbers didn't change...
My digital black book surfs the Internet...
More contacts now then I need or can imagine...
Voice mail, call waiting, conference calling, text messaging and email addresses...
There are so many ways to contact me, just let me be...
Rotary phone, what has happened to my dial tone...?

The house phone was a privilege; now an obsessed utility...
I can phone you in the desert, cave, plane, bathroom or elevator these days...
Physical lines no longer separate us...
The expense of one is the addition of others...
Our world used to be so intimate...

Beautiful Spring Day

I make enough to pay the consequences...
Selah, thank you Lord...!
Sometimes I write within my past tenses...
Testimony quenches congregations...
Sak pase to the foreign nations...
In the caves is where I study...
Deep within the caves I engage...
Traversing amongst myself and eliminating rage...
Ignoring substance of thought...
Continuing to walk throughout the pollen filled spring day...
There is no common sense in a liberal society...
The Lord giveth and taketh away...
There is no reason to complain...
Life is short and sure to change...
Continuing to walk throughout the pollen filled spring day...
The Sun is beautiful...
I am thankful for spiritual renewal...

Aluminum Man

Aluminum Man pushes the metallic shopping cart...
Plastic Woman shuffles nearby...
North, south, east, west...
Summer, spring, winter, fall...
Collecting empty cans and plastic, sorting them between his bags...
Twenty bottles redeemable for one dollar...
One thousand cans redeemable equals one hundred bucks...
Hermit crab with a cart for a shell...
Tragic, people can be rude and nomadic...
Without gloves he rummages throughout the disease filled trash for recyclable treasure...
He can assess and break down any metal no matter the condition...
Redirecting traffic throughout the urban streets...
His chariot wheels fall off; he acquires another cart...
Twenty-four seven collecting within the day and throughout the dark...
Territorial about their locations...
Hoarding blue recycling bins and trash depots...
No discrimination, no persuasion...
At the beach, in the park, perusing sidewalks, subway corridors and all sorts of outdoor public affairs...
The candy peddler passes by with no chocolate...
Seems everyone has a hustle...
Collecting their cans and not bothering a soul...
The Billionaire Bum maintains his space while shrugging numbers...
For convenience, there is a can collection machine that tallies and receipts their earnings...
Sipping sloppy seconds from unknown residents...

We could feed the world if we were not so greedy...
Shelter the homeless if we were not so needy...
Live longer lives if we were not so speedy...
The world could be clean if we weren't so mean...
Peeking out the window, there is a can chariot bordered alongside my neighbors' building...
That cart should be in the shopping lot; it is not, it is really close to where I dwell...
Aluminum Men are in my city; homeless or in despair...
Several life changing events have put them there...
Scantily clothed but not naked; neither barefoot nor shod...
Aluminum man religiously does his job...
Just to get a bite to eat; a bit of shelter, or maybe some drugs...
Parking at the local soup kitchen for a dish…
No conversation and then keeps it moving...
At times, slightly more or less than minimum wage...
Recycling a green world's agenda just for some cash…
I do not think things will change…
Aluminum Man…

The Operations

My boss said save your vacation time, so I did...
That was the beginning of operation 10 weeks...
Finding out I was entitled to more time...
Operation 10.8 weeks...
Pay me if I leave...!
Plus, I want my vacation...
Either way, pay me...!
I can sacrifice for years; you don't understand my situation...
Waterman that Jones Greene Champion...!
Operation 50...
Save 50 thousand bucks a year...
Operation 2...
Bank two years' worth of salary...
Operation House...
Have a nice place to move my young family...
Operation 40...
Rise to the top of my profession...
With God's blessings; one of the best in the nation...
Operation 45...
Be set for retirement, since credit means nothing to me...
Operation 50...
Settle on my Green Acres in North Carolina;
Riding a black horse named China; hands high reaching out to Hosanna, rocking on my porch...
Operation 55...
Travel the world and enjoy the sunshine...
Live Mortally Immortal...!
Operation Life...
Keep moving forward allowing my family more opportunities than I ever had...
To be the best...!

This is my vision…
These are my operations…

Wooden Parachute

Dedicated since I finish my tasks...
Patiently internalizing, doing my math...
Dictating progress, evaluating the path...
Time is valuable and subject to change...
I am separating my world from time...
Preparing my wooden parachute...
I will be ready for when it is time to leap...
Like a cat, Waterman will land on his feet...
These chains keeping me for a while make me smile;
keeping me safe and focused...
I did my trial with no denial, literally...!
Working to get paid and enhance my trade...
See, my parachute is wooden...
Building and preparing the great escape for years...
Gold is emanating from my eyes...
Reaching higher altitudes with the end goal in mind...
The vessel will crash, but I will not be in it...
I am in the air bursting through the clouds...
Gravity is a nominal thought...
I cannot help all the people that are falling from the
sky...
My mind is not confused; but it is bruised and focused...
Picking and choosing words with caution; fighting
emotional tension...
Sometimes coming out my face and displaying my rage...
No need to cause commotion since my true work is
almost done...
We kill what we are...
I will no longer live in desperation...
I will continue to move forward...
The Sun shines on every point of reflection...
Needed but I just do not fit...

It is almost time to remove myself from the establishment...
Was the world we had worth living...?
The Lord said all I have to do is endure; there is much in store for me...
Do not exceed your life in a day...
I knew who was guiding you before you started watching me...
First one in, but the last one out...
See, your lack of confidence is killing you...
Do what you have to do...
Imagine the idea while becoming the concept...
Asking life for a better explanation...
I have a parachute, a wooden parachute, which is better than none...
I will land on my feet...
My parachute will break on impact...
The new vessel will be a wooden home; like my wooden bones, which is stronger than steel...
The bars I am scratching at are steel...
My parachute is wooden...
My life in this world is real...

Whoa Verses the Fool and Sacrifice

The soldier cut off my ear...
Re-attaching my ears I hear the words of my Lord...
The fool cannot stop me from being real...
I did not need a ride; you see I walked...
The fool cannot tell me how I feel...
I did not choose your words; I could have talked...
The fool does not know when or how I will heal...
Managing my punishment; I did not need the fool's pity...
Thou shall not steal...
I needed your love; the fool chose to be reckless...
I cannot tell the fool right from wrong...
Once I was blind...
Restoring my sight I saw the beautiful works of the Lord...
I did not need the fool's money; I shined floors when needed...
Pass the harmonica and sing the song...
I did not need the fool's bed; I have slept on rocks...
Mankind is driven by cheap motives...
See, I did not need the fool's praise, one day I will be gone...
Sold, hopeless and selfish...
I did not need the fool's food; I grew my own instead...
I needed your help; the fool chose to be helpless...
She broke my heart; I needed something real...
He broke my hand; the Lord showed me I could heal...
I needed direction; the Lord is my shepherd...
I know my world is changing...
I know my last breath more than death...
The fools are killing each other for unexplainable reasons...

2009 Chickahominy Pow Wow

Ever since I can remember I was told about Charles City Indians. Having both parents and their ancestors born in Charles City, Virginia. On September 28th, 2009 I attended my first Pow Wow. Before entering the presentation area I was stopped by a lady at a trailer, she was a Chickahominy Indian and she thought I resembled someone she knew.

Once Pop and I were at the presentation, we immediately took part in the honoring American veterans. Pop being a World War II vet and myself a Vietnam vet. I was able to talk with many Chickahominy Indians as well as Cherokee and Sioux. Dan, a Sioux Indian and a Desert Storm vet discussed with me the difference between Vietnam and Iraq. I was very impressed by the outfits worn and the pride of heritage

I have found reference to the Bradby surname in both the Pamunkey and Chickahominy tribes. While I do not know if there is any relations to my great great grandmother Nancy Bradby it's worth pursuing.
Also worth pursuing is the link between my great great grandmother Parkie Kaziha Langston and the Pamunkey tribe.

2009 Chickahominy Pow Wow : Charles City, Virginia (Lawrence I. Greene)

Baby on the Balcony

Steel bars on the balcony ledge...
No bars for the high-rise windows...
Insulated fireproof front doors...
Bodegas, skate boarders, gun slingers, pedophiles, child prostitution and arsonists...
Baby clinches his fist...
Baby looks down from the balcony bars...
Daddy needs a job...
Daddy's tracking ankle bracelet annoys him...
Baby on the balcony, watching someone getting robbed...
Why is Baby on the balcony by himself...?
Soiled diapers, no formula and clinching to the bars...
The apartment is a rancid mess...
The Sun is scorching Baby's exposed head, feet and chest...
Baby waves at the passing subway transit and commuter buses...
Pray Baby does not fall and the bars are tightly situated...
Where is mommy...?
Crouched in the corner shaking from a dramatic street drug session...
Baby does not tear...
Old weathered soul maintaining a young naïve body...
Staring at stained glass windows which no one can see through...
Young world, what does it all mean...?
No one is watching Baby...
It is beautiful to be young, loved and cared for...
Bang, Bang, Bang...!
With police supervision the Division of Youth and family services bangs down the door ...
Army ants stealing colonized worker ant larva and eggs...

Now Baby's with a foster family; mistreated and
underestimated...
Defeated without a chance...
Street life is cruel and the victims are our children...
Baby on the balcony...

Empty Strangers

Empty strangers...
Searching for a lost love in a familiar world...
Mahogany and golden bronze solar swirls...
Harmonized emotions directing the innocent...
Platinum mustangs crossing the sea...
Botanical gardens doused by the spring rain...
Tattooed by a simple memory...
Hang gliding in heaven...
See...dreams come true when you are awake...
Two paths crossing each other repeatedly...
Daring inclinations to speak; frustrated without completion...
By-passers on a busy street...
Lifeless without connection...
Lonely evening crossings...
Living life without the air...
Just talk to her; she is meant for you...
The world is theirs plus or minus the pain...
Splitting hairs in the dark; combing them in the day...
Grabbing hold to the moment...
Till the day they meet...
Greeting beyond any words...
Mutual satisfactions tied into the universe...
Beautiful treasures of peace and deva-vu...
Impregnated by fate, dancing with transcendence, generating legacy...
Dedicated to the unknown companionship...
Creating new branches, for when leaves fall from trees...
Everything means nothing till that time...
Till the day they separate...
Just talk to her...
She is meant for you...

Hey Clown

Hey clown, I see you missed a spot...
Walking around with your big colorful clown shoes on...
Don't make me happy dance on you...!
Caked up with makeup...
Do you know your face...?
Bewildered with fake parts and glow in the dark accessories...
Funny two toned wig and braid extensions...
Do you know your hair...?
Do you love yourself...?
Are you confused...?
Why do you want to be someone else...?
Job interviews must be interestingly humorous...
Clown talk is broken and hilarious...
Hey clown, your pants are on the ground...
Hey clown, your perfume layers are bringing me to tears...
Dancing in the nightclub, walking the streets, flamboyant in the mall...
Sporting your 8 inch high-heel sneakers...
Little kids are scared to honk your nose...
Joker supremacy...!
Strutting with glossy lips and girly hips, man...!
Tragic to say the least...
Happy clowns...
Sad clowns...
Funny clowns...
Nice clowns...
Class clowns...
Scary clowns...
Fancy clowns...
Retarded clowns...

Nasty clowns...
Political clowns snickering at the podium while lobbying carnival legislation...
Juggling social dysfunction; cackling and creating ruckus...
I see you are full of tricks...
It is like a movie scene, better yet a circus...
Scenes nightmares are made of...
Scenes ancestors would turn in their graves for...
Pulling up in your uninsured loud colored clown car...
Watching all the clowns frolic out the vehicle like a rainbow tornado...
These clowns come in all sorts of sizes and disguises...
Socially some may be your friends...
I was never a fan of clowns...

Seriously

Take what you do seriously...
Do not see yourself as a joke...
I have been through everything I have written...
I will live beyond what I wrote...
Life is short and by no means a game...
You are what you create...
See, tomorrow is never promised...
Do not listen to the fool; they scorn the wisdom of your words...
In life not one thing is impossible...
Dream your goals and manifest your reality...
The world is yours for the taking...
Know who you are...

Just Thinking

I was just thinking. I was thinking about the past. I was thinking about where I came from. I was thinking about my parents and where they came from; a place with so much history about me. I was surfing the net trying to get information. Information about WHERE I come from. It is something, just thinking. My mother has a history that is very interesting. Charles City County, Virginia, a place where segregation was a way of life. She looked White; but had Chickahominy Indian in her blood, and could have passed.

They say that the darker the berry the sweeter the juice. I guess that she may have believed in the saying. I was just thinking. My father was from the same place as mom but with a different flavor. He was born on a plantation not during slavery; just 2 generations before. They lived in a place where it is so far from the city. Their worlds became one world and they relocated from the rural to the suburbs. I was just thinking (thoughts) something to do! There were six of us in 15 years. Eight in all and now only 5 are left. I miss the 3! I miss having all of us all together, there is a void.

I was just thinking can't go back! I would love to do it again. I am surfing on the Internet looking for answers. There are not any not now. I have grand-children, three to be exact. One on the way, wow! What do we do, when do I stop thinking. Not now; maybe tomorrow, not now when? Just thinking...thoughts. SIGNPOST HILL THIS IS WHERE YOU CONNECT! LET'S DO THAT, OKAY! (signposthill.com) : 12/12/08 - 12:52:59 by Perry Greene

My Mother

I remember my mother for all the things that she told me about the world and how people are. I did not believe her when I was a youngster, but know I know she was right on the money!

Making me a man at 20 years old, telling me God bless the child that has his own. Tell me how unfaithful people are and the only one you can depend on is Jesus! Thanks mother; thanks for all the things that you showed me and taught me about people. The older I get the more I understand! You told me I was going eat shit before I died, and I thought you were ridiculous. Now I know what you mean; so much I understand. I love you for all the good things you taught me, and I love you for all the bad things I thought you were telling me. Make your bed hard you have to lay in it! I understand today. Thank you mother thank you very much! Oh, I forgot one. What goes around comes around!

Things I Remember- 04/19/10 - 22:47:58 by Perry Greene (Uncle)

Grandma Jones' Teacakes Recipe

A. <u>Ingredients</u>:
- 2 Eggs
- 1/2 stick of melted butter or margarine
- 1 cup of granulated sugar
- 1/8 teaspoon of ginger
- 1 teaspoon of vanilla
- 1 cup of self-rising flour
- 1 cup of all-purposes flour

B. <u>Mixture</u>: Add eggs, sugar, ginger, vanilla flavor and margarine together into a large bowl and mix well with spoon. Then slowly stir the flours into the mixture. Once all the ingredients are blend and form into dough substance, then you start to squeeze and press dough with your hands. This process is called kneading. You continue this process for about five minutes. Finally you roll the dough into a ball. At this point you can make a flat teacake or teacake cookies.

C. <u>Bake</u>: Bake until golden brown at 350 degree on a cookie sheet or in a pie pan.

The General (Inspired By Waterman)

The troops moved into position...
The tanks flanked every side...
Fox holes where dug and fortified.
The soldiers were poised and ready...
"Lt. Where is the General?"
"He sleeps..."
"You mean to tell me he does not see?"
He does not hear the bombs bursting; the rockets launching, and cries of our brothers...?
Why does the General not aid us in our time of need...?
Please Lt. it isn't time to wake him...?
Please Lt. should I send someone to shake him...?
Do nothing....
The General dreams...
The General foresees what most people will never believe.
When the General sleeps he gathers his nerve.
When the General sleeps, he stock piles his courage...
When the General speaks we listen...
When the General points North we move forward.
For the General is a not a man...
He is our salvation and our command...

By Earl L. Greene (Brother)

I See Purple

I see purple.
Every time I close my eyes; that is the color I see.
It is so amazing how many colors the veil exposes to me.
Yesterday, yellow shaped my visions.
Yet, that was then and now today it is purple...
Purple...
Such a rich color; absolutely regal, totally mysterious...
I always wonder how the Lady of the spectrum will embrace me...
Will the Orange light change me; perhaps morph me into an average being.
Then again, the green hue could soothe my eyes and put my mind at ease.
That would be much needed; as the red wave swirls with heat and rage.
Now I am thirsty and no water will sate my thirst.
I pray the blue light of hope will quench my search.

By Earl L. Greene (Brother)

By
A new defect-revealing etchant for GaAs

J. Appl. Phys. 48, 3739 (1977);
http://dx.doi.org/10.1063/1.324291 (3 pages)
(Received 28 February 1977; accepted for publication 2 May 1977)
A new defect-revealing etchant for GaAs
L. I. Greene
Bell Laboratories, Murray Hill, New Jersey 07974

Abstract:

A new etchant for n and p bulk GaAs is described. Etching is accomplished through an electrochemical anodic process which uses NH_4OH?:?H_2O at a pH of 10.6–13.4. Etching rates depended on the current passed through the solution, while conductivity in turn depended on the pH of the solution. A large number of n+ GaAs polished wafers were characterized with this etching method. Samples etched showed growth-induced striations, dislocations, and twin lamellae. Etching was done on {111}-, {111}- {211}-, {511}-, and {110}- as well as {100}-oriented substrates with comparable results.

By: Lawrence I. Greene (Father)

In Your Dreams

Lottery prediction winner...
Numbers call for me to speak them, then I peak them...
Call me goat mouth...
Deliberately traveling through scenes in your dreams...
Knowing my destiny, helping to direct yours...
The Green Diamond in the Sky sparkling your eyes...
Whoa, my meta-abilities...!
Declaring the bars I would scratch; lit a match and puffed
a cigarette...
Staring into the mirror I saw my face change...
Pharaoh, king, general, master...
No longer needing my eyes I laughed at déjà vu...
My power is vibrating through...
Piercing the Internet and guiding radio waves...
Midas touching what I feel into gold...
I cannot; or will not, touch everything...
When I enter your dreams have no fear...
I journeyed beyond tomorrow...

Sandy 2012

Wait for the waves...
Surf and turf before the storm...
Evacuate the state before it is too late...
Where can we go...?
Hunkered in we waited for the wind...
Pass the sandbags and raise the levies...
The water talks to me and the sky is jealous...
Irene was a tease compared to what's to come...
President Obama is in our state between debates;
bipartisanship through recovery relief...
Utopia cannot exist without the concept of fear...
LEG declared the great oak would fall; and it did...
The calm before the storm we patiently waited for it to come...
Freezer stocked with ice; we charged the laptops and cell phones...
The Four Winds hit in unison...
Inland, the rain was not so bad...
Sixty mile per hour winds snapped tree limbs like twigs...
The approaching hurricane was hard to explain...
Sandy was her name...
New Jersey and New York were in her direct path...
The night sky hue was an electric blue...
Power lines and transformers explode then the neighborhood goes dim...
Water and toilet paper; the most important staple to have throughout the storm...
New Jersey residents were pounded throughout the night...
High tide swallowed the jersey coast line; heavily flooding residents and business...
Sayreville toppled, Sea Bright severely crippled, Atlantic

City borders without the boards...
Countless townships are humbled...
Roller coasters in Seaside monument the ocean floor...
The state is broke; boats corralled on transit train lines...
Millions without power; what is the state to do...?
The gas crisis of 1977; reincarnated in 2012...
Odd verse even license plates dictate the day you can wait
for a quarter tank...
Neighborhoods totally destroyed...
Untimely death, displacement, interstate utility support....
Grocery stores are in distress; no meat, bread or dairy...
FEMA steps in; diagnosing mass impact...
Ten days later a five unit Mississippi electric company
convoy restored power in our building...
The worst domestic storm I have witnessed in my life...
New Jersey is strong; our rebuild will be magnificent...

Bored

Early I rise...
The train runs out of steam...
The conversation is boring...
Pursuit of the American dream; landlocked and un-enthused...
Overall System Conformity when the Invisible Class System clashes...
Work to get paid, weekend to rest, vacation to reset your mind...
Growth is uncomfortable...
30 years to retire and pay off your mortgage...
The routine is boring...
Early I depart to sleep...

Crabbing in Sea Girt

I love crabs and lobsters; juicy when steamed and in hot butter...
I have family that resides near the shore...
Driving down to see them; ice cooler and net in hand...
Basketball shorts, tall black sweat socks and a pair of outdated hi-top sneakers...
My cousin Elliot is a seasoned crabber...
We wade in brackish water from dusk to dawn...
Positioning our rods into a circumferenced perimeter; chicken parts tied to the end of strings...
Sipping beer and smoking Newport cigarettes; we laughed and crabbed all day...
Watching the water ripple; waiting for the poles to twitch...
Lightly tugging on the string; towing the tied chicken closer to the net...
Swoop goes the net; I have captured a blue crab...!
Sometimes collecting two or three within a swoop...
Wading in the water catching crabs...
Necessary, fun and relaxing...
Walking through thigh high water; learning the terrain, avoid sinking into softer ground...
Placing our crabs in the ice cooler...
A crab in the bucket has new meaning to me...
Try filling the bucket with what's caught on your own...
Count how many empty buckets there would be...
Crab verse fisherman mentality; too many fish in the sea...
No cages, spears or fishing rods...
Catching crabs with chicken attached to the string...
Eels surprise us as the tide arises; they love chicken too...!
We would crab till the night greeted us...

When done; we would split the crabs up like a pirates'
booty, cooler filled to the brim...
I would drive home with my treasure; cooler packed of
blue and red crabs...
Pots of crabs I would distribute to the family...
I love crabs and lobsters; juicy when in butter...
I did not go crabbing this summer...

Election Tuesday 2012

Obama Incumbent; let's keep it that way...
Waking up early to do our part...
Sandy broke us into pieces but we still must represent...
Hunkered in waiting for the Nor'easter to hit...
Lights out and still no heat; chilly outside but colder in here...
Climactic calamity will not cause retreat...
Our voting booths reside at the community senior center...
The country is so divided; red and blue states, Bloods and Crips...
Political gang violence at its finest...
Independent and my colors are neutral...
A multi-millionaire Republican Mormon will not run America...!
Not one yellow, brown, red or tan person at the convention; disregard the hired help...
America, the greatest nation ever to be outsourced...
I needed to vote; there is too much at stake...
Volunteer seniors patiently move the line along...
In the booth the senior literally votes for me, seriously...!
Patiently waiting for voting districts to close...
Corralling the big screen watching the media commentate...
The last four years have been interesting...
Blame game, racial slurs and utter disrespect...
This congress is not built to make laws...
The process is not about the individual; it is about us, the people...
I voted for change; now it is time to move forward...
People distort truth and complain...
Very few get out and make it happen...

Republican's do not have a clue how to produce a relevant candidate...
You cannot chop down the cherry tree with a cotton bat...
The world glued to their radios and televisions...
Obama's multicultural mix verse Romney's Caucasian constituency...
Media distorts the facts; shenanigans at its finest...
There are more states in red and my stomach is in knots...
Florida, Virginia, Ohio...
Amazing how 2 - 3 states can determine an election outcome...
Never underestimate the Hispanic population...
Popular verse electorate; I know my vote counts...
Rich people do not be greedy...
We have an opportunity to make real change...
Globally, this election is important...
Immigration, healthcare, economy and unemployment...
Tax the rich and feed the poor...
This land is our land; not that of a chosen few...
Notice how the states are gaining blue momentum...
Anti-Republican politics and economics...
Massachusetts, Michigan and Mexico...
Your governing state; where you were born, and your Mama...!
Romney's state was painted blue...
The nation began to dance; as the last remaining states entered their underappreciated votes...
President Barack Obama reelected as the 44th President of the United States...!
The POTUS is back on the block...!
Sadly, many were not prepared for this win...
See, the cherry tree has strong roots...
When you cut it down it will grow back again...

Comfortable Growth

People ask me, so I try to explain...
Cooperation...
The more people you know the less help you get...
Ambition...
The more you do the less you appear to want...
Drive...
The distance is far so you decide to avoid the trip...
Emotions...
The more you love the more hate you have to carry...
Honesty...
The more trustworthy you become the more clandestine your actions appear...
Knowledge...
The more you know the less you want to confront...
For every action there is an equal and opposite reaction...
Growth does not occur comfortably...

Diary of a Waterman

I will not crack; I will withstand the temperaments of time...
Not giving up, I will continue to move forward...
I have written this diary through thick and thin...
Stayed humble and prayed for grace; throughout my life I sought the Lord's face...
Titles tell a story; from beginning to end...
Volume covers are scenes from recurring dreams...
The books are architected like a pyramid; perfected in every way...
I will not run or hide; blessed throwing Green Diamonds in the Sky...
I will not crack; the foundation is strong, the temple will be magnificent...
Diary of a Waterman...

Mark Martel/Illustrator

Mark Martel's years as an illustrator, designer and writer reach back to the days of hand-crafted graphics and forward to the Internet era. Over the years he has done work for Dayton companies like Iams, Lexis-Nexis and Mead as well as pro bono projects for the Dayton Opera, Philharmonic and Theatre Guild. Recent work includes book illustrations, storyboards for video and film projects, comic book art to promote the New York City water supply, and AIDS prevention artwork for Africa. He has worked in most media including print, direct mail, comics and ads. His fine art includes figures, portraits and landscapes in a range of painting and drawing media. Today through the Internet he serves clients in over 20 states and a dozen countries around the world via MartelArt.com.

"I like working in mixed media—acrylic, pastel, watercolor, Photoshop, Word, print, web, film… About the time we switched from magic markers to computers at work I started doing more painting and drawing in my free time. I used to draw more from my imagination, but real life is far richer, more unpredictable and immediate. There's not much better than painting outdoors on a beautiful day. It becomes a mixture of puzzle, exercise and meditation when you really get in the flow."

Visit MartelArt.com or email Mark@MartelArt.com

Lawren's Bio

Lawren was born in Summit, but raised in the neighboring towns of Plainfield, North Plainfield and Piscataway. A native of New Jersey he currently resides in Elizabeth with his wife Magdalena Greene. Attending College in Greensboro, at the University of North Carolina A&T State he obtained his BS in Economics in 1999. Upon graduating from NCATSU he felt the need to embark on a journey of higher learning and Graduated with a Master's of Science in the field of Management Information Systems at Kean University in Union, New Jersey while working full time and attending night school. He currently is completing his Masters of Science in Human Resource Management at Thomas Edison State College in Trenton, New Jersey. Lawren is internationally certified by the Project Management Institute as a PMP (Project Management Professional), ACP (Agile Certified Practitioner), RMP (Risk Management Professional) and SP (Scheduling Professional) designation.

Throughout his college years he realized he had a love for writing and expressing his inner thoughts through poetry. His desire to write poetry was influenced at NCATSU and he quickly started to gain momentum as the years transpired. Born in an era of spoken word and coffee shop ambiance Lawren quickly grabbed a hold of his writing style and began expressing his everyday life, struggles and campaigns in the form of poetry and spoken word.

As an Internet pioneer; Lawren also owns his own internet development company, where he is able to meet the growing online development demands of existing and potential customers, friends, family and associates. He formed his online business (www.elwci.com) with his father Lawrence I Greene and brother Earl Greene in 1996. Their operations are based in New Jersey and business spans globally and throughout the United States. A creative man by nature Lawren through his writing identifies with the hustle and bustle of urban life.

After many years of dedication; on 10/29/2012, Lawren successfully launched www.transactioncity.com.

2022 Update: Prime Michael Greene (1st Son) was born on 1/20/2022 to Lawren and Magdalena Greene. Lawren Greene acquired his PhD in Information Technology Project Management from Capella University.

LAWREN: "Diary of a Waterman"

Or you're considering having Lawren as a guest for your next event please contact at www.lawrengreene.com

lawrengreene@gmail.com

Lawren E. Greene
32849 Natural Bridge Road
Wesley Chapel, FL 33543

www.ingramcontent.com/pod-product-compliance
Lightning Source LLC
Chambersburg PA
CBHW042319090526
44583CB00029BA/2998